GEOPOLITICAL ALPHA

*An Investment Framework
for Predicting the Future*

By

Marko Papic

WILEY

Published by John Wiley & Sons, Inc., Hoboken, New Jersey.
Published simultaneously in Canada.

For general information on our other products and services or for technical support, please contact our Customer Care Department within the United States at (800) 762–2974, outside the United States at (317) 572–3993, or fax (317) 572–4002.

Wiley publishes in a variety of print and electronic formats and by print-on-demand. Some material included with standard print versions of this book may not be included in e-books or in print-on-demand. If this book refers to media such as a CD or DVD that is not included in the version you purchased, you may download this material at http://booksupport.wiley.com. For more information about Wiley products, visit www.wiley.com.

Library of Congress Cataloging-in-Publication Data:
Names: Papic, Marko (Geopolitical strategist), author.
Title: Geopolitical alpha : an investment framework for predicting the future / by Marko Papic.
Description: Hoboken, New Jersey : John Wiley & Sons, Inc., [2020] | Includes bibliographical references and index.
Identifiers: LCCN 2020025448 (print) | LCCN 2020025449 (ebook) | ISBN 9781119740216 (hardback) | ISBN 9781119740230 (adobe pdf) | ISBN 9781119740223 (epub)
Subjects: LCSH: Investment analysis. | Geopolitics—Economic aspects. | Economic forecasting. | Investments.
Classification: LCC HG4529 .P37 2020 (print) | LCC HG4529 (ebook) | DDC 332.67/253—dc23
LC record available at https://lccn.loc.gov/2020025448
LC ebook record available at https://lccn.loc.gov/2020025449

Cover Design and Illustration: Tata Wijana Warsita
Author Photo: © Steven Drobny

Printed in the United States of America.

SKY10033926_032322

This book is dedicated to the country that no longer exists.
Pjevaj nek te čuju, ko ne sluša pjesmu slušaće oluju!

Contents

Foreword

Montreal. February 2017.

A cold, dark, and ice-stormy night.

    I met Marko Papic for the first time over dinner at a spot he enthusiastically called "the coolest restaurant in town." Upon entering, I found a dark and empty restaurant save for a bartender, a waiter, a *mâitre d'*, and a lone customer sitting in the back corner. I started strategizing a polite early exit. But the food and drinks were incredible, and we proceeded to have an excellent, wide-ranging conversation. We stayed late and got totally blasted. It was the first of many times I would observe Marko make a correct, out-of-consensus call.

    Within minutes of meeting Marko, I knew he was unique. My singular skill is sniffing out quality from crap and gathering the good ones around me — be it finding new money managers to run capital for our institutional clients, bringing together smart investors on a deal, backing founders of new financial technology companies, or convening the most interesting people in the world at an event in some far-flung location. I also seek out those with unique skills and try to persuade them to join the Clocktower Group team.

By the time I met Marko, I'd been looking for a chief strategist for a while. I needed someone to act like a basketball center, a big man in the middle to gel the team. I was looking for a beautiful mind to sit on top of our unique and exclusive information flow, then channel it into a coherent form for our clients. At first, I looked for the typical economist. Over the past 40 years, bond markets, central bankers, and finance ministers drove markets – and the world. It was the Lords of Finance and the Committees to Save the World who pulled the puppet strings, and the *alpha* lay in correctly forecasting their next move.

Enter 2016.

The passing of the Brexit referendum and the election of Donald Trump marked a sea change in the macro game. Populist movements in developed countries drove home the point that the era of the economist and the interest rate soothsayer was over. In the post-Trump, post-Brexit era, geopolitics are all that counts. With interest rates pegged to the zero lower bound for the foreseeable future, the Lords of Finance and Committees to Save the World have run out of ammo.

As such, Clocktower's chief strategist needed not be an Ivy-trained economist with a perfect résumé coupled with a PhD, CFA, MBA, and other meaningless acronyms. We needed someone not locked on the movements of the Fed & Co., but focused on international and domestic politics. The battles and power players of today (and tomorrow) are Trump versus Xi, the UK versus Europe, Putin versus world, MBS, Macri, Bolsanaro, etc.

Enter Marko Papic: a geopolitical expert who grew up getting chased by packs of wild dogs in collapsing Yugoslavia; who subsequently moved to Iraq, Jordan, Switzerland and Texas; and who married a *Tejana* and settled in Canada. Whispers of an unorthodox geopolitical thinker with out-of-consensus market views drifted from clients and prospects. A strategist out of Montreal who more often than not, turned out to be right. For many, Marko, the nihilist Serbian, was their favorite strategist. I realized he was just the stateless, unbiased, enthusiastic, unique idea generator that the team in Santa Monica needed to fill out our global macro squad.

After following Marko's calls for a year and test-driving him at a few client events, I spent the better part of 2018 convincing him that the beaches of Southern California are a better place than the slopes of Mont-Tremblant. In December 2018, Marko signed on to join Clocktower Group as our chief strategist. In 2019, he crushed it. In January 2020, I said, "Marko, that was great, but now it is time to take the training wheels off," and made him write this book. I've written two books about global macro and was halfway through writing my third: the final installment in my trilogy. Contract was signed, chapters were in the can, and an advance was paid. Halfway through, the world changed. It was time to pass the ball to the big man in the middle.

Marko took the pass and ran with it. Like his childhood hero Kobe Bryant (RIP), he approached this book with insane focus. He wrote chapters faster than I could read them. He did this all while producing reports and talking to clients, seeds, founders, and partners on top of a torn ACL/meniscus (which he ignored), working from home and homeschooling his three kids due to COVID-19. Mamba-style.

Marko has a lot to say about this brave new world that revolves around politics and geopolitics. People deserve to hear it — not just Clocktower clients and friends but anyone who wants their eyes opened to the invisible barriers that dictate the future. In *Geopolitical Alpha*, Marko models how to make well-researched, actionable forecasts using his constraint-based framework. Along the way, he gifts you, the reader, with funny stories, anecdotes, and historical examples coupled with invaluable insights on relevant geopolitical trends: the state of US–China tensions, the future of Europe, the implications of the COVID-19 pandemic, US elections, and other schisms that will drive world markets. I hope you learn and enjoy. You're welcome.

Steven Drobny
CEO and Founder of Clocktower Group
Author of *Inside the House of Money* and *The Invisible Hands.*
March 2020
Currently under "Shelter-in-place"
order in Malibu, Claifornia

Introduction

"The German president just resigned. We are selling everything. This is it."

I t is May 31, 2010, and Horst Köhler, the president of Germany, has resigned.

I saw the news flash across my inbox in one of the hundreds of news items that I skimmed every morning, but I ignored it. I had triaged it, along with most articles that day, for the sake of sanity; I thought it was irrelevant.

Several hours later, I stare at the Polycom in the middle of the boardroom at Stratfor, the Austin, Texas–based geopolitical analysis firm that gave me my first job. My decision to ignore this one news item is about to cost me that first job. The knot in my stomach has knots.

The saleswoman whose client – a large Connecticut-based hedge fund – is on the line bores a hole in the side of my head with her gaze. I almost hear her thinking, *Oh my God … this foreign kid is out of his depth.*

I have no idea why the German president resigned or why it is market-relevant to a hedge fund (I have only a vague idea of what a hedge fund is in the first place). I have no idea who the German president even is!

* * * * *

By May 2010, the Euro Area sovereign debt crisis was already in full swing. The 2008 Great Recession had come and gone without the collapse of Western civilization, but things were still touch-and-go. People were on the lookout for the next shoe to drop. In October, 2009, incoming Greek Prime Minister George Papandreou revealed that the previous government had massively underreported the budget deficit. Instead of 6.7%, the figure was 12.7% (later revised to 15.4%!). The shoe *dropped*. By December 2009, the greatest economic crisis in the developed world since the Great Depression was afoot.

Nobody at my firm really cared. It was not the fault of the folks running the place; the firm was simply not designed to care about financial markets. For most of the past three decades, the investment and geopolitical communities rarely communicated, in part because they struggled to understand each other. They had become over-professionalized, erecting barriers to entry largely for job security, like medieval guilds.

When the Euro Area crisis hit, my marching orders at the firm were not to spend too much energy on it. I was told to focus on US ballistic missile defense in Europe and some other geopolitical matters that nobody outside the Beltway cared about. We had no edge in covering capital markets – few of the firm's analysts understood their own credit card statements. But as the firm's Europe analyst, it was impossible to ignore the evolving imbroglio. Not only did it flood my inbox with scary headlines and client emails, but I also sensed that this was the career opportunity of a lifetime.

By early 2010, my own career had stalled before it had even really begun. I was on leave from a PhD program at the University of Texas at Austin. Political science coursework and research ware easy, but not interesting. I would have coasted for the rest of my life teaching Poli Sci 101, but the oversupplied labor market in social science PhDs meant that I had to take whatever job was available, even if it deposited me and my family in some academic colony in the middle of nowhere.

I took the job at Stratfor because it was based in Austin. I got lucky. The place was fast-paced, young, and brutal. It taught me not to waffle, to digest information quickly, and to create knowledge shortcuts. But I was still missing the sense that I was making a difference in anybody's life.

My feeling of inadequacy was, in large part, a product of my job description. At the start of the decade, Europe had not produced geopolitical risks for a quarter of a century. The fall of the Berlin Wall, the dissolution of the Soviet Union, and the rise of the world's largest trading bloc were all epic events, but they were all tailwinds in the sails of the global economy. There was a sense that history had ended in Europe and that Jean-Claude Juncker was its Last Man.

At the same time, I was expressly hired to be the firm's Europe analyst. Given Stratfor's roots in "Great Power geopolitics," my position was the equivalent of being the admiral of the Swiss Navy. Most of the all-hands meetings were about Tomahawks, car bombs, and *jihad*. I usually got to fight with the Africa analyst for the scraps left over by the Middle East, counterterrorism, and East Asia analysts.

"But … the Lisbon Treaty … " I could feel the sneers before I finished my sentences – sneers from the "real analysts" who subsidized my EU-watching.

Thankfully for my career – and sadly for 400 million European citizens – the Euro Area crisis hit with a vengeance. Even though I couldn't navigate my credit card statement either, I knew that this was my moment to add value.

That said, all this was not clear on the morning of May 31, 2010. I was ushered into the conference room by the salesperson who handled the firm's financial relationships. I tangentially knew what these clients did for a living. Most were passive in their use of the firm's services. They read the analyses we posted online. They gave little feedback. Most of the time I didn't know if anyone cared what I was writing. But over the course of the next 12 months, I would have the most professionally intense period of my life. I realized *a lot* of people who *definitely* understood how interest rates worked were reading my research.

* * * * *

"The German president just resigned. We are selling everything. This is it."

I look at the Polycom. I have a choice to make. Do I waffle my way out of the conversation, or do I bite the bullet?

Something about the accent on the other end of the line instills fear. I think it is a Long Island accent. I cannot tell precisely, as I'm a Serb living my fourth year in the US. Before arriving, all I really understood about America came from movies and *The Simpsons*. My gut tells me not to waffle "Long Island"; *he will know*. So, I take a deep breath and 'fess up.

"Guys, I don't know who the German president is."

Silence. Uncomfortably long. I glance at my colleague; she is revising her résumé in real time. I imagine my boss decapitating me on the same boardroom table at the next all-hands meeting.

"What do you mean? Aren't you the Europe guy at this shop?!"

Ok, here we go. Long Island is angry. The man pays for a service and is not getting it. I respect that. But the Serb in me now starts to come out. I get irrationally confident for no good reason.
"No ... sorry, I apologize. You misunderstood me ... yes, I am *the* Europe guy. And if *I* don't know who the German president is ... " Silence on the other line ... *time to go on the offensive.*

" ... Then it is not a significant piece of news. The president of Germany is the equivalent of Queen Elizabeth; he cuts ribbons, kisses babies, and shakes hands at the airport. I don't know why he resigned, but this event has zero relevance."[1]

* * * * *

This was a risky move. The resignation *could* have been related to the Euro Area crisis.

---

[1] German President Horst Köhler resigned because, in 2010, it was still not acceptable for a German statesman to say that Berlin would use its military to protect its economic interests – such as to keep trade routes open. He was widely respected and a popular, nonpolitical leader. Ironically, his successor (who also resigned) later said much the same thing with little fanfare and no pressure to resign, showing how quickly the world was evolving in the early part of the 2010s.

The conventional view at the time was that Germany would not bail out the EU member states. Germans were obsessed with fiscal austerity, risks of inflation, and that "the Swabian housewife saved every *pfennig*." Maybe the president was a "hard-money" zealot who objected to bailing out profligate Euro Area peers like Greece. Maybe he thought that the crisis was an opportunity to "liquidate everything" – in the words of former US Treasury Secretary Andrew Mellon, who almost single-handedly turned a severe recession into the Great Depression.

And yet ... I had a reason for dismissing this news. I had a *framework*, and it had taught me to push hard against the Eurosceptic narrative for months. This view on Europe would become a successful investment theme, and the proto framework that I had developed would become my profession and passion over the ensuing decade.

This framework – which focuses on the material constraints policymakers face – is what this book is about.

The framework boils down to this: Niccolò Machiavelli was wrong. No amount of *Virtù* will help the Prince overcome *Fortuna*. So don't study the Prince. Study his constraints.

* * * * *

Back in 2010, I take a gamble because "Long Island" pushed my buttons. It is an educated gamble. Long Island's singular focus on relevance – the "so what?" – forces me to make a call. Not to waffle, not to talk about "on the one hand" and "on the other hand," not to split hairs about "hard-to-estimate probabilities," but to give him an investment-relevant view in three sentences. *The resignation of the German president does not matter. Go back to making money.*

"Oh ... got it. Thank you. We'll talk later."

Click.
Exhale.
I straighten up and turn to my colleague, chest flexed, a "What's up?" look on my face while maintaining an air of "I had this the entire time." (I did not.)

In a slow, staccato voice, she says, "These guys don't know what they are doing."

Boom. There it is. My Jerry Maguire moment. If we were in a cartoon, a lightbulb would have pulsated above my head and burst. I reply:

"They're not stupid. That guy could literally ... buy me ... to tutor his kids for the rest of my life. These guys are not stupid. They are just ... busy."

* * * * *

And human. And over-professionalized. To become an investment professional in 2010, one had to be confident in a lot of subjects, but a basic grounding in political science was not among them. This failing is not because investors suddenly became ignorant of global affairs and history but because those skill sets had not mattered for most investors since at least 1985.[2]

That moment led to a career-altering decision for me. I decided that I wanted to devise a framework for geopolitical forecasting rooted in the real world. Not based on conversations with "wise men in smoke-filled rooms" or on a narrow, inflexible view that geography and history predetermine outcomes, but on actual research and fundamentals. A framework that was not only easy to use but that was replicable by others who sought insights into the future.

There were two reasons I felt confident to declare that the resignation of the German president was irrelevant, both rooted in material constraints. First, the president was constrained by Germany's constitutional irrelevance. Second, I already had a framework for what German policymakers and voters would be forced to accept in the Euro Area crisis. Even if I had been wrong about this particular news item, I had a structural, macro view of what would happen next in the Euro Area crisis, one that was unlikely to unravel due to a single resignation. As I explain in

---

[2] Most does not mean all investors. Many of the greatest macro hedge fund minds of the past three decades made smart calls based on correct geopolitical insights. For example, George Soros "broke" the Bank of England in 1992 by understanding that the Bundesbank may burn deutschmarks defending the lira and the peseta, but not the pound. Aside from the occasional story of an astute geopolitical insight leading to fame and fortune, most professional investors have not had to care about geopolitics in their daily lives for a very long time.

Chapters 4 and 5, the Euro Area crisis illustrates how material constraints impact not only policymakers but also voters. European integration is not only going to continue, it will accelerate over the next decade due to these epochal constraints.

After downloading the constraint-based framework, the reader will be able to stop relying on the news flow for analysis. Much as an anchor keeps a ship from being blown out to sea, constraints anchor the smart investor to a subjective probability grounded in material reality.

I take one chapter to describe this framework. The punchline: investors (and anyone interested in forecasting politics) should focus on material constraints, not policymaker preferences.

Preferences are optional and subject to constraints, whereas constraints are neither optional nor subject to preferences.

The era of geopolitical ignorance is over. The days when investors and corporate decision-makers could be successful without much understanding of politics will be a footnote in the annals of history. In the first chapter, I go over these paradigm shifts rather quickly because, at the time of this writing, the idea that "we're not in Kansas anymore" is obvious.

At the same time, not everyone needs to rush to enroll in political science courses. The constraint framework has worked well for me by providing the tools sufficient to make sense of politics. As such, I hope to offer professionals who must take politics seriously a shortcut – not a foolproof, scientific method – to forecasting geopolitics.

The focus of the rest of the book is on the framework itself. While I initially built the constraint framework to help investors make sense of geopolitics – and make money in the process – the C-suite can also use it to make long-term investment decisions. Journalists can use it to find the right buttons to push in an interview, and voters to become more politically informed.[3]

Chapter 2 describes the inspiration for the constraint-based framework. It is a mix of political science, political theory, intelligence analysis, and social psychology – as well as voodoo and trial and error.

Why read beyond the first part that describes the framework? It is one thing to hear the framework described; it is another to see it in action.

---

[3] By the way, if you have *that* relative at every family gathering, this is a perfect book to get them for the holidays!

It would be like telling a budding skier that skiing comes down to balance and reading the terrain. Sounds awesome. Now plunge yourself down a double black slope. I therefore take the framework for a spin, using recent geopolitical and political events as the racetrack. The book concludes by operationalizing the framework in a process that gives us the title: *Geopolitical Alpha*. Alpha, in the context of this book, refers to a return on an investment against a benchmark, in finance-speak, rather than the leader of a pack or someone spending too much time in a gym.

There are three things this book does *not* aim to do.

First, it cannot teach you about the world. To wield the constraint-based framework competently, you must know a lot. For instance, that the German president = Queen Elizabeth. If you don't know, speak to experts. That potential absence of a knowledge base is why I include a chapter on how to use expert judgment.

Second, this book will not tell you the future. This is a methods book. I offer up my framework because many investment professionals have found it useful. But I am not a prophet, nor will focusing on constraints make anyone else a prophet. This book is simply my attempt to share what has worked for me. There are other frameworks out there that work for other investment strategists.

Third, this book will not tell you what I think *should* happen.

I don't care. Not in this book, not in my field. I am a professional nihilist. And if you analyze politics for a living – especially if you have a fiduciary duty to your investors – you should be the same! To competently use my framework, meditate on your biases and bathe yourself in indifference. If you are not up to it, you should not be in the forecasting business, let alone finance.

Part One

SCAFFOLDING

Chapter 1

We're Not in Kansas Anymore

The world is undergoing paradigm shifts on multiple fronts: political, geopolitical, generational, and technological. What these changes are and their implications for the future are beyond the scope of this book. Instead, I present a framework that has helped me make sense of the world over the past decade. I hope it will prove helpful to navigate the paradigm shifts to come.

I use the term "framework" because it is less deterministic than a theory and not as prescriptive as a method. It is messy, full of contradictions, and much more art than science. It fits with forecasting geopolitics and politics because forecasting is similarly messy. There is nothing parsimonious about the constraint framework I present.

In the past 25 years, geopolitics and politics have switched from being tailwinds to the global economy and markets to being headwinds. For many in business and finance, it feels like a rug has been pulled out from under them. I know the feeling; I saw it happen to my family firsthand when I was eight years old.

3

Cut off from the Yellow Brick Road

In 1986, my 36-year-old dad joined General Export (Genex), the *crème de la crème* of Yugoslavia's corporate world. For my dad, it was the equivalent of landing a job at IBM in the 1950s-era United States.

Dad had *made* it. His life – and by extension my life – was going to be pure *kajmak*.[1] Step one: a four-year stint in the London office ("so you and your sister can learn English"). Steps two and beyond: an upgrade to our 505-square-foot "condo," then maybe a car with more than two cylinders, a house on the Dalmatian coast, a year at a foreign university … culminating in an entrée into the upper echelons of socialist society.[2]

What was so great about Genex? At the end of 1989, the conglomerate controlled 12–13% of Yugoslav foreign trade and nearly a third of Serbian trade with the rest of the world.[3]

What did it manufacture? What services did it export?

Nothing and none. What Genex "manufactured" was pure geopolitical *alpha*.

The Soviets did not believe in running a trade deficit. So, every year, the USSR would produce a list of goods that it was interested in exchanging for barter. Because Yugoslavia was a promiscuous communist country – it played both sides of the Cold War – a company like Genex would sell Yugoslav and foreign goods to the Soviets in exchange for what the USSR was willing to export (mainly commodities). Genex would then sell the Soviet commodities in the global market, pocketing a hefty profit in hard currency.

Unfortunately for Genex, but fortunately for almost everyone else on the planet, the Berlin Wall fell on November 9, 1989. Two years later, the Soviet Union disintegrated. The geopolitical gravy train ended and Genex's edge with it. The firm's entire corporate strategy was leveraged to the geopolitical status quo. In fact, my homeland was basically living off the Cold War. When the geopolitical winds shifted, the end was nigh for both Genex and Yugoslavia.

---

[1] Like "gravy," but cheese … and *much* worse for your cardiovascular system, if you can believe it.

[2] From which there is no sliding back into the proletariat!

[3] "Rise and Fall of Genex: To Have and Not to Have," *Transitions Online*, April 25, 1998.

Thanks to the combination of a massive geopolitical paradigm shift and epic mismanagement, Yugoslavia in the 1990s was worthy of a chapter in Jared Diamond's *Collapse*. The near-first-world life that my family built in Belgrade descended into hell in weeks.

The country's currency, the dinar, was devalued 18 times in seven years, with 22 zeros erased from its value.[4] The monthly rate of inflation peaked at 313,000,000% in January 1994 – at the time the second-highest recorded rate of inflation.[5] Between February 1992 and January 1994, the price level in Yugoslavia rose by a factor of 3.6×10^{22}.[6] I have an academic footnote to prove it.[7]

My hometown of Belgrade came fourth in the 1986 vote for the 1992 Summer Olympics. But by 1992, it had descended into an episode of *The Walking Dead*. In May 1994, my family left Belgrade with two suitcases. Destination? Amman, Jordan.[8]

Thankfully, my dad saw it coming, so he quit Genex a few years before the deluge. He got a job in a direct sales company selling cooking pots. He went from faux IBM to essentially Tupperware.

Many years later, whenever I fretted about my grades or school in general, he told me, "Relax. Why are you stressed? Do you know what Marx and Engels have to say about direct sales? Nothing. All my university exams and work experience are useless for the damn job I do today."

If you are a CIO of an institutional investment fund, a portfolio manager in an asset management firm, or a C-suit executive, you also face geopolitical paradigm shifts that will, at best, make your work more challenging. At worst, they will collapse your civilization like they collapsed my father's. In this book, my intention is to offer you a framework with which to prepare yourself for the former possibility. For the latter, I've got nothing.

---

[4] Steve H. Hanke, "The World's Greatest Unreported Hyperinflation," *Cato Institute*, May 7, 2007, https://www.cato.org/publications/commentary/worlds-greatest-unreported-hyperinflation.

[5] Only behind the Hungarian record from 1945–1946, until – to my somewhat perverted disappointment – Zimbabwe beat out both countries in 2008.

[6] What does that even *mean*!?

[7] Pavle Petrović, et al., "The Yugoslav Hyperinflation of 1992–1994: Causes, Dynamics, and Money Supply Process," *Journal of Comparative Economics*, July 31, 2013.

[8] Yes, you read that right. We ran away from war by going *to* the Middle East.

Investors are all in the same predicament that my dad faced at age 36. The training, certifications, and experience of the past 35 years have woefully underprepared the West's financial and corporate communities for the paradigm shifts that are occurring.

The End of the Goldilocks Era

Politics and geopolitics have shaped investment and business decisions for centuries. In his seminal work, *The House of Rothschild*, Niall Ferguson describes how the Rothschild family – well-versed in geopolitical analysis – became the richest and most powerful family of the nineteenth century. Adam Smith named the bible of economics *An Inquiry into the Nature and Causes of the Wealth of Nations*. Not people, not companies, nor corporations, but *nations*. And while John Maynard Keynes is most renowned for *The General Theory of Employment, Interest and Money*, he showed the range of his genius in *The Economic Consequences of the Peace* (1919), where he correctly forecasted the rise of the populist right, the Second World War, and even the European Union.[9]

For centuries, success in business and investing required the skills of both long division and sensitivity to political and geopolitical change. Yet today the curricula of most MBA programs – *and* the CFA curriculum in its *entirety* – ignore the latter.

For the better part of a quarter-century, between 1985 and 2008, election results in most large markets made little difference to the price of assets or company earnings.[10] For the vast majority of investors, politics and geopolitics were worthy of a one-hour meeting at the start of the year or, at most, a small expense on the research/consulting budget.

Politics and geopolitics still played a role, but in the background, working as a tailwind in the sails of investors. Events and paradigm shifts played out into the hands of the multinational corporate and

---

[9] John Maynard Keynes, *The Economic Consequences of the Peace* (New York: Harcourt, Brace, and Company, 1922).

[10] I would argue that the last election of any relevance to the financial markets in a major developed market economy in the 1980–2010 stretch was the 1981 French election, in which socialist François Mitterrand won an upset over the center-right Valéry Giscard d'Estaing. I am open to a debate on this question.

financial communities. As a result, a new crop of investors emerged out of this Goldilocks Era who were overquantified, while the gray-hairs and their cautionary tales receded into neglect.

Since the collapse of the Soviet Union, American hegemony meant that wars either occurred in investment-irrelevant countries – Rwanda, Armenia, Azerbaijan, Moldova, Somalia, Bosnia and Herzegovina, Lebanon, etc. – or were finished quickly, such as the First Gulf War or the 1999 North Atlantic Treaty Organization (NATO) air war against Serbia.

By the time I entered the financial industry in 2011, few if any of my clients and colleagues had ever had to make an investment decision based on geopolitics. The world's premier political risk consultancy – Eurasia Group – announced in its very name that its focus was on the fringes of the corporate world. By "Eurasia," Ian Bremmer – the firm's founder and a visionary in the field of political risk analysis – meant the frontier markets of the former Soviet Union. In 1998, Bremmer's vision was that political risk analysis would matter for "the Stans" and few others.

Why?

The answer lies in Mikhail Gorbachev's 1985 "Leningrad speech" – the one where he lambasted the Soviet leadership and launched *perestroika* ("restructuring").[11]

By the late 1970s, the Soviet Union was in the midst of a deep economic malaise. Living standards had stopped improving throughout the decade, and the Soviet Union fell far behind the US in terms of technological advancement. Gorbachev threw in the proverbial towel in the contest between a statist-planned economy and a free-market one.

By conceding the defeat of communism in the Soviet Union, Gorbachev undermined it in the rest of the world. The consequence of this ideological capitulation was the Third Wave of democratization and the adoption of free-market policies across the globe. Within a decade of Gorbachev's speech in Leningrad, free-market capitalism became "the only game in town," and within two decades, 90% of the global population was living in capitalism (Figure 1.1).

---

[11] Bruce Steinberg, "Reforming the Soviet Economy," *Fortune*, November 25, 1985, https://archive.fortune.com/magazines/fortune/fortune_archive/1985/11/25/66654/index.htm.

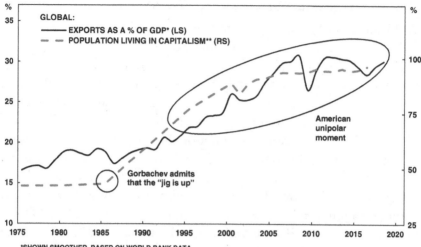

Figure 1.1 *Perestroika* launched the largest supply-side revolution.

The strategic victory of the US over the Soviet Union complemented the ideological victory of the free market. With the dissolution of the Soviet Union, the US became the sole superpower capable of enforcing norms of state behavior on a global scale.

The US did so by challenging revanchist regimes that were willing to challenge the new status quo, such as Saddam Hussein's Iraq and Slobodan Milošević's Yugoslavia/Serbia.[12] It also supported the new capitalist orthodoxy by encouraging international economic institutions to promote macroeconomic reforms, dubbed the "Washington Consensus."

The defeat of demand-side policies in the Thatcher–Reagan revolution of the 1980s occurred alongside the Soviet defeat. Profligate fiscal policy, politicized monetary policy, and an inflexible regulatory regime had saddled developed markets throughout the 1960s and 1970s, culminating in dramatic inflation that was only exacerbated by the "oil shock" following the 1973 Yom Kippur War.[13]

---

[12] As a child, I had the "pleasure" of living under both regimes!

[13] A popular misconception is that the 1973 oil shock caused the stagflationary environment of the 1970s. This is not true. Commodity prices ex-oil were already on the rise well before the Yom Kippur War, signifying that inflation was coming one way or another.

In response to this economic malaise, UK Prime Minister Margaret Thatcher instituted her neoliberal shock therapy. While the initial outcome was a recession and elevated unemployment, her policies eventually led to an economic recovery in the late 1980s. Thatcher's tax cuts, privatization, and deregulation became the pillars that would underpin the Washington Consensus – and *laissez-faire* economics in general – that countries would replicate across the developed and later the developing world.

One country that rejected the supply-side revolution was France. In 1981, in the midst of the rightward policy turn in the UK and the US, France elected socialist François Mitterrand. Mitterrand ran on an unabashedly left-wing policy package called the "110 Propositions for France." The package of reforms included price controls, reregulation of industries, minimum-wage increases, public works programs, a massive public-sector job program, nationalization of major industrial groups, reduction of the working time, a wealth tax, and an extension of trade union powers. Mitterrand's surprise electoral win led to two major runs on the franc in the year after his victory and the resulting near ignominy of contemplating aid from the International Monetary Fund (IMF).

In the battle of ideas, the Thatcher/Reagan supply-side – *laissez-faire* – won as decisive a victory over Mitterrand's demand-side – *dirigisme* – as one could imagine. Voters and policymakers across the developed world took note and adjusted behavior accordingly.[14]

By the mid-1980s, the twin tailwinds of *laissez-faire* economics and American geopolitical hegemony created the ultimate Goldilocks scenario for investors and C-suite executives alike.

On the geopolitical front, hegemonic stability – in the words of Charles Kindleberger – prevailed.[15] The George H.W. Bush and Bill

---

[14] The victory of supply-side policies in the early 1980s over demand-side was not absolute but rather contextual. With runaway inflation caused by excessive fiscal and monetary stimulus in the 1960s and 1970s, as well as capacity constraints built up through over-regulation, supply-side solutions were the correct suite of policies … for the era. This does not mean that adding more supply is always the correct solution. Policymakers have learned this the hard way in today's secular stagnation era, where arguably it is not supply, but rather demand, that is lacking.

[15] Charles Kindleberger, *The World in Depression* (Berkeley: University of California Press, 1975).

Clinton administrations enforced that stability when they engaged with the rest of the world.[16] The US foreign policy establishment, staffed mainly by foreign policy hawks who cut their teeth on the Cold War, favored an activist and engaged foreign policy, one that ensured the US would continue to provide the expensive global public goods necessary to grease the wheels of economic globalization.

The Tornado Hits Kansas: Geopolitical Paradigm Shifts

Hegemony sows the seeds for its own decline. America's policing freed up other countries to strengthen their own economic independence. By ushering in stability and globalization, the US allowed countries to set aside their challenges to US hegemony and focus on economic development. But those material gains ultimately allowed these challengers to get to the point where they could challenge the US for hegemony. This is the story of the rise and fall of empires; stability breeds collapse.[17]

In the wake of the Great Recession, a messy, multipolar world has replaced American hegemony.

Multipolarity is a concept from political science that describes a world in which no single entity (unipolarity) – and no two entities (bipolarity) – possess a preponderance of power with which to impose order in an otherwise anarchic system. Instead, multiple countries pursue their national interests independently, an arrangement that forecasters know – from history and political science theory – produces high geopolitical volatility (Figure 1.2).[18]

---

[16] To this end, the decision by Bush Sr. to intervene in Somalia at the end of his term was an attempt to bind the incoming Clinton administration – seen as isolationist and domestically focused – to an internationalist foreign policy. A debate was raging in Washington among policymakers and academics over whether the US should remain engaged. Many Cold War warriors worried that the US may abandon a leadership role as it did after its previous unipolar moment: in the 1920s when it decided to turn its back on the League of Nations. This proved to be a misplaced fear, as Clinton's eight years in power definitely reinforced America's hegemonic role.

[17] Robert Gilpin, *War and Change in World Politics* (Cambridge: Cambridge University Press, 1995).

[18] John Mearsheimer, *The Tragedy of Great Power Politics* (New York: W. W. Norton & Company, Inc., 2001).

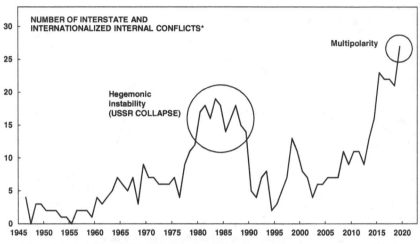

Figure 1.2   Multipolarity begets disequilibrium.

Think of the 2014 Russian annexation of Crimea or China's militarization of the South China Sea since 2012. Both would have been unthinkable during the post–Cold War era when the US was invested in maintaining a global balance of power.

Without a single hegemon to enforce rules of behavior, globalization reached its apex in the past decade. This sequence of events did not require the election of a populist to divine. Deglobalization is structural and thus difficult to reverse. For globalization to persist, one or more states need to bear the high cost of global public goods, such as defense of trade routes, global economic policy coordination, the role of a consumer of last resort, and the continued defense of rules of behavior, such as state sovereignty and noninterference. It was difficult to imagine any country filling this void in the 2010s, and it still is in the coming decade.

Finally, the Great Recession of 2008 and rising income inequality in the developed world undermined the *laissez-faire* economic system. While globalization lifted billions out of poverty across the world, it also expanded the global supply of labor, weighing on wages for the middle

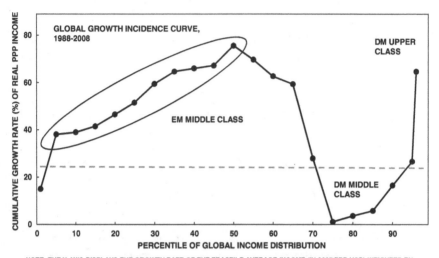

Figure 1.3   Developed world middle classes stagnated amid globalization.

class across the developed world (Figure 1.3).[19] Wage stagnation is not the only source of malaise in advanced economies, but it is a powerful one.

That said, the political reaction is not uniform across the developed world. In the US and the UK, the populist backlash was the strongest, in part because the two countries most enthusiastically adopted *laissez-faire* in the 1980s and 1990s. These policies left their middle classes the most exposed to the winds of change after 2008.

The end of American hegemony, multipolarity, the apex of globalization, and the erosion of *laissez-faire* economics defined the 2010s. These trends also changed the nature of political and geopolitical risk, which had been localized in emerging and frontier markets and thus largely relegated to commodity prices.

---

[19] Christoph Lakner and Branko Milanović, "Global Income Distribution: From the Fall of the Berlin Wall to the Great Recession," *The World Bank*, December 2013, http://documents.worldbank.org/curated/en/914431468162277879/pdf/WPS6719.pdf

The Nail in the Coffin: COVID-19

When historians look back at the 2020s, they will remark that the COVID-19 pandemic had a dramatic influence on the West, that it was the final nail in the coffin of the Washington Consensus and its mutation into something else ... a Buenos Aires Consensus, perhaps (more on this in Chapter 4).

I vehemently disagree. The pandemic has simply accelerated the paradigm shifts that began in the 2010s: geopolitical multipolarity, deglobalization, and the end of the Anglo-Saxon *laissez-faire* consensus.

When the COVID-19 market sell-off began in February 2020, I was in Miami at a gathering of top macro minds in the industry. Few there expected policymakers to react to the pandemic as dramatically as they did: with unlimited credit lines to businesses, massive quantitative easing (QE) programs, and even "helicopter money" – deficit-financed cash handouts to the public. The consensus at the event was that Speaker of the House, Democrat Nancy Pelosi, would play politics and delay the stimulus to hurt President Trump in the election. Policymakers would be "behind the curve."

The reason policymakers were not behind the curve when it came to monetary and fiscal stimulus had little to do with the nature of the crisis. They were already primed to respond with extraordinary measures by the paradigm shifts of the last decade, particularly shifts away from the Washington Consensus.

Fiscal prudence? Who cares? The US had already blown the budget deficit under the Trump administration at the top of the economic cycle. Why would anyone worry about the size of the stimulus when they were already past the point of no return?

The COVID-19 crisis may have accelerated the inevitable, but America's turn from a *laissez-faire* economy into a *dirigiste* one had begun much earlier. For investors and businesses, geopolitical analysis became more important than ever.

Getting the market right, from here on out, is as much about the politics and geopolitics as it is about valuations, interest rates, and earnings. And yet, our epistemic community of financial professionals has no real framework with which to navigate this new paradigm.

Welcome to Oz

The quarter-century between 1985 and 2010 was a great time to be an investor. With geopolitics and politics on autopilot, running a business or a portfolio became routine, iterative, and mathematical. The Goldilocks Era allowed for the professionalization of the investment industry in unprecedented ways.

But the same skill sets required to conduct financial analysis do not always lead to cogent political analysis. During a quarter-century of self-selection, hiring managers favored industry entrants who were comfortable with quantitative modeling and engineering. As a result, the 2010 financial industry – and the business world as a whole – found itself inadequately staffed for the paradigm shifts to come.

There are three particular weaknesses in the 2020 financial industry that make it poorly prepared for the geopolitical and political paradigm shifts afoot:

1. **The Quant Obsession:** By the late twentieth century, a PhD in political science could be awarded to a student who knew very little about actual politics. I realized that an academic career was not for me when I encountered a young professor at the University of Texas, only a few years my senior, who was supposedly a NATO expert. But he did not know the basic fundamentals of how that military alliance made its decisions. The young professor became a "doctor of politics" thanks to the mathematical elegance of his dissertation, not his depth of understanding of the subject matter. By the 1990s, economics had won the war of social sciences. It dominated academia to the point that political scientists no longer produced research that any policymaker, business person, or investor paid attention to.[20] Meanwhile, with politics and geopolitics stuck in their Goldilocks settings, the finance profession turned to modeling based on macroeconomic and market inputs, because exogenous factors like elections and wars largely ceased to matter for the most liquid markets.
2. **Self-selection:** As investment decisions became more and more akin to engineering problems, the industry stocked up with

---

[20] Don't believe me? Peruse the pages of the discipline's flagship academic journal, *International Organization*. Try to stay awake.

engineers. I call this hiring flood the ascendance of the "Newtonian Investor." The Newtonian Investor is a finance professional who bests his peers through a superior understanding and manipulation of mathematical rules. This investor is like the engineer who constructs the most durable bridge by best accommodating actual Newtonian laws of physics. But the laws of economics are not so fixed, and they are subject to change along with everything else when a paradigm shift occurs.

3. **Ideology:** The 1980s electoral defeats of demand-side policies gave *laissez-faire* mythical and religious staying power in the financial industry. Investment professionals became ideologically wedded to a set of policies. However, *laissez-faire* ideology often comes with a disdain for government and politics that denigrates the very act of political analysis. As such, a true investment professional came to be someone who read the *Wall Street Journal* and did not bother with the political world because it was beneath him or her to do so. But one's fiduciary responsibility as a custodian of others' assets demands a nonideological, nihilist approach to investing and politics.

Of course, investors should still use quant tools and approach their craft with scientific rigor. But the Goldilocks Era of geopolitical tailwinds allowed investors to become overly focused on macroeconomics and the markets. Investors would benefit from applying that same rigor to politics. There is an empirically driven framework for analyzing politics that does not involve cozying up to policymakers at cocktail parties.

Further, investors were generally blind to a major irony in their own ignorance of politics. It was politics and geopolitics that played a major role in the "Great Moderation," which saw inflation tamed and economic volatility dissipate. But instead of recognizing the important role of politics, the financial industry universally credited and praised a committee of academics setting interest rates. That such moderation was actually underpinned by globalization, massive expansion of the global labor supply, adherence to *laissez-faire* policies, and global stability enforced by American hegemony is a heretical view.[21]

In 2020, it is obvious to most of us in finance that *we're not in Kansas anymore*. Merely reading the Fed minutes, waiting for the ISM print,

---

[21] It is at this point that most PhDs in economics will stop reading this book.

and scanning the pages of *The Financial Times* is no longer enough to do one's job. Unlike academics, investors cannot be rigid. Our performance is measured in real time. As such, finance has picked up on the need to complement understanding of economics and the markets with political analysis. The demand for cutting-edge geopolitical forecasting is rising.

Beware of the Wizards

In this book, I present a macro, top-down, framework to analyzing politics. There are other approaches to geopolitical analysis. They all have their time and a place. The difference between my approach and that of the political risk industry is that I think that the constraint-based framework can be replicated by investors on their own time and with their own resources. In fact, there are components of the framework where an investor skilled in macro fundamentals and markets can best a seasoned political analyst.

Selling political analysis is not new. Henry Kissinger set up Kissinger Associates soon after he got out of government, in 1982. The aforementioned Eurasia Group has been around since 1998, and Stratfor, the shop where I began my career, opened its doors in 1996.

In my experience, the political consultancy business is dominated by advocates of the "intelligence model." The major consulting firms hire former technocrats and occasionally former policymakers. While such professionals can provide good context and background to most of the world's problems, they are rarely analysts or researchers. They do not personally get down in the trenches of research. Furthermore, the moment political consultancies hire them, they disconnect from the network of classified intelligence and analysis provided in their previous posts. They can also overemphasize their own expertise – say epidemiology in the case of the COVID-19 pandemic – and misunderstand how policymakers will react to such crises.

The intelligence model suffers from two additional weaknesses.

The first is the "statistical significance" problem. To make a reasonable forecast or net assessment, public (government) agencies rely on signals from electronic and human signals (data points), creating a mosaic of information and sources that approaches some reasonable level of statistical significance. This massive data collection is beyond the scope of any political consultancy, which, by definition, is a for-profit business that cannot rely on endless state resources to collect intelligence. Instead of a mosaic of intelligence, the investor quite often gets an over-the-hill technocrat looking to cash out. The technocrat sits across from them in the boardroom, at best giving them useful background on a particular issue, at worst regurgitating *Wall Street Journal* and *Financial Times* op-eds.

The second limitation of the intelligence model is that today's geopolitical and political risks are no longer only investment-relevant to frontier and emerging markets (EMs). An intelligence-led model of political analysis might work in a simple political system, where access to the key decision-makers is all that one needs. Similarly, getting (legal!) policy intelligence on a particular regulatory matter may indeed generate *alpha*. But in complex political systems of the most liquid markets – the US, China, the EU, India, and other large EM economies – access to power does not guarantee insight. This is because power is diffuse and checked by constitutional and bureaucratic constraints.

I will spend a lot more time on this question of "supply" of political analysis – and how to talk to "experts" – in Chapter 3. The political analysis community – including experts and political consultants – has enormous value for investors. The point of this book is not to get the reader to cancel their political research providers and put seasoned analysts out of business. But the only way to make an investment decision in 2020 is to think of political analysis as part of the investment process itself, not to merely outsource it to external research providers.

For now, the point is that investment-relevant political and geopolitical analysis is not something that should be outsourced to a former State Department deputy assistant secretary of European and Eurasian affairs.[22] Political and geopolitical analysis is not exogenous to the investment process. It is inherent to it.

This book provides investors – and anyone else interested in political and geopolitical forecasting – a framework with which to conduct their own analysis. Yes, you can and should still read newspapers and rely on outside political analysis (and I'd love to give you tips on which consultants to use), but my goal is to share a simple precept that has worked for

---

[22] Who probably struggles to understand his own mortgage statement.

me (most of the time). By using this framework, you can make better use of the outside advice and research and, hopefully, get better at separating the signal from the noise in the news.

But let's get something out of the way right at the top. The fact that I, Marko Papic, have a job in finance is conspicuous. None of my four university degrees are in finance, business, economics, or any mathematical science whatsoever. In my eight years studying at the university level, I spent maybe forty hours in total begrudgingly learning math.[23]

That I am now a chief strategist of an alternative asset management firm is a foreboding outcome for the world of finance. It means that we are no longer in the Goldilocks Era, where the twin tailwinds of American hegemony and globalization allowed investors to ignore the messy world of geopolitics.

Just because politics and geopolitics are not easy to quantify does not mean that they are (complete) voodoo. At the core of the constraint framework that I present in this book is my belief that investors should focus on the material world of constraints, rather than the ephemeral word of policymaker preferences and beliefs.

The world of constraints is measurable and quantifiable whereas the world of preferences is not. It is the constraints that are ultimately predictive, actionable, and *alpha*-generating.

This is because of the Maxim That Shall Forever Be Bolded: **Preferences are optional and subject to constraints, whereas constraints are neither optional nor subject to preferences**.

---

[23] To be clear, most of the math I studied in graduate school is not even considered math by my natural science friends. It is just statistics.

Chapter 2

The Constraint Framework: Three Pillars

I n the finance world of 2020, politics matter. However, investors still disagree whether political research gives them an edge in terms of performance. Some remain skeptical, while others merely use geopolitics as a retroactive excuse for poor performance.[1]

The criticism I've heard most often is that "political analysis is a *nice*-to-have, but it is not a *must*-have." It is marginal to the decision-making process — at best, a handy tool when an exogenous event threatens one's strategic decisions. Another way to put it is, "We will cry geopolitics when something blows up, just so we have a scapegoat to blame for our faulty predictions."

---

[1] The year 2019 was a tough one for factor investing in part because there is no way mathematically to reproduce the "Trump factor." If I had a dollar for every time I had to sit through an "apology tour" by a factor investor claiming, "My models worked, but then geopolitics scuttled them," I wouldn't have to publish a book to pay for Santa Monica day care!

My answer to this view is: "Don't bother. When something blows up, buy everything."

Other than the 1973 Yom Kippur War, few geopolitical events since the Second World War have been disastrous for the markets (Figure 2.1). That near-perfect predictability is why this book is not about Black Swans or hoarding gold for an impending apocalypse.[2] It is about incorporating geopolitical analysis into your investment process, as you would any other macro factor.

Geopolitics Is Not a "Nice-to-have"

In 2011, I arrived in Montreal to start a job at the world's oldest and most-respected independent investment research firm: BCA Research. Since 1949, BCA Research has offered its clients an interesting proposition: getting the macro forces in the economy right is more effective than trying to pick individual stocks. In the 1950s, this big-picture approach was novel. I owe a lot to the firm and my colleagues, as they taught me everything I know about macro investing.

The macro DNA behind BCA's success is credit cycle analysis. Getting the credit cycle right is still the backbone of macro investing. Most investors pay attention to it, and a few – like the $160 billion behemoth Bridgewater – have turned it into a moneymaking science.

When I joined BCA Research, I hardly knew what a credit cycle was. Nor did I understand much about finance or economics. I was hired for a simple reason: the CEO saw the geopolitical paradigm shifts coming and wanted someone on staff to speak on it.[3]

Several colleagues taught me the basics of macroeconomics and the markets. They probably contemplated self-immolation as I struggled

---

[2] Gold is a wrong hedge against an apocalypse anyway, as the COVID-19 pandemic has taught everyone. Gold is a great hedge for inflation, which may ultimately be the outcome of the pandemic. But when disaster strikes, investors want *cash*, which is why King Dollar appreciated at the height of the COVID-19 panic even though it is likely to be nuked in the subsequent orgy of fiscal and monetary stimulus.

[3] Besides having the foresight that geopolitics would matter, the CEO was also ... uhm ... cost-conscious and took a low-risk chance on a cheap 29-year-old kid!

EVENT	DATE	MAX S&P 500 DECLINE*	1 MONTH LATER	3 MONTHS LATER	6 MONTHS LATER	12 MONTHS LATER
Hungarian Revolution	1956-10-23	−10.78%	−2.12%	−2.71%	−1.02%	−11.69%
Cuban Missile Crisis	1962-10-16	−10.52%	5.40%	13.30%	21.13%	27.84%
Prague Spring	1968-01-05	−10.04%	−4.24%	−2.76%	5.18%	8.39%
Tet Offensive	1968-01-30	−9.31%	−3.80%	5.06%	5.22%	10.40%
Nixon Shock	1971-08-15	−9.38%	4.26%	−4.05%	9.76%	17.11%
Yom Kippur War/1st Oil Shock	1973-10-06	−16.10%	−4.45%	−9.97%	−15.33%	−43.25%
Iranian Revolution/2nd Oil Shock	1979-01-16	−6.32%	−0.79%	1.67%	3.30%	11.65%
Soviet Invasion of Afghanistan	1979-12-25	−10.86%	5.53%	−7.87%	8.42%	26.21%
Tiananmen Square Massacre	1989-06-04	−2.32%	−1.93%	8.67%	7.95%	12.87%
Berlin Wall Collapse	1989-11-09	−10.23%	3.60%	−0.88%	1.87%	−6.78%
Gulf War 1	1990-08-02	−19.92%	−8.23%	−11.28%	−2.40%	10.16%
Coup Against Gorbachev	1991-08-19	−3.62%	2.95%	0.78%	8.44%	11.08%
Dissolution of USSR	1991-12-26	−0.23%	2.63%	0.75%	−0.34%	8.63%
US Bombing of Chinese Embassy In Belgrade	1999-05-07	−5.97%	−0.78%	−3.32%	1.88%	6.52%
US-China P3 Incident	2001-04-01	−19.69%	9.14%	5.52%	−10.50%	−1.19%
9/11	2001-09-11	−23.10%	0.45%	4.05%	6.93%	−16.76%
George W Bush UN speech	2002-09-12	−25.11%	−5.82%	1.66%	−9.33%	14.85%
Operation Iraqi Freedom/Gulf War 2	2003-03-20	−8.96%	2.05%	13.71%	18.34%	26.73%
Madrid terrorist attack	2004-03-11	−6.36%	2.94%	2.68%	1.55%	8.43%
Ukraine Orange Revolution	2004-11-22	−1.72%	2.75%	0.59%	1.02%	7.13%
London terrorist attack	2005-07-07	−2.09%	2.38%	−0.16%	7.31%	5.64%
Lebanon War	2006-07-12	−6.88%	0.65%	8.28%	13.68%	22.97%
First North Korean nuclear test	2006-10-09	−0.24%	2.05%	4.55%	6.96%	15.88%
Lehman Collapse	2008-09-15	−44.68%	−23.88%	−27.18%	−36.57%	−11.74%
India Mumbai attacks	2008-11-26	−42.85%	−1.68%	−15.19%	2.55%	25.12%
EU Debt Crisis	2010-01-13	−7.87%	−6.12%	4.51%	−4.39%	12.05%
ROKS Cheonan sinking	2010-03-26	−10.54%	3.90%	−7.70%	−1.54%	12.62%
Senkaku rare earth embargo	2010-09-08	−2.56%	6.03%	11.78%	20.29%	7.92%
Arab Spring (Mubarak steps down in Egypt)	2011-02-11	−5.44%	−1.87%	0.97%	−11.78%	1.01%
NATO intervention Libya	2011-03-19	−5.78%	2.61%	−0.60%	−5.87%	10.21%
US Debt Ceiling 2011	2011-08-02	−19.25%	−6.39%	−1.29%	5.70%	8.85%
Netanyahu red line on Iran	2012-09-27	−7.67%	−2.43%	−2.01%	8.00%	16.90%
US Fiscal 2013	2013-01-01	−2.41%	6.10%	9.53%	13.24%	29.60%
Ghouta, Syria chemical attack	2013-08-21	−4.63%	4.09%	9.32%	11.78%	21.28%
Debt Ceiling and Government Shutdown	2013-10-01	−4.06%	3.93%	9.05%	11.24%	14.82%
China ADIZ East China Sea	2013-11-23	−3.48%	1.29%	1.74%	5.31%	14.34%
Crimean Invasion	2014-02-27	−2.08%	−0.28%	3.11%	7.86%	13.49%
Islamic State (Fall of Mosul)	2014-06-04	−0.95%	2.99%	3.62%	7.47%	8.71%
Greek bailout referendum	2015-07-05	−12.35%	1.11%	−4.32%	−2.89%	0.57%
Russian intervention into Syria	2015-09-30	−9.78%	8.30%	7.46%	7.50%	12.93%
Paris Terrorist Attacks	2015-11-13	−13.31%	−0.53%	−7.82%	1.17%	6.99%
North Korean Nuclear Test	2016-01-06	−13.31%	−5.54%	3.84%	5.50%	14.41%
BREXIT Referendum	2016-06-23	−5.60%	2.92%	2.43%	7.12%	15.38%
North Korean Nuclear Test	2016-09-09	−4.79%	1.22%	6.19%	11.14%	15.68%
Trump's election	2016-11-08	−2.31%	4.98%	7.25%	12.14%	21.26%
Hwasong-14 North Korean Test	2017-07-04	−1.78%	1.97%	4.48%	12.14%	11.70%
Trump declares trade war	2018-03-01	−10.13%	−1.37%	2.13%	8.36%	4.71%
US-China trade war escalates	2018-05-29	−3.47%	1.06%	8.33%	1.78%	3.46%
US sanctions on Iran	2019-05-02	−6.84%	−5.67%	0.50%	5.12%	−2.98%
US-China trade war escalates	2019-08-01	−6.12%	−0.92%	3.84%	9.21%	10.75%
Iran strikes Saudi refinery	2019-09-14	−4.57%	−1.37%	5.37%	−9.85%	
US strikes Iran's Soleimani	2020-01-03	−31.32%	0.43%	−23.07%	−3.24%	
Coronavirus Outbreak	2020-01-20	−32.80%	1.31%	−15.21%	−2.34%	
Russia-Saudi Oil Price War	2020-03-08	−33.92%	−7.48%	8.75%		
MEAN GAIN/LOSS		**−10.67%**	**0.06%**	**0.70%**	**3.51%**	**9.46%**
MEDIAN GAIN/LOSS		**−7.28%**	**1.09%**	**1.94%**	**5.31%**	**10.92%**

*RETURNS ARE CALCULATED BASED ON PEAK-TO-TROUGH MARKET DRAWDOWNS AROUND THE CITED EVENTS FOR A MAXIMUM WINDOW OF THREE MONTHS BEFORE AND AFTER EACH EVENT.
REPRINTED WITH PERMISSION BY BCA RESEARCH INC (WWW.BCARESEARCH.COM).

Figure 2.1 If something blows up, just close your eyes and buy.

with basic financial concepts such as valuation, discount rates, and log-ging into a Bloomberg terminal.[4]

I learned a ton in the first six months on the job. But perhaps the most eye-opening experience was navigating the firm's library and archives. Yes, even in 2011, BCA Research had "stacks" of academic journals and books, some going back over a century. I asked the librar-ian on staff to give me a collection of BCA Research reports, some of which were penned in the 1950s. I slowly moved through the decades. I felt like an archeologist exploring the records of some long-lost civi-lization. Each decade's core theme took shape while hints of impending paradigm shifts came into focus.

At the end of this apprenticeship period, I sat down with the mild-mannered gentleman who was my mentor. It was time to sell my strategy and earn my place at the shop.[5] I was full of ideas on how to incorporate geopolitical and political analysis into the firm's process, as I had just consumed hundreds of BCA reports (and thousands of Investopedia pages).[6] But the business plan my mentor proposed was a letdown:

> "Every time something blows up, you should whip up a piece. Focus on events – 'Black Swans' – that can upend the firm's major asset allo-cation views."

I was disappointed. I had a gut feeling that most Black Swan events were irrelevant, a feeling later confirmed by quantitative research. I had also come to BCA with a Jerry Maguire memo in hand. I had proof of

---

[4] I owe these patient mentors, especially David Abramson, Martin Barnes, Arthur Budaghyan, Francis Scotland, and Chen Zhao. They were my first mentors in the world of finance. Without Martin, in particular, I would not have a career in finance.

[5] BCA Research is on the "sell side" of finance. It *sells* its services to firms managing assets of their clients, the "buy side." Sell-side workers are the Willie Lomans of finance. They have to pen their research and then physically get on the road to sell it, like some clothing salesman from the 1940s. Those on the buy side are the patricians, as they have the resources to *buy* sell-side services. Sell side is not academia. Some education-minded institution wasn't going to fund me to write interesting research that nobody read. My job was to both produce investment-relevant research, then hit the road and sell it. Door-to-door.

[6] Shout-out to Investopedia.com!

concept: the 2010 Euro Area sovereign debt crisis proved that geopolitical analysis could get ahead of the narrative flow that moved markets and generated constant *alpha*.

Most critically, I had just spent the entire Quebec winter (all six months of it) reading through BCA Research's archives.[7] From my noneconomist perspective, the firm's own research confirmed that geopolitics were integral to most major economic trends of the past fifty years.

> "But that would mean that I am an appendage … extraneous to the firm's process."

My mentor's reply was wreathed in ice: "Well, yes. But this is how you get paid here. After all, your research has to sell. Otherwise … "

He left the rest unsaid, but I let my imagination fill in the blank.

To this day, I am glad I said no. I mean there I was, in finance. I'd leveled-up from a glorified blogger job and a dead end in academia. If this guy wanted me to write about Black Swan events, why rock the boat? That job is simple enough: take my colleagues' view of the markets as a *fait accompli* and apply some probability profile from the geopolitical risk smorgasbord.

Say the house is bullish on the economic growth outlook and recommends investors short duration (i.e., sell long-dated bonds). What do I add? Got it: a random pandemic is a threat to that view as US Treasuries will rally on risk to global growth. Done. Get paid, go home, watch the kids grow!

But BCA's own archives screamed for a more sophisticated approach. Each decade's research had an unspoken geopolitical anchor, even if the macroeconomic analysis danced around it:

1945–1961[8]: The immediate post–World War II years saw five recessions in quick succession. The Great Depression and the calamity it

---

[7] I've long thought that the firm's competitive advantage is that Montreal is frozen for half a year. It means that finance nerds have nothing better to do than go underground and produce world-class investment research.

[8] No, this span is not technically a decade, but its postwar sensibility binds it together.

birthed was still raw in policymakers' minds. As such, they relied on private-sector relevering to get out of each slowdown. Their over-reliance ushered in what BCA Research later called the "Debt Supercycle" (which, incidentally, didn't end until 2008).[9]

1960s: The 1960s saw a period of secular stagnation. Policymakers grew complacent as inflation failed to react to low unemployment, so they became emboldened to pursue fiscally profligate policies. Between the fiscal outlays of the Vietnam War and President Johnson's Great Society entitlement expansion, deficits soared outside of a recession for the first time since World War II. Sound familiar? In 2020, we are living in a 1960s rerun with the COVID-19 pandemic putting the last nail in the coffin of the Washington Consensus and one of its central tenets: prudent fiscal policy.

1970s: The 1960s' demand-driven policies led to the stagflation of the 1970s. Yes, the 1973 oil crisis contributed to inflation – the rare example of a significant geopolitical Black Swan – but political and geopolitical decisions made in the 1960s had the most lasting impact on 1970s economic woes. An oil price spike in a deflationary context would have had only a fleeting impact.

1980s: The disaster of demand-driven policies in the 1970s caused a political revolution at the end of the decade. As noted in Chapter 1, Reagan and Thatcher gave supply-side policies a chance, while the academics running central banks had a popular political mandate to crush inflation.

1990s: The geopolitical paradigm shift of the Soviet Union's collapse complemented the 1980s' supply-side political revolution. These events combined in the 1990s to form the twin tailwinds of global-ization and American hegemony. Together, they tamed inflation and altered the political power balance between labor and capital. Great Moderation ensued.

---

[9] Tony Boeckh, head of BCA Research, coined the term "Debt Supercycle" in the early 1970s. It is at the core of the firm's DNA. Intriguingly, the supercycle is a deeply political concept, but nobody really tried – in the 70-year history of the firm – to frame it as such. John Mauldin, "The End Game of the Debt Supercycle," *Forbes,* June 19, 2010.

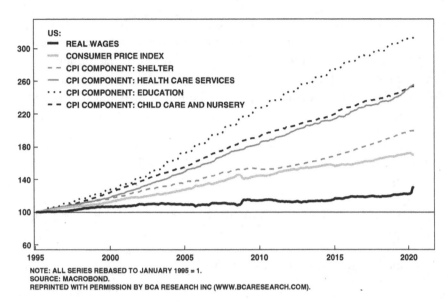

Figure 2.2   Middle-class goods inflation.

2000s: The party did not end with the 2001 recession. Policymakers reinflated the Debt Supercycle with gusto, due in part to fear that the 9/11 terrorist attack would stifle consumer confidence. But growing income inequality – which, yes, was present before QE, to the surprise of many investors waking up to inequality only today – led to a massive levering-up by the household sector. Households overspent to keep up with the Joneses and maintain their present buying habits, given the ever-higher cost of middle-class goods (Figure 2.2).[10]

From the above decade trends, I concluded that treating politics and geopolitics as an externality to markets made no sense. The only way to incorporate geopolitics was to recognize its pervasive influence. It affects

---

[10] Adam Seth Levine, et al., "Expenditure Cascades," *SSRN,* September 13, 2010, https://papers.ssrn.com/sol3/papers.cfm?abstract_id=1690612.

everything it touches – from market forces down to the individuals who analyze them. I realized it was important to investigate my investment views – to assess whether the political assumptions that underpinned them were correct. Seeing this entanglement and determined to untangle it, I declined to pursue the proposed business plan and suggested an alternative:

> "We are going to make market calls and forecasts based not on what policymakers want to do, but on what they *must* do given their material reality."

My mentor flashed me a look like he was the Cheshire cat gazing at Alice from his tree perch.

> "And how do you intend to do all that?"

The First Pillar: Materialist Dialectic

Niccolò Machiavelli's *The Prince* is the foundational text of modern political theory. Machiavelli posits that governance is an interplay between *Fortuna* – fate and all things beyond the control of the Prince – and *Virtù* – the Prince's ability to navigate *Fortuna*.

Fortuna is a river "which, when enraged, inundates the lowlands, tears down trees and buildings, and washes out the land on one bank to deposit it on the other. Everyone flees before it, everyone yields to its assaults without being able to offer it any resistance." But not all is lost. If the Prince prepares for the flood and makes "provisions during periods of calm by erecting levees and dikes to channel the rising waters when they come," the Prince can restrain *Fortuna*.[11]

Machiavelli saw *Fortuna* and *Virtù* as equals: " ... since our free will must not be denied, I estimate that even if fortune is the arbiter of half our actions, she still allows us to control the other half ... "[12] The Prince has the free will to manipulate fate.

The Prince is not a treatise on forecasting politics and geopolitics. It is a manual for the acquisition and preservation of power. In its original

---

[11] Niccolò Machiavelli, *The Prince* (New York: Bantam, 1981), 84. A totally hypothetical example of this interplay between *Fortuna* and *Virtù* would be preparing for a pandemic by having a team on staff that exclusively plans for such a calamity.
[12] Ibid.

context, *Virtù* is important, but I never understood how to incorporate it into a forecast. Furthermore, while following global events in my early career, I realized that policymakers of even the highest quality succumb to the material reality of *Fortuna*. On the other extreme, even the most *in*competent policymakers are ultimately pushed to do the right thing by the constraints of the market, economics, and politics. As economist Herb Stein said, "if something cannot go on forever it will stop."[13]

Machiavelli's analogy of *Fortuna* and the river has stayed with me since I first read the book 25 years ago. If forecasters could predict the flow of that river, would they not be more than halfway to predicting policymaker behavior?

Imagine a giant holding a large mug of ale over a hill. The giant tips the mug over and allows the beer to gush down the decline. If I know the hill, I can predict the ale's course: it will follow the path of least resistance, because it is influenced by the material reality of the hill's terrain.

As Machiavelli claims, the flow of *Fortuna* may be equally as important as the Prince's *Virtù* in determining the final outcome. But the forecast must start with its course – *Fortuna*, rather than the policymaker's reaction to it; the reaction is a derivative of the flood. And the only way to know the flood is to know the terrain.

And Karl Marx knows the terrain.

Marx – as an analyst, not a prophet of doom – is an essential teacher in analyzing the terrain upon which *Fortuna* flows, and his analysis is the first pillar of the constraint method.[14]

In *Das Kapital*, Marx explains how the post–Industrial Revolution world works. He takes a complicated and somewhat nebulous

---

[13] Full quotation: "I recently came to a remarkable conclusion which I commend to you and that is that if something cannot go on forever it will stop." Joint Economic Committee, *A Symposium on the 40th Anniversary of the Joint Economic Committee: Hearings Before the Joint Economic Committee, Congress of the United States: Ninety-Ninth Congress: First Session: January 16 and 17, 1986* (Washington: US Government Printing Office, 1986), 262.

[14] I recognize the irony in referencing Karl Marx in a book about political forecasting. His most well-known prediction – that capitalism would collapse in a proletariat revolution that would eradicate all private property – may be one of the world's greatest "swing-and-a-miss" forecasts ever. Not only was it spectacularly wrong – Beijing, Hanoi, and Moscow all embrace capitalism today – but it led to a century of misguided policies. While Marx cannot have foreseen how the conflict of economic systems would end, his theory of capitalism and materialist dialectic still enabled him to predict a conflict of economic systems. From the mid-nineteenth century, he predicted the chief political dynamic of the twentieth century. This successful prediction illustrates his importance as a thinker in the social sciences.

concept – capitalism – and breaks it into its most basic components. Using this materialist approach, he rarely delves into the qualitative world of ideas. In the first nine chapters of *Das Kapital*, Marx decomposes capitalism into its constituent, *material*, elements. He focuses on the material realities that underpin capitalism: price, money, labor, means of production. After exposing the system's inconsistencies, Marx concludes with a forecast: a crisis is coming.

While the conclusions of *Das Kapital* are interesting, and much ink (and blood) has been spilled debating them, it is the engine that powers these conclusions that is most relevant to the constraint framework. This engine is "dialectical materialism."

Marx's dialectic stands in opposition to the Hegelian dialectic, which many know as the oft-quoted adage "thesis, antithesis, synthesis." Both dialectics are an attempt to make sense of human history and how society defines "truth." For Hegel, the starting point of the search for truth is human thought: ideas. Like Machiavelli, Hegel sees the human actor as possessing agency. According to Hegel's worldview, the ideological preferences of both the powerful few and the masses influence history.

Or, as John Keynes famously said,

> The ideas of economists and political philosophers, both when they are right and when they are wrong, are more powerful than is commonly understood. Indeed, the world is ruled by little else. Practical men, who believe themselves to be quite exempt from any intellectual influences, are usually slaves of some defunct economist.[15]

The innovation of Marx's *Das Kapital* is that it rejects the notion that ideas dictate human history. Marx and his collaborator, Friedrich Engels, posited that the material world, not ideas, must be the starting point of analysis.

What makes the materialist dialectic a *dialectic*? In Marxist thought, the material world – the society's modes of production – is the concrete foundation upon which all thought, norms, values, and institutions ultimately rest.[16]

---

[15] John Maynard Keynes, *The General Theory of Employment* (Youcanprint, 2017), 239.

[16] "Modes of production" determine how societies are organized, given technological capacity, to interact with the material reality around them.

According to Marx, the European feudal system was not a product of human thought but of the means of production available in the Middle Ages. All nonmaterial aspects of feudal society – the culture – reinforced the hegemony of thought created in service of material modes of production. Ideas serve materials. If Hegel's theory says the idea egg came before the chicken, Marx's counters that it was the material chicken that got the idea egg rolling.

For the sake of not putting anyone to sleep, I kept this discussion brief, and it is woefully inadequate to meet the standards of graduate courses in political theory.[17] The bottom line is that the material dialectic is the main pillar of the constraint framework. The framework's starting point of analysis is the *material* world, not the world of *ideas*. Material conditions create human reality. Thought systems (philosophy, religion, political parties, etc.) develop around this material condition and are therefore a derivative of it. People cannot "think" or "prefer" their way out of material constraints.

As for Marx's forecast of a proletariat revolution, he was not entirely wrong. His description of capitalism remains cogent, particularly the tension between what employees earn, what employers accumulate in profit, and what that does to the aggregate demand level in an economy. Some – including myself – would say that the world is at an unsustainable extreme between the share of the economy going to corporate profits and the share going to labor (Figure 2.3).

By focusing on the material world, Marx forecasted the tumult that would dominate the twentieth century. Yes, he got the final outcome wrong, and he was hopelessly prescriptive, but he correctly surveyed that the status quo of the nineteenth century – in which laborers had scant protections or political power – would not last.

Second Pillar: Diagnosticity of Constraints

For investors used to quantification, a focus on the material world should be welcome. Constraints are observable and therefore empirical.

To find these constraints, investors should observe as much as possible about the real world, right? Wrong. Not all observable data is created

---

[17] To my former professors and academic professionals all over the world, I apologize.

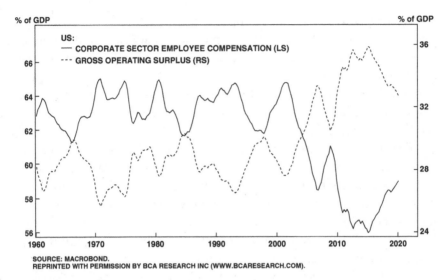

Figure 2.3 What is unsustainable will stop.

equal, and more information often does not produce superior forecasting results. The quality of the data matters more than its quantity, especially in circumstances where a complete data set is impossible to obtain.

Richards J. Heuer, Jr., author of the CIA methodology manual *Psychology of Intelligence Analysis,* spent his life improving the judgment of intelligence analysts: "Judgement is what analysts use to fill gaps in their knowledge. It entails going beyond the available information and is the principal means of coping with uncertainty." Heuer goes on, "While the optimal goal of intelligence collection is complete knowledge, this goal is seldom reached in practice."[18]

Heuer dealt with political analysis and forecasting throughout his nearly 50-year tenure at the CIA. He thrived on uncertainty, paucity of high-quality information, and concept-driven (as opposed to

---

[18] Richards J. Heuer, *Psychology of Intelligence Analysis* (Washington: The Central Intelligence Agency, 2015), 31–32, https://www.cia.gov/library/center-for-the-study-of-intelligence/csi-publications/books-and-monographs/psychology-of-intelligence-analysis/PsychofIntelNew.pdf.

data-driven) analysis. His career in intelligence forced him to rely on the fuzzy, the qualitative, and the soft, as opposed to the clear, the quantitative, and the hard, data. Instead of shying away from these challenges – or trying to fit the qualitative square peg into a quantitative round hole – Heuer developed a systematic approach to intelligence analysis.

While Heuer does not address material constraints directly, he rightly asserts that the intelligence analyst rarely has complete information.

Given this limitation, Heuer introduces two concepts for all political and geopolitical analysts to keep in mind. First, having more information does not necessarily help one's forecast. More information sometimes only contributes to a higher level of conviction, not necessarily forecast accuracy.

Second, the quality of data is what matters. And the key determinant of quality is diagnosticity, the second pillar of the constraint framework. Diagnosticity is "the extent to which any item of evidence helps the analyst determine the relative likelihood of alternative hypotheses."[19] To illustrate, Heuer uses the example of a patient with a fever. Because a body temperature in excess of 38 °C is consistent with so many reasons to be ill, it has limited diagnostic value.

Paucity of information and diagnosticity of intelligence are critical concepts for investors and those without access to government-funded intelligence agencies. Without access to near-unlimited budgets, satellite imagery, mass surveillance, and a web of assets across the world, agency outsiders always operate with limited information. As such, it is all the more important to understand what information is actually diagnostic.

Diagnosticity helps analysts eliminate unlikely, or competing, hypotheses (a process known as "competing hypotheses analysis"). A nondiagnostic variable is one that does not help eliminate any of the hypotheses.

Preferences are not diagnostic variables because they are optional; the policymaker chooses whether to act on them. Such variables are nondiagnostic because it is impossible to eliminate hypotheses based on a variable that may not affect the outcome at all. In contrast, constraints are

---

[19] Ibid., 45.

the gatekeepers that determine whether preferences affect the outcome. Constraints have high diagnosticity because preference-based outcomes are subject to them.

Diagnosticity in Practice

Take President Donald Trump's preference to have the Affordable Care Act, "Obamacare," repealed. In 2017, analysts could easily conclude from Trump's statements that he had a strong preference on this topic. However, it was impossible to gauge his sincerity, commitment, and pain threshold for pursuing such a policy. Furthermore, Obamacare is an entitlement, and American policymakers' track record of repealing entitlements is poor.

Trump's preference to repeal Obamacare was subject to two material constraints: the risk of losing popular support, and congressional math. In 2017, President Trump did have a majority in the Senate, allowing him to repeal Obamacare.[20] However, it was not a large majority. Due to the political risk to moderate Republican senators – and likely Senator John McCain's animosity toward Trump – the repeal bill failed 49–51 in the Senate.

By the summer of 2017, Republicans had tried to kill Obamacare 70 times since its 2010 implementation. And yet, when all the stars aligned – when they held both chambers of Congress and the presidency – they fell short.

Given the preference of President Trump and the Republican party to eliminate Obamacare, this outcome surprised most investors. They miscalculated because they overestimated the importance of preference and failed to consider its low diagnosticity. As Heuer posits, it is extremely difficult to eliminate a hypothesis based solely on policymaker preferences.

Material constraints, on the other hand, have high levels of diagnosticity. They are diagnostic because they are not optional. President Trump could change his mind about Obamacare, but he could not

---

[20] Trump's majority allowed him to use the budget reconciliation process, which disallows a filibuster in the Senate.

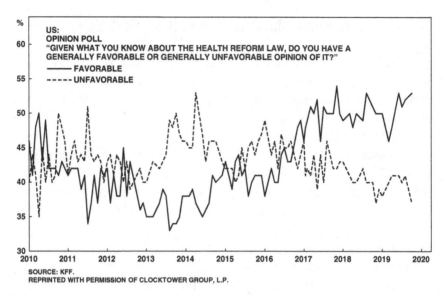

SOURCE: KFF.
REPRINTED WITH PERMISSION OF CLOCKTOWER GROUP, L.P.

Figure 2.4   Popular support for Obamacare became a material constraint.

wish away moderate Republicans Susan Collins, Lisa Murkowski, and
John McCain in 2017. Furthermore, Obamacare became popular in
mid-2017, right when Republicans finally held the political capital to
extinguish it. By the time the GOP circled back to thinking about
healthcare in 2018, the midterms were upon them, and support for
Obamacare surged (Figure 2.4).

Diagnosticity is the second pillar of the constraint framework.
Beyond diagnosticity, Heuer also briefly mentions the third pillar. Later
in his book, he points out that "when observing another's behavior,
people are too inclined to infer that the behavior was caused by broad
personal qualities or dispositions of the other person and to expect
that these same inherent qualities will determine the actor's behavior
under other circumstances. Not enough weight is assigned to external
circumstances that may have influenced the other person's choice of
behavior."[21]

---

[21] Heuer, *Psychology*, 135.

Third Pillar: The Person versus the Situation

The third pillar supporting the constraint framework is the idea of the fundamental attribution error, borrowed from the field of social psychology. I draw the most from *The Person and the Situation* by social psychologists Lee Ross and Richard E. Nisbett.[22]

While Ross and Nisbett drew many insights from social psychology experiments, the one that best illustrates the material constraint framework is their discussion of the Princeton Seminary experiment. In the early 1970s, behavioral scientists John Darley and Daniel Batson constructed a fascinating experiment.[23] The setting of the study was the Princeton Theological Seminary. The subjects? Students studying to become ordained priests.

Seminary students were asked to deliver a sermon in a classroom across campus, where senior members of the faculty would evaluate their performance. They were given some time to prepare the speech. At the conclusion of their preparation, a third of the students were told that they were very late, that their superiors were already waiting on them, and should leave immediately; a third that they were going to be late if they did not leave soon; while a third were told that there was no rush and that they could proceed to the meeting at a leisurely pace.

Darley and Batson designed the experiment to test how time pressure influences behavior. On the way to the sermon, each student encountered a victim in need of help (an associate of the experimenters). Out of the time-stressed cohort of students, only 10% stopped to aid the victim. Out of the cohort that was in a hurry, but not really stressed, 45% offered to help. Finally, 63% of the students in no rush stopped to see if they could help.

Remember: the test subjects are young men looking to dedicate themselves to the service of God and thus presumably predisposed to being good Samaritans. The character and preferences of these students were as conducive to offering aid to a stranger as one was going to get on a college campus.

---

[22] Lee Ross and Richard E. Nisbett, *The Person and the Situation* (London: Pinter & Martin, 2011).

[23] J.M. Darley and C.D. Batson, "From Jerusalem to Jericho: A Study of Situational and Dispositional Variables in Helping Behavior," *Journal of Personality and Social Psychology* 27, no. 1 (1973): 100–108.

What was the topic of the sermon they were asked to perform? The story of the Good Samaritan (Luke 10:29–37 in the New Testament). They had specifically been primed to "do the right thing."

Ross and Nisbett offer other examples and research to prove their overall point that time and time again, the situation is a better indicator of the outcome than the person. The context in which an individual finds himself has more influence on his behavior than his character, background, religion, upbringing, etc.

Given their career paths, the majority of test subjects probably had a preference to help a fellow human in need. And being a Good Samaritan was top of mind, as they had just prepared a sermon on it! However, when subjected to the material constraint of time, their preferences succumbed to the constraint.

Using this and other examples, Ross and Nisbett introduce the concept of the "fundamental attribution error," a mistake analysts make when they attribute real-world outcomes to characteristics, personality, and moods of individual actors. The individual's psychological profile is given primacy over the external context; the person takes precedence over the situation.

Political analysis provides fertile ground for the fundamental attribution error. The news media is partly to blame because it personalizes events and tells human rather than situational stories. To be fair, stories don't sell well without individual actors in them. Journalists are giving their readers what they want, which is a reaffirmation that people matter and that human agency can triumph over the determinism of the situation. Geopolitical analysts have no such excuse.

Fundamental Attribution Error in Practice

Examples of this attribution error abound in both the media and what passes for geopolitical analysis:

"Kim Jong-un Is a Wild Card": In early 2013, the US media obsessed over the potential danger of a confrontation between North Korea and the US. The young leader of North Korea, Kim Jong-un, was an unknown entity at the time, and analysts feared Kim would do something dramatic to cement his leadership. Rhetoric from Pyongyang certainly fueled the uncertainty and backed up the personality-driven analysis.

However, focus on the situation would have revealed considerable constraints on Kim Jong-un's preferences, whatever they were. In 2013, North Korea had limited ballistic missile technology. Its conventional military capability – aside from artillery – was (and remains) paltry. An equally restrictive constraint came from its nominal ally, Beijing. China opposed – and continues to oppose – any confrontation with South Korea. Such a confrontation would give the US an excuse to establish a greater military presence in Northeast Asia. In addition, the geography and demographics of South Korea make it extremely difficult for North and South Korea to engage in a limited military conflict, as any engagement would expand rapidly. This landscape prevents an escalation in tensions to the point of war. Because Seoul is effectively unprotected from North Korean conventional artillery, South Korea would have to preemptively attack the North at the first sign of conflict, likely ensuring the end of the Kim dynasty. The same logic – and constraints – held during the showdown between President Trump and Kim in 2017. While the media breathlessly accused President Trump of playing with fire, the White House bluff ultimately worked precisely because Kim Jong-un was never holding a strong hand, and his preferences – and even potential irrationality – ultimately could not overcome his constraints

"Israeli Hawks Want to Bomb Iran": Since at least 2011, a unilateral Israeli strike against Iran has been one of the greatest tail risks to the markets. In early 2012, the media ramped up Israeli rhetoric and oil markets exhibited a considerable risk premium. Investors accepted the rhetoric at face value. They assumed Israeli Prime Minister Benjamin Netanyahu headed a "hawkish" government that considered Iran's nuclear program an existential threat. Observers of the situation made a big deal of the personalities of both Prime Minister Netanyahu and Iranian President Mahmoud Ahmadinejad. The former would never allow a regional rival to threaten Israel's existence; the latter was trying to hasten the return of the Mahdi by causing an apocalypse.[24]

---

[24] Serious publications, such as the *New York Times* and the *Wall Street Journal,* pandered to the apocalypse narrative by alluding to Ahmadinejad's references to the Mahdi – the "Twelfth Imam" – even though they likely knew that the Iranian president is constrained on military, religious, and foreign policy matters by the supreme leader. But the "Armageddon and the Mahdi" headline is far more likely to get clicks than "Highly Constrained President Threatens Apocalypse While Senior Shia Clerics Laugh at Him." Masood Farivar, "Armageddon and the Mahdi," *The Wall Street Journal*, March 16, 2007, https://www.wsj.com/articles/SB117401728182739204.

Investors placed too great an emphasis on the rhetoric coming from both sides, ignoring constraints. Israel did not (and does not) possess a strategic air strike force (i.e., bombers), the lack of which would complicate a military strike against Iran. And the Arab Spring unleashed forces that would ultimately coalesce into the Syrian Civil War and the rise of the Islamic State. Both were much more proximate threats to Israel than an illogical Iranian nuclear strike. The final constraint formed when Iran became an implied nuclear power once its underground – and impenetrable to Israel – Fordow facility went fully operational in December 2011. At that point, an Israeli attack would have all but guaranteed that Tehran would eventually produce a nuclear device.

"Vladimir Putin Wants to Recreate the Soviet Union": The most obvious example of the fundamental attribution error in the last decade is the prevalent analysis of President Vladimir Putin's strategic thinking. The flawed argument is that since coming to power in 1999, the Russian president, enamored of the Soviet Union, has wanted to recreate the communist empire. Evidence for this argument: the 2008 invasion of Georgia, the 2014 annexation of Crimea, and the subsequent interference in domestic affairs of former Soviet states. The Baltic states must, by this analysis, "be next."[25]

Even if Putin's nostalgia motivated Moscow's policies, Russia faces numerous constraints. Its symbiotic economic relationship with Europe is a major constraint. While most pundits see Moscow dominating that relationship, it is actually Berlin that has Russia by the ... pipelines. With at least 80% of Russian natural gas exports headed for the EU in 2019 – and about half of that going to Germany alone – it would be economic suicide to turn off the tap to Europe.[26]

Another subtler constraint is the state of Russia's military. While much improved since the 1990s, Russia's military does not have the

---

[25] Ted Galen Carpenter, "Are the Baltic States Next?" *The National Interest*, March 24, 2014, https://nationalinterest.org/commentary/are-the-baltic-states-next-10103.

[26] Which is why Russia was so quick to sign a massive natural gas export deal with China – on Beijing's terms – following the annexation of Crimea in 2014. President Putin is smart enough to know that he needed an alternative market to Europe. Unfortunately, the natural gas infrastructure required to export a meaningful amount of natural gas to China will take over a decade to construct. So, for the time being, Europe and Russia are in an uncomfortable economic symbiosis. This issue is extremely crucial and yet vastly misunderstood. For all of President Putin's supposed strategic genius, he allowed his country to become addicted to Europe's natural gas demand.

capability necessary for the massive power projection required to maintain the borders of a vast empire. It barely had the capacity to intervene in Donbas, where Ukrainian troops held Moscow's mercenaries and unofficial volunteers in check. Ukraine has one of the least equipped and motivated militaries in Europe.

The third pillar of the constraint framework is the recognition and avoidance of fundamental attribution error. To forecast politics and geopolitics, analysts have to avoid the fundamental attribution error and focus on the situation, not the person.

The Three Pillars of the Constraint Framework

The constraint framework has helped me make sense of the world, though it is not scientific or quantitative. It is a blend of the materialist dialectic, intelligence methodology, and social psychology. And yes, some voodoo to boot!

My framework's uncertain origins and inexact nature are caveats that I will repeat often, lest someone accuse me of claiming to have invented sliced bread.

And yet, the framework did not come out of thin air. There is a philosophical (materialist dialectic), practical (hypothesis testing), and empirical (social psychology) method in the madness.

To review, the three pillars of the constraint framework are the following:

- **The Materialist Dialectic:** The starting point for geopolitical analysis must always be rooted in the material world. While that reality does not necessarily need the Marxist emphasis on "means of production," it does need to be empirical. Investors should always seek the immutable reality – the constraints – in a situation. While the economic constraint is not always the most important one, some other tangible barrier will be.
- **Diagnosticity:** Given paucity of information and poor data quality, investors (and others seeking to forecast politics) must focus on the data that is concrete and iterative, rather than ephemeral data locked away in someone's brain. To properly falsify a hypothesis,

investors should focus on data that has a high level of diagnosticity. Policymakers' preferences are not diagnostic. Constraints are.

- **Social Psychology:** Social psychology makes a strong case that the context and the situation, not the person, drive human behavior. Therefore, investors and others seeking geopolitical insights should focus on constraints over preferences.

These three pillars support the Maxim That Shall Forever Be Bolded:

Preferences are optional and subject to constraints, whereas constraints are neither optional nor subject to preferences.

And Now for Some Math

No book about forecasting can be without math. Math is often overused in both finance and academia, and I don't want to fall into the trap of giving my framework a false veneer of science. But I feel obliged to have some formal logic in the book if only to preserve my street cred among fellow forecasters. As such, I have decided to load one section of the book with enough mathematics to fill the required quota.[27] In this section, I "formalize" the above maxim.[28]

In the *preference model*, the probability that a decision-maker, X, will accomplish the preferred outcome, Y, is expressed as $P(Y)$. The equation to solve for $P(Y)$ is

$$P(Y) = p_X(y)\, p_y(Y)$$

where $p_X(y)$ is the probability that X prefers action y, and $p_y(Y)$ is the probability that taking action y leads to X's preferred outcome, Y. I call

---

[27] Why the general disdain for formal theory? My main point of contention is that using formal, mathematical expression produces knowledge without the particulars of context. This is fine if you're trying to publish a paper in academia. But if the point is to actually apply the knowledge to real-world problems, it could lead to massive errors.

[28] Two additional reasons for the mathematical "flex" here: first, formulae are cool. Second, my dear friend Dan Green, a professor of physics at UC San Diego, offered to help with this model (by "help," I mean Dan wrote the whole thing).

this the "preference model" because the decision-maker can control her actions, y, but the action is not the direct, sole variable in determining the outcome. The decision-maker's preferences also determine the outcome by influencing her actions.

The *constraint model* introduces variables that constrain the decision-maker from taking action y. These constraining variables are Z. For instance, constraint Z – rain – will likely influence an athlete's preferred action, y – to go out for a run. Citing a single preference, $p_X(y)$, associated with an action, $p_y(Y)$, ignores the hidden variables, like weather, that influence the athlete's decision.

A world in which the preference model holds true would look like this: a toddler prefers to take the action of buying a pony. The outcome – $P(Y)$? She buys a pony, because material constraints – driving age, parental permission, access to forms of revolving credit, literacy, etc. – don't inhibit her preference from affecting the outcome.

To account for the role of material constraints in the decision-making process – and the final outcome – the second model is

$$P(Y) = \sum_Z p_X(y|Z)\, p_y(Y|Z) p_Z(Z).$$

In the above model, I add up all the possible constraints (Z), while $p_Z(Z)$ is the probability that Z is true and affects the outcome, Y. The other factors remain the same but now depend on these additional constraints.

What is the point here? The additional factors – the constraints – mean that these two equations are not the same, and thus predict different outcomes.

If I think of the preference model as just adding up the preferences alongside each constraint – $p_X(y) = \sum_Z p_X(y|Z)$ and $p_y(Y) = \sum_Z p_y(Y|Z)$ – then the probabilities, $P(Y)$, in the two models would only produce the same outcome when the constraints are irrelevant ($Z = 0$, or the total constraints have zero influence on decision-making).

I'll illustrate this with an example.

I am a big fan of basketball – the National Basketball Association (NBA), to be exact. I've watched it since I was a kid. Back in the day, players used to take swings at one another all the time. Shaquille O'Neal once almost decapitated Charles Barkley. Chris Childs landed a combo on the great Black Mamba (Kobe Bryant). And those were just the 1990s. If you go even further back in history – the 1980s in particular – the brawls were vicious.[29]

There are lot of situations in the NBA today where it appears that a fight is about to break out. And yet, there are few fights. Instead, there are a lot of "hold-me-back" incidents that only appear aggressive. In fact, they involve two players jawing aggressively but patiently waiting for their teammates and referees to separate them so that they can yell at each other from a safe distance.

How do the two models account for this?

- **Preference model:** In the preference model, y is X's preference to be in a fight, and Y is the final outcome of an actual fight breaking out. From the frequent posturing, it seems that players really want to fight. So $p_X(y) = 1$. However, the final outcome is rarely a fight. So $P(Y) \approx 1$. This disparity between preference and outcome suggests that it is difficult to go from wanting to fight to actually fighting, so $p_y(Y)$ must be close to zero ($p_y(Y) \approx 0$) for the model to balance. But there is no place in this model to explain *why* $p_y(Y)$ should be 0, when preferring to fight should lead to a fight outcome (think 1980s basketball). The preference model has no means to describe the teammates who stop the fight, despite X's strong preference to fight.

- **Constraints model:** The preference for a basketball player, X, to fight is actually related to whether or not his teammates are there to stop him. If $Z = 0$ (there are no teammates nearby), then $p_X(y|Z = 0) = 0$, which means that the bold professional has no desire to fight. If there are teammates present ($Z = 1$), then $p_X(y|Z = 1) = 1$. However, through years of dedicated observation, I know that when teammates are nearby, there is no fight because they "hold X back," so that $p_Y(Y|Z = 1) \approx 0$. When teammates are not near – $p_Y(Y|Z = 0) = 1$ – there *can* be a fight if that is X's *preference*. Unlike the

---

[29] Compare 2020 to the 1980s, where fighting was not just common but encouraged. Rumpel Stiltsky, "1984 NBA finals game 4: Celtics at Lakers (McHale Clotheslines Rambis) Larry Goes to Hollywood Pt. 2, *YouTube*, 1:02, July 22, 2017, https://www.youtube.com/watch?v=qmIA61zEcfg.

preference model, the constraints model enables me to accurately describe what is happening on the court:

$$P(Y) = \sum_{Z=0,1} p_X(\gamma|Z)\, p_y(Y|Z); = p_X(\gamma|Z=0)p_y(Y|Z=0)$$

$$+ p_X(\gamma|Z=1)p_y(Y|Z=1); = 0.$$

In the NBA, there are no fights because the preference to fight is anticorrelated with the probability of a fight outcome. Or, to put it bluntly, "*Hold me back* …"[30]

Wait, does that sound familiar? It should! There are "hold-me-back" moments *all the time* in the world of geopolitics. Leaders taunt each other and signal aggressive policy when they may have no intention to follow through on their threats. Sometimes the intention of the rhetoric is the exact opposite – to get one's opponent back to the negotiating table.

I have shown that merely knowing the preference of an actor is insufficient to determine his ultimate action. **Preferences are optional and subject to constraints, whereas constraints are neither optional nor subject to preferences**. As such, investors need to study the constraints, not the preferences.[31]

Where Do We Go from Here?

As illustrated in the above equation, the constraint framework leaves room for the potential relevance of decision-makers' preferences, including their ideologies, upbringing, culture, and religion. The framework allows for respect of those who delve deep into policymakers' minds. A good biography or a history book is always the first place to start when contemplating a forecast. In order to practice the constraint framework, one has to *know things*.[32]

---

[30] If you think this is a waste of time, you have not perused the pages of modern political science academic journals.

[31] Professor Dan Green and I will now clear our calendars for the Nobel Prize ceremony. You're welcome.

[32] And to know things, one has to read a lot. Other forms of information consumption seldom have the same staying power as information gleaned from books. So read, people!

But the constraints put on this knowledge create much-needed objective distance between the analyst's and actors' personalities. The problem with personality-based (preference-based) analysis is that it is difficult to be empirical about preferences. It is also difficult to operationalize them. I can read *The Art of the Deal* once to download the supposed crucial insights on President Trump's preferences, behavior, and temperament. But with this task complete, it is difficult to accurately apply that information to forecast whether he will bomb Iran, pass corporate tax cuts, repeal Obamacare, impose tariffs on China, invade Canada, or let COVID-19 burn through the population like a fever. It is difficult because he may have a preference to do all of those, but I do not know the limiting factor that determines what he can and cannot do: material constraints.

As such, a preference-based analysis is the starting point of a forecast. But it is something that analysts need do only once or twice per public figure. It is not an iterative process.

In the next section of this book, I delve into the actual constraints. I define five material constraints that are particularly crucial in forecasting events: *political, economic, financial, geopolitical,* and *constitutional/legal,* as well as the constraint wild cards: *terrorists* and *pandemics.* I arranged them in order from the most salient to the least. Each chapter discusses how each constraint operates, how to measure it, how it helped make an important forecast in the past, and how it may help investors do so in the future.

But before I embark on the analysis of material constraints, in Chapter 3 I survey the "other" framework of forecasting geopolitical events – the one that focuses on intelligence, or insights.

Chapter 3

The Wizards of Oz

"The most valuable commodity I know of is information."
— Gordon Gekko, *Wall Street*

When it comes to politics and geopolitics, most investors take the Gordon Gekko view to heart. To gain an edge, the consensus is that having insight from the ground is critical. Or, even better, to "know somebody." Because politics, from this viewpoint, is unpredictable, the only path to clarity is through intelligence-gathering. Billions are exchanged each year for fireside chats with wise old men (almost always men, almost always old – but rarely as wise as advertised) who spin a good yarn from their experiences or extensive Rolodex.

You have met these storytellers. You know them by the speed with which they name-drop from your very first encounter. Like peacocks spreading their plumage to attract a female, they try to lure the frameworkless victim with a verbal display of their networking prowess.[1] My rule of thumb is that if a political consultant drops three names before drawing his next breath, I daydream about basketball for the rest of the conversation.

While this chapter lays out the limitations to the intelligence model, I do not think that political analysis is truly possible without it. A top-down, macro approach to geopolitics is clearly my wheelhouse. But without actual understanding of issues at hand, the investor cannot ascertain what constraints are real and actionable.

I personally consume plenty of on-the-ground research from political consultants. And I have a fairly strong opinion on which ones are actionable and value-added and which ones are not. I therefore do not intend to discourage anyone from seeking the advice of consultants. This chapter simply cautions investors where the usual failings of the method are.

I aim to give the investor and businessperson the tools to break open the black box of consultants, to be able to differentiate a stellar one from a substandard one. The constraint framework allows investors to critically evaluate and wield the insights from experts and frees them from blind dependence.

Overview: Intelligence and Investing

There are five limitations of intelligence-based political and geopolitical forecasting. Investors should definitely rely on outside expertise, but they need to do so knowing what to expect.

First, no matter what the person across your conference table tells you, he is not in actual intelligence. If he was a government agent, or if he shared information gained through top-secret clearance, he would be committing a felony. Consultants' lack of an official "intelligence agency" label does not mean that their information is incorrect or useless – far from it! But they do not have access to the volume of insights that intelligence agencies peruse. Intelligence-driven analysis is therefore

---

[1] Also known as: bullshit.

not statistically significant. Very few do a good job.[2] Intelligence agents working for the government have nearly unlimited funds to throw at a question, whereas your consultants don't. People "in the know" are not the same as public intelligence organizations with unfettered access to a mosaic of human, electronic, and signals intelligence.[3]

The way to differentiate a good political consultant from the bad is humility. Not necessarily humility of behavior, but intellectual humility – doubt – built into his or her analysis. If your consultant gives you a high-conviction view without a scenario analysis or a probability decision tree, he is not humble and is likely overstating his statistically insignificant insights. The real experts will present you with either a set of scenarios and data points to monitor or a decision tree with probabilities.[4]

Second, political and geopolitical paradigm shifts discussed in Chapter 1 have moved the market-relevant questions from the frontiers of economic development to the core. In a small, underdeveloped economy, it may make sense to base a business decision on a single piece of insight from the president's second cousin, once removed. But in the complex political and economic systems of the most liquid markets – the G20 economies – the constraints to power are too great. In fact, a highly connected person in such an economy may mislead the investor; the contact's view can waylay the insight-reliant investor by reinforcing his pre-existing bias – giving him artificially high conviction in an inaccurate forecast.

Third, intelligence-driven forecasting can lead to "funneling," the oversimplification and mass dissemination of information from a handful, or even just one, source. People with actionable intelligence rarely share it with just one end user. The incentives are stacked for them to scale their insights and provide them to as many investors as possible. This dynamic means the investor loses, whether or not the forecast is sound.

---

[2] Only one, in my opinion. Read the acknowledgements to see which one.

[3] To quote the movie *Wall Street* again, Gekko chides his young understudy, Bud Fox, with a question: "I guess your dad's not a union representative of that company, huh?" The consultants you hired may have great intelligence from Malaysia, but they may be stumped if you asked them for help with Indonesia.

[4] In the last third of this book, I present what such analysis should look like.

If the information is correct, the market will have already priced some of the gains ahead of the event. If it is wrong – as insights "from the ground" in Argentina were in 2019 – the result of funneling is carnage in the markets.

Fourth, policymakers and the markets enjoy a reflexive relationship, meaning policymakers often use the markets to force action from their political counterparts. For an investor to get helpful intelligence during Greece's and Germany's game of chicken in the Euro Area crisis, speaking to their policymakers was useless. Each side wanted the global public's favor, and so employed bravado to shape the narrative. Policymakers often "talk their own book." As such, what they say – and what political consultants report they said in smoke-filled rooms – should be taken with a large grain of salt. If you wouldn't believe a CEO's spin on a quarterly call, why would you believe a government official?

Finally, are you sure you are speaking with an expert? The person you are watching on CNBC or Bloomberg – are you sure he knows what he is talking about? Are you sure he is not some 27-year-old kid who quit his PhD program and is making $42,000 in an intellectual sweatshop?

I start with that last problem first.

The False Expert

I spent six years in Austin, and Bayless Parsley is one of the best things that happened to me while in the Republic of Texas. He and I worked together at Stratfor, the geopolitical intelligence firm that gave me my first job. While I manned the Europe desk, he was in charge of the North Africa desk.

I use the term "desk" liberally. Stratfor already had a sub-Saharan analyst,[5] so when it was time to promote Bayless for his hard work and enthusiasm, he was given the North Africa assignment. Bayless is intelligent, perceptive, and has otherworldly interpersonal skills – of no little value in the intelligence-driven approach. But he was a beginner on North Africa.

---

[5] The excellent Mark Schroeder of Geomarkets Africa today.

Then, on December 17, 2010, Mohamed Bouazizi set himself on fire. This act of desperation set off the Arab Spring … and unleashed Bayless Parsley upon the world.[6] Within months, he was quoted by all the major news agencies on the enveloping crisis. For example: here,[7] and here,[8] and also here[9] and here.[10]

Three years later in December 2014, Bayless was interviewed on the radio about some renewed fighting in Libya. His insight:

> The reduction in Libyan oil production since 2011 has clearly been quite stark. I mean, depending on who you believe today, they are producing between 180,000 and 350,000 barrels per day. It was 1.6 million before and they were exporting 1.3 million barrels per day of that amount. So, that is where all the cash comes in, in Libya. It will be harder to distribute wealth if you are the central government and keep people in line. But that is sort of a moot point as there is no central government in Libya today. It is a completely chaotic state of affairs. Whoever has the guns at any particular time in any particular region are the de facto rulers of that country.[11]

The response was a low-calorie blurb recounting what everyone, by 2014, already knew about Libya. The content is not what is intriguing,

---

[6] Sorry, man. It's true.

[7] Lisa Mullins, "Who Is Leading Libya's Revolution," *Public Radio International,* March 21, 2011, https://www.pri.org/stories/2011-03-21/who-leading-libyas-revolution.

[8] Stratfor, "Dispatch: Egyptian Elections in Doubt as Violence Returns to Tahrir," *YouTube,* 4:21, November 21, 2011, https://www.youtube.com/watch?v=bI7Mv0vlaK8&app=desktop.

[9] Mark Gollom, "Analysis: Post-Gadhafi Libya Faces Enormous Challenges," *CBC News,* August 23, 2011, https://www.cbc.ca/amp/1.1022710.

[10] Uri Friedman, "The Libyan Stalemate Suggested by Google Earth," *Yahoo! News,* July 15, 2011, https://news.yahoo.com/amphtml/libyan-stalemate-suggested-google-earth-215655107.html.

[11] I could not find this interview anywhere on the internet, but Bayless supplied me with the audio and the correspondence from the media organization that conducted it. It is legit. It was played on the radio to millions of listeners worldwide. If you want a copy, feel free to reach out! Bayless Parsley, audio recording heard by author, December 20, 2014.

however. Talking heads say less substantial things on TV and radio all the time.[12]

What *is* intriguing is that by December 2014, Bayless had moved on from Stratfor and was head of sales for a software company specializing in stadium and sporting venues. Yep, the closest my friend had come to North Africa that year was ordering couscous. Given his affinity for a good practical joke, he thought it would be hilarious to do the radio interview on Libya when a news organization approached him with the opportunity – even though he had taken a break from the world of geopolitical consulting.

Surely this must have been some college radio station! Some freckle-faced youth failed to conduct due diligence on my friend Bayless, i.e., to check whether his consultancy, "Papić & Parsley," was a front for a phone prank of global proportions.[13]

False. It was the British Broadcasting Corporation (BBC) World Service.

My buddy Bayless pranked the BBC World Service radio broadcast that goes out to hundreds of millions of people.[14]

Now look, it is not my intention to embarrass the fine folks at the BBC. We all make mistakes. Nonetheless, this entire episode serves as a cautionary tale to consumers of world news: beware the talking heads.

---

[12] For the most part, this is not always the fault of "talking heads." I've said vacuous stuff on TV myself, many times. The problem is the format: you try fitting earth-shattering information into 30 seconds of airtime.

[13] Do you notice my last name in this fake consultancy? Bayless thought that this would be doubly hilarious if he dragged me into the joke. I did not. I prayed that none of my BCA Research colleagues found out. Thanks to Bayless, I was moonlighting as a partner in a geopolitical consultancy that gives vacuous comments on the Libyan unrest.

[14] Here I briefly hand the proverbial pen to Bayless, who wanted to share something with my readers: "I also think it's relevant to point out that BBC called me out of the blue, clearly because I was in some database. I didn't go out of my way to trick anyone. I just answered the phone, was asked if I wanted to do an interview on the Libyan oil industry and said, "Absolutely!" Only lie I told was about Papić & Parsley. That needs to stay in the book because it makes you an accomplice of the scheme and is therefore hilarious. As to why I did not say anything to BBC, well, a simple LinkedIn search would have shown that I worked in an entirely different industry."

Journalists have deadlines. Often the person on TV is not their first choice or the best choice but the most readily available. I have also been in virtual green rooms the moment before the "hit," where the anchor and the interviewee exchange pleasantries. In that time crunch, I was specifically directed to "be punchy." One anchor told me, "we are going to have images and video of Greeks burning shit up and just generally going nuts, so try to match the visuals with your views."[15]

The media sells narratives, yet another reason to consume with caution. If the narrative in place is that COVID-19 will kill millions around the world, the one epidemiologist who disagrees will probably not see his quotes lead the story. They will either be edited out or buried in paragraph 14 as a dissenting voice. Journalists know how to craft and push narratives. Not because of some conspiracy cooked up in a French château, but because narratives generate "clicks," the all-important currency they depend on now that Google and Facebook have starved them for ad revenue.

Journalists' treatment of the less marketable perspectives creates a problematic trend in who gets the most airtime. Research shows that the more an expert appears in the media, the less likely he is to produce accurate forecasts. Philip Tetlock, the expert on experts, stresses in his book *Expert Political Judgment* that analysts who frequently appear in the news media are especially bad at forecasting. Because the media's endgame is entertainment, clicks, and eyeballs, it wants its experts to be pithy, glib, extreme, and highly confident.

In addition to sharing Tetlock's disregard for forecasters in news media, I also disdain those who publish opinion pieces. A geopolitical forecaster with a weekly column is unlikely to claim that the world is not ending or the crisis everyone is freaking out about is irrelevant.

A special circle of forecasting hell is reserved for analysts who go beyond opinion pieces to write policy recommendations. The moment

---

[15] The name of the network? Look … I don't want to get sued, but I think you can figure it out.

forecasters pollute their analysis with policy prescription, I no longer take their forecasts seriously.

The Connected Player

In the summer of 2019, odds of a "no-deal Brexit" implied by the political betting markets reached a peak of 45%, essentially too close to call (Figure 3.1). A no-deal Brexit meant the UK would have crashed out of the EU without a deal to regulate its economic relationship with the bloc. It would have unsettled the financial markets and raised tariffs on goods and services.

I spoke with several contacts throughout that summer. Those that quoted sources close to Number 10 Downing Street were bearish. There were two personality-based theories, neither of which helped predict the eventual outcome. The first: that the new prime minister,

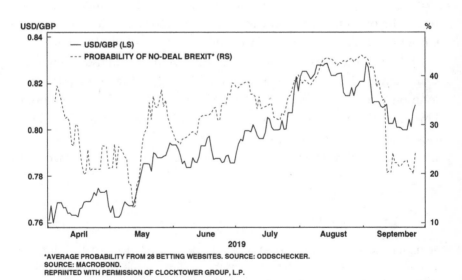

Figure 3.1   No-deal Brexit hysteria.

Boris Johnson, was incompetent and could lose sight of the big picture as a result. The second theory was that his Rasputin-like advisor, Dominic Cummings, was hoping for a hard break from the EU. On September 5, Boris Johnson confirmed the bearish thesis by stating he'd "rather be dead in a ditch" than ask for a Brexit delay from the EU.[16]

In retrospect, Johnson's comment was a buy signal. The market soon sniffed out that his bravado was focused elsewhere, that he was "selling his own book."

There were multiple benefits for Johnson to signal hawkishness across different audiences. These benefits remained, regardless of whether his later actions matched his hawkish preference. Because of that disconnect between stated preference and action, his statements were nondiagnostic, as were the whispered concerns of his cabinet members to journalists and intelligence-gathering geopolitical analysts.

At the time, Boris Johnson was playing a *three*-level game, which is highly unusual and challenging.[17] He was not only trying to navigate trade negotiations with an external adversary – the EU – and a domestic one – the opposition. He was also trying to resolve an internal conflict within the Tory party between the "deal" and "no-deal" Brexiters.

UK commentators criticized Johnson and his advisor Dominic Cummings for their mess of a party line. I disagreed with the criticism. Johnson had a very difficult problem. Figure 3.2 shows that, throughout June, the Brexit Party commanded the lead in national polls. This lead was a political earthquake, given that the party was founded merely six months earlier. If it had gained anywhere near 20% of the national

---

[16] "Boris Johnson: 'I'd Rather Be Dead in a Ditch' Than Ask for a Brexit Delay," *BBC News*, 0:33, September 5, 2019, https://www.bbc.com/news/av/uk-politics-49601128/boris-johnson-i-d-rather-be-dead-in-a-ditch-than-ask-for-brexit-delay.

[17] Robert Putnam, "Diplomacy and Domestic Politics: The Logic of Two-level Games," *International Organization* 42, no. 3 (Summer 1988): 427–460.

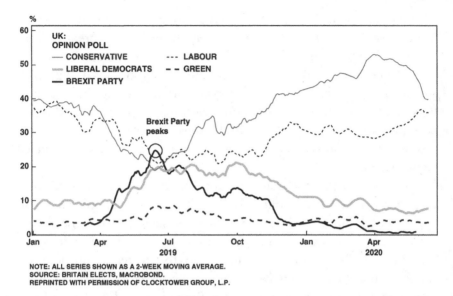

NOTE: ALL SERIES SHOWN AS A 2-WEEK MOVING AVERAGE.
SOURCE: BRITAIN ELECTS, MACROBOND.
REPRINTED WITH PERMISSION OF CLOCKTOWER GROUP, L.P.

Figure 3.2   The real reason for Johnson's bravado.

vote, it would have wounded the Tories, considering the UK has a first-past-the-post electoral system.[18]

Through most of the modern history of the UK, Tories have benefited from the first-past-the-post model. It is on the left of the ideological spectrum that votes traditionally split. The Labour Party, Liberal Democrats, Scottish National Party, Green Party, and Welsh Plaid Cymru all compete for voters who are, to varying degrees, left of center. The rise of the Brexit Party to about 20% of the vote would have been a tectonic shock to the Tories, who never really had to deal with competition.[19]

---

[18] In the UK, each electoral district conducts an election. The winner of that election, regardless of the level of support, heads to Westminster. There is no threshold for the winner and no second round. As such, a conservative-leaning district where the Tories and the Brexit Party split 60% of the votes equally among them could still go to a left-leaning candidate who won the plurality of the vote. Because of this quirk, parties are wary of bleeding support to smaller parties.

[19] The similarly populist and right-leaning UK Independence Party's best performance was 12.6% of the vote in 2015.

Johnson's rhetoric – and the on-the-ground intelligence reporting his seriousness – makes more sense when put into the context of Tory internal politics. If the Brexit Party's peak at 26% of the vote represents the height of no-deal Brexit support, it means Johnson was dealing with an electorate in which over a quarter supported severing EU relations. Pursuing a policy that *only* 26% of the electorate supported would have been folly and extremely dangerous. However, it made sense in the context of a pre-election campaign, which is what Johnson probably realized he was facing.

Seen within the constraints of Tory politics, Johnson's game theorizing was rational; he politically benefitted from disclosing hawkish preferences. Johnson's bravado and aggressive stance made sense within the context of trying to bring the minority of no-deal Brexit voters back into the Tory fold. Once they were Tory voters again, Johnson could capture a majority in Westminster. This scenario is precisely what happened, as Johnson monopolized the Brexit issue and the Brexit Party received just 2% of the vote and no Members of Parliament (MPs) at the December 12, 2019, election.

The episode represents a successful real-world application of the constraint forecasting method, so I will return to it in Chapter 4. Here it merely illustrates how policymakers get stuff done. Johnson's bravado gave him more maneuverability to pass a Brexit deal – where his predecessor, Theresa May, failed.[20] To get a deal on Brexit done, Johnson had to convince Britain and the world that he was a hard-liner.

In June, this potential internal party strategy was not the intelligence I was getting out of London. I spoke to several connected hedge fund

---

[20] The original Brexit deal failed because Prime Minister Theresa May failed to win a majority in the 2017 election. *That* was the original sin of the Brexit crisis in 2019. May was forced into a coalition with Northern Ireland's Democratic Unionist Party (DUP), which was highly sensitive to any arrangement that cleaved Northern Ireland away from the UK ("unionist" being the operative word). Because of the objections of the DUP and their 10 parliamentarians (representing a whopping 2% of UK's total population), May changed her original backstop proposal – which had applied only to Northern Ireland. Her new one encompassed the entire UK in the EU customs union for the duration of the post-Brexit transition period. Once Johnson got his majority, he immediately threw the DUP and Northern Ireland under the proverbial bus.

managers who assured me that they spoke with people either close to, or actually inside, 10 Downing Street. Their message was one of doom and gloom. Most connected political consultants had the same message: the odds of no-deal Brexit were rising substantially.

It is not that I did not believe the intelligence, sourced from people close to the new Johnson administration. I truly did accept that members of his administration saw no-deal Brexit as a rising probability. I just ignored what they thought was going to happen. They were prisoners of their own material reality and unaware of how powerless they were to change it. Given Johnson's constraints, the increase in no-deal probability was something to bet against. While the Tory Party had a new leader with potentially radical preferences, the material constraints against a no-deal Brexit remained – chiefly, that such an outcome had neither popular support nor a commanding majority in Westminster.

Johnson's bravado was nondiagnostic. It was a brilliant piece of election campaigning, but it had nothing to do with his ultimate decision on a Brexit deal.

The Funnel

How sure are you that the information gathered "on the ground" gives you all sides of the story? Are you sure that it is unique? That you are the only one in possession of it?

The hottest emerging market investment theme of 2019 was Argentina. President Mauricio Macri ushered in a period of painful structural reforms when he came to power in the October 25, 2015, election. Investors and journalists love 180-degree turnaround stories, but they rarely happen in politics. Macri was such a story.

Every investor knows the old adage that at the turn of the twentieth century, Argentina was "one of the 10 richest countries in the world." In 1950, Argentina's gross domestic product (GDP) *per capita* was eight times greater than that of South Korea (Figure 3.3).

After half a century of economic mismanagement and unfulfilled promises, Macri's 2015 victory signaled a turnaround. He pushed

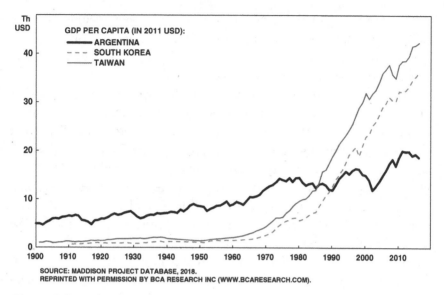

SOURCE: MADDISON PROJECT DATABASE, 2018.
REPRINTED WITH PERMISSION BY BCA RESEARCH INC (WWW.BCARESEARCH.COM).

Figure 3.3   Argentina – promise vs. performance.

through "shock therapy" that dragged on growth and drained his political capital. There was a reduction of government subsidies, elimination
of export restrictions on agriculture, foreign exchange controls, and
import restrictions, tax reform, and pension reform.

But the global growth context in which these reforms took place
was not kind to his administration. In 2017, China implemented its
own structural reforms that saw policymakers favor deleveraging and
macroprudential regulation over stimulus. These reforms hurt commodity exporters, highly leveraged to global growth because China contributes more to the annual incremental change in global growth than the
US, EU, and Japan combined. Given that emerging markets are highly
leveraged to global growth, they experienced tough times in 2018 and
2019.

Despite these contextual constraints on Macri's new policies, the
buzz in financial circles throughout 2019 was that he would win another
term and double down on reforms. Most investors I spoke with had

close contacts with Macri administration insiders, and some even had access to his campaign team. The insight from the Argentine Treasury was positive, and most political consultancies confirmed the story. One consultancy (that will forever remain nameless) was particularly confident.

I am no expert on Argentina. As such, I have no comparable story akin to the Brexit debacle to hang my hat on. I therefore did not offer a counternarrative to my clients – a failure on my part. I did, however, point out two things:

First, the Argentine "misery index" spiked in 2019 – a lot (Figure 3.4). On its own, the misery index is a crude measure of political risk. Its main flaw is that some countries chronically experience high levels of unemployment and inflation. It does not necessarily mean that they are on the precipice of collapse. But paired with Argentina's recent lackluster results from politically driven reforms, it was conceivable that the public would turn against Macri. And yet, the "intel from the ground" suggested otherwise.

Second, I noticed a strange lack of public opinion polling around March. Bloomberg caught the same thing and published a piece in June titled, "Argentina Election More Uncertain as Pollsters Go Dark."[21] Nobody I talked to in the financial industry thought this was strange. They claimed that they had polls from inside the country, either conducted by the Macri campaign itself or by big data aggregators – ones that correctly predicted Jair Bolsonaro's 2018 win in neighboring Brazil. I was uncomfortable with their responses because campaign polls almost always overstate how well the candidate is doing. And the aggregators conducted noniterative, one-off polls, which are usually a poor replacement for iterative polls conducted by agencies that have covered elections in a particular country periodically.

---

[21] Patrick Gillespie, "Argentina Election More Uncertain as Pollsters Go Dark," *Bloomberg*, June 26, 2019, https://www.bloomberg.com/news/articles/2019-06-26/argentina-s-election-faces-more-uncertainty-as-pollsters-go-dark.

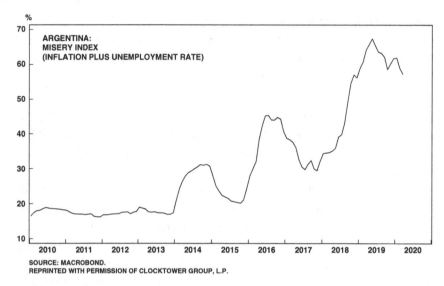

Figure 3.4   Misery index doesn't lie.

There was something fishy going on in Argentina, and nobody seemed to care. When the primary elections showed that Alberto Fernández and Cristina Fernández de Kirchner smoked Macri by 16%, markets vomited. In the week following the primary election, the Argentine peso fell 26% against the dollar while the main equity market index fell more than 43%. A major hedge fund lost $1 billion in August alone.

Over the next several months, I read hedge fund client notes that tried to explain why they took such a massive gamble on Macri. Most blamed a polling Black Swan event. Nobody admitted they had fallen victim to insiders who sold them a great story laced with potent "insights from the ground."

In the Argentina narrative, the financial community got swept up in a story of dashing supply-side reforms that would overcome obstacles to vanquish populist, demand-driven policies and save the beautiful market in distress, to live happily ever after. Ideological bias played a role in this carnage. I was nearly thrown out of a large hedge fund's office because the CIO thought I was a socialist who did not believe in reforms when I dared cast doubt on Macri's prospects.[22]

The already-primed financial community needed little convincing from consultants with contacts on the ground. This intelligence-buying is where "funneling" comes in. Though I do not have hard evidence, my working theory is that the majority of Argentina bulls were talking to the same handful of people, both in Buenos Aires and abroad. Every time we spoke, hedge fund managers assured me they had Argentina covered.

I enjoy a nice Argentine steak with a glass of Malbec in Buenos Aires as much as the next guy. And even beyond good food, gathering information from the ground is a worthwhile errand – when done with an objective eye. But one did not have to be in Buenos Aires to see that Argentina's misery index was flashing red.

The Insider

Throughout 2017, investors fretted that the Trump administration would not be able to pass a corporate tax cut for two reasons. First, Republicans' failure to repeal Obamacare proved the party's general incompetence. They adjusted the probability of tax reform passage and justified it with the failure of "repeal and replace," even though the two were discrete events. The other reason? The Tea Party.

The 2010 Tea Party rebellion was supposedly all about government profligacy: with the US budget deficit at nearly 10%, comparisons of the US to Greece became talk show fodder. And now the "socialist" President Obama was going to expand healthcare benefits to the poor.

From 2010 to 2017, the Tea Party dominated political punditry. Some claim that Donald Trump's victory was the culmination of their activism.

Except that Trump did not really campaign on cutting the budget deficit.

---

[22] See Chapter 11 – after you've read the chapters in between.

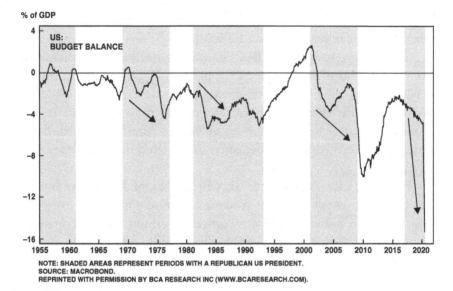

% of GDP

Figure 3.5   Republican presidents expand budget deficits.

Then, there is the overwhelming evidence that, contrary to conventional thought, Republican presidents do not cut budget deficits – they expand them (Figure 3.5). The American public becomes less concerned with government profligacy the moment a Republican president steps into the White House. While Democrats are not very concerned about deficits, Republicans limit their concern to Democrat deficits (Figure 3.6).

I hit the road in early 2017 with these two theory-disproving charts in my deck, and pounded the pavement with one forecast: corporate tax cuts are coming. They will be profligate, and thus stimulative.

Investors did not want to hear it because the memory of the Tea Party was still fresh in their mind. How could Trump pass a corporate tax cut without offsetting spending cuts, after seven years of Republican voter activism about the budget deficit? In addition, investors' memory of the failed Obamacare repeal suggested that Republicans were incompetent. Chances of anyone heeding my forecast died when clients with access to

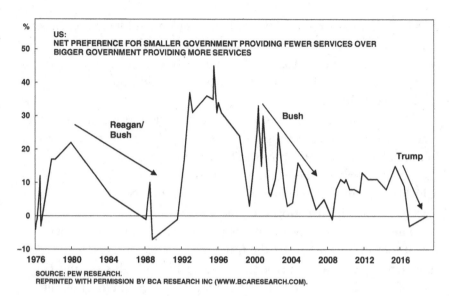

SOURCE: PEW RESEARCH.
REPRINTED WITH PERMISSION BY BCA RESEARCH INC (WWW.BCARESEARCH.COM).

Figure 3.6 Voters welcome Republican profligacy.

DC insiders claimed the opposition to profligate tax cuts was too great among the rank-and-file party members.

Nonetheless, the evidence for tax cuts grew, particularly after Mark Meadows (now the White House chief of staff, then a Republican representative from North Carolina), chair of the Tea Party–linked Freedom Caucus, confirmed that the tax reform plan did not have to be revenue-neutral.[23] His tacit permission was a crucial bellwether. If the leader of the congressional Tea Party faction was cool with blowing out the budget, what was all the consternation about?

A lot more went into the forecast, including boring stuff like examining how the reconciliation procedure would allow Republicans to pass

---

[23] Lindsay Dunsmuir et al., "Republican Meadows: Tax Plan Does Not Have to Be Revenue Neutral," *Reuters,* March 26, 2017, https://www.reuters.com/article/us-usa-obamacare-meadows/republican-meadows-tax-plan-does-not-have-to-be-revenue-neutral-idUSKBN16X0L9.

the tax cut on a razor-thin majority in the Senate, a subject for Chapter 7. But Meadows was critical. Once Meadows and other Freedom Caucus members came out in August 2017 supporting a clean increase to the debt ceiling, I knew no House Republicans would oppose blowing out the budget deficit.

Despite confirmation of the view, my conviction was shaken when I attended a small gathering of investors, policymakers, and general "shot-callers" in the Hamptons in the summer of 2017. It was precisely the type of an event where conspiracy theorists expect elites to exchange valuable information necessary to maintain the New World Order. Except that the information was comically wrong.

The last speaker at the event was a White House insider. Not a member of the administration (at the time), but as close to President Trump as it gets. The insider proceeded to share his thoughts on the priorities of the administration. I was itching to ask a question about my highest-conviction view of the year: that corporate tax cuts would happen and that they would be stimulative – by blowing out the deficit. After the insider wrapped up his remarks, my hand shot up and I asked my question. His response crushed me:

> "No way. I'm telling you, there is zero chance that tax reform will be allowed to increase the budget deficit. Look, our government debt is above $15 trillion. We are worse off than Greece. There is no way that President Trump is going to add to it. The only way corporate tax cuts happen is if we find offsets in the budget for them. So I am sorry to crush your hopes, but you are way off."

It was a real gut punch. My analysis was so elegant, so thorough, and the charts – oh the charts ... – so punchy! I went up to the insider after the talk and begged him to reconsider. As if changing his mind would change the verdict of his insight: "Marko, you are wrong."

I went home from the Hamptons crushed. I was not refreshed by the soft Atlantic breeze, the pastel-colored polo shirts, or the elegant canapés. The manicured golf club did nothing to lift my spirits, nor did the hobnobbing with billionaires. I came into the office, gathered my team, and said, "Hell, we may be wrong."

Were we? Hell no!

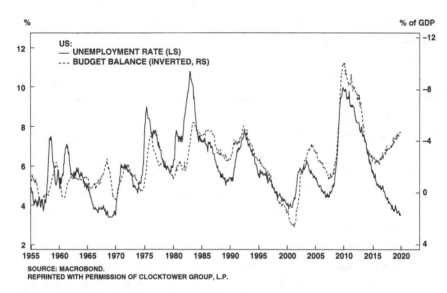

%   % of GDP

Figure 3.7   The Tea Party allowed this to happen.

The Senate passed the deficit-widening bill 51–48 on December 19, 2017. The S&P 500 responded by rallying 7% over the course of a month, peaking at 2872.87 points on January 26, 2018. Getting the corporate tax call right was key to catching this rally.

As for the budget deficit, it has nearly doubled since President Trump came to power. In early 2020, it stood at the highest level in a non-recessionary environment (and thanks to the bipartisan COVID-19 stimulus, it will balloon to dizzying heights that I approximate to be a shade under 30% of GDP). Figure 3.7 shows how extraordinary this situation is. I stop the data right before the COVID-19 recession so as not to obfuscate the novelty of the Trump administration fiscal profligacy. It began well before the pandemic.

Normally, the budget deficit is correlated with the unemployment rate because every time a recession happens, the government steps in to offset the decline in private demand. For the first time outside of the late 1960s – and to a much greater extent than at that time – the US government was blowing out its deficit despite the fact that there was no macroeconomic justification to do so. This behavior leaves the US woefully short on fiscal space to stimulate when the next recession hits – which, thanks to the COVID-19 pandemic, will be precisely when this book goes to print.

For nearly a decade, the Tea Party harangued the Obama administration about the elevated budget deficit. Once a Republican got into the White House, it flipped. The insight is not that Republicans are hypocrites, but that all policymakers are. They push the envelope as far as their constraints allow them, which sometimes results in contradictory actions.

The passage of the bill demonstrates that complex political systems, such as the US, cannot be analyzed as if they are banana republics. Even a close confidant of the president with daily access to the White House gave disastrously wrong intelligence.

As for the insider I met in the Hamptons: he runs a political consultancy that provides forecasts to investors. He continues to flout his access to the president, continues to make disastrously wrong predictions, and continues to remain in business. Unlike true intelligence analysts, he provides no scenarios and no probabilities, just high-conviction calls.

The Spy

No private company can come close to the roughly $60 billion that the US government spends on intelligence agencies, of which roughly a third goes to the CIA.[24] The CIA can make forecasts based on actual intelligence because it has so much quality data that it becomes statistically significant. It can check its assets' insights against quantifiable data including financial transactions and signals intelligence like wiretaps. Crosschecking creates a mosaic of data that a CIA analyst has access to. And even then, equipped with the maximum amount of high-quality data, public spy agencies like the CIA still make mistakes. It is why Heuer, introduced in Chapter 2, dedicated his career to helping the CIA train its analysts to stop obsessing about getting more data.

---

[24] In 2013, the Snowden leak confirmed that the CIA received around a third of the intelligence budget. Richard McGregor, "Size of CIA's Budget Slice Revealed in Edward Snowden Leak," *Financial Times,* August 29, 2013, https://www.ft.com/content/31997218-10f6-11e3-b5e4-00144feabdc0.

Once these expert analysts leave the public sector, their value to private firms is uncertain. Even a briefing from high-profile, retired policymakers or intelligence operatives is tricky. Are they actively engaged in the issue you are speaking to them about? Do they have access to the mosaic of intelligence that helped them in their government job? If so, can they share it with you legally? Are they writing a book instead of rolling up their sleeves and spending sleepless nights on the question you posed to them?[25]

These questions are impossible to answer.

Most intelligence operatives are at least trained in understanding the uncertainty of their forecasts. A true professional will be humble and focus on a scenario-driven approach to analysis. A scenario-driven approach allows the analyst to provide you, the client, with a set of factors to monitor. These are variables that will either confirm or disconfirm the different hypotheses or scenarios.[26] These experts will downplay their unique sources and insights. They will provide you with a framework from which you can follow the developing forecast and exercise your own judgment. A subpar analyst will instead emphasize his personal network of "sources," inserting himself as much as possible into the forecast so as to appear indispensable. Because who else knows the president's cousin, twice removed?

You Cannot Outsource Your Fiduciary Duty

The first time I introduced myself to the sales force at BCA Research, one saleswoman – the best at the firm, I was later told – asked, "Where do you get your information? Who do you speak to?" Her tone of voice told me not to mess around. I was embarrassed to be put on the spot, until I realized that she was doing me a favor.

Most investors think that the way to political or geopolitical insight is through access to intelligence. No matter how many times they

---

[25] Yes, I see the irony in this statement!

[26] Recall Heuer's competing hypotheses analysis from Chapter 2 – this kind of pivotal data is the most useful in forecasting.

get burned, they keep buzzing back to dive-bomb the "intelligence" streetlamp.

I have never met an investor who listens to quarterly CEO calls and expects to hear the truth. And every time a big hedge fund manager goes on Bloomberg to proclaim that a certain company is *the* stock to buy, my more experienced colleagues scoff that they are "selling their book." Investors should not treat chats with policymakers and political insiders any differently.

For an epistemic community that has its bullshit detector set at high when it comes to the markets, investors are awfully gullible when it comes to insight from smoke-filled rooms in DC.

That said, I don't think investors should wall themselves off in their office and draw decision-tree diagrams with no contact to the outside world. They just need to approach all aspects of that outside world with healthy skepticism. There are three types of experts that I recommend seeking out as much as possible:

- **Academics**: Academia is filled with undervalued and underappreciated assets. Instead of talking to some slick geopolitical consultant over an overpriced meal at a Mayfair restaurant, email an academic who spent the last 20 years of his life researching the topic at hand. Academics are open to interacting with the private sector. Don't just reach out to the top academics with a hot reputation; they are most likely publishing more op-eds than original research. Reach out to the ones passionate about their research and willing to take the time to connect the dots for you. Just be careful to put their views into your own constraint-based net assessment. Don't let the actual expert tell you what the market is going to do. They do not know.
- **Technocrats**: Talk to retired policymakers and insiders, but adjust your expectations. Know it is impossible to create a mosaic robust enough to have a statistically significant intelligence-driven forecast. If you intend to speak with former government officials, go for the second- and third-tier technocrats and bureaucrats rather than the top dogs. The top personnel are often ideological, legacy-driven, and disconnected from the analysts and information that made them valuable forecasters. Instead, reach out to the technocrats behind the

big names that really know how the world works – or at least how their small slice of it does.

- **Regulators**: Sector-specific insights do exist and are valuable. If you need sector intelligence, hire a consultant that specializes in regulatory analysis. These are usually people who worked in regulatory agencies and understand those archaic webs. Steer clear of consultancies that claim they can predict regulatory churn through big data. I don't buy it, though I'm willing to be proven wrong. Talk instead to the old hands who know how the regulatory sausage is made.

Insights from experts are incredibly useful, and this chapter is not meant to discourage investors and businesspeople from seeking such information. Keep spending money on consultancies to know the stuff you don't have time to learn.

This book presents a framework for how to assess insights and intelligence. It equips you with the tools to evaluate the insights of even the most well-placed sources you come across. You can call their bullshit and discern diagnostic information from funneled insights. Armed with the constraint framework, you will become a much smarter consumer of intelligence.

As investors, we cannot outsource our fiduciary duty to someone else. The ultimate forecasting buck stops with us.

Part Two

THE CONSTRAINTS

Chapter 4

Politics

"You may have all the money, Raymond … *but I have all the men with guns.*"

— Frank Underwood, vice president of the United States
of America in *House of Cards*

I n *Expert Political Judgment*, Philip Tetlock calls on over two decades of psychology research to argue that those who professionalize "commenting or offering advice on political and economic trends" are no better at making predictions than anyone else.[1]

His conclusion leaves me with mixed feelings.[2]

---

[1] Philip Tetlock, *Expert Political Judgment* (Princeton, NJ: Princeton University Press, 2005), 239.

[2] Tetlock's book is a must-read for anyone who deals with forecasts for a living. I do have one critique: instead of studying professional political forecasters – those who work in the private sector making bets on geopolitical events for a living – he picked 284 media personalities, think tankers, journalists, and academics. I have never read a piece of news, op-ed, academic study, or think-tank analysis expecting to find a good forecast. His sample is skewed. Not to mention that his favorite whipping boy – *The McLaughlin Group* – is a debate show meant for entertainment (and unfamiliar to anyone under the age of 75). I don't doubt Tetlock's conclusions, but I wish he would not use the term "expert" so liberally.

Tetlock's book is encouraging because it means laypeople don't need insights from smoke-filled rooms to make actionable forecasts. Due to experts' forecast inaccuracy, everyone else has high odds of making a comparable prediction. Which means everyone – "experts" included – can improve their predictions by reading my book.

His book is discouraging to *me* – a forecaster – because it suggests that clients may also be wasting their time with this particular expert!

Yet I find solace in Tetlock's conclusion: the worst forecasters are those who "know one big thing," who base their forecasts on a singular approach or theory.[3] Instead of seeking the right answer, they seek time- and theory-saving ones.

For Tetlock, the high scorers are those who "know many small things (tricks of their trade), are skeptical of grand schemes, see explanation and prediction not as deductive exercises but rather as exercises in flexible 'ad hocery' that require stitching together diverse sources of information."[4]

If accurate forecasts via "ad hocery" is what you want, you came to the right place. There is plenty of it coming up! This book is about to shower you with it!

This book is light on theory and absolutely incapable of the parsimony practiced by those who apply only one theory to seek the truth. Sure, in Chapter 2 I reference plenty of theory: Marx, Machiavelli, social psychologists, and the CIA's intelligence analysis manual. These all form the scaffolding of the constraint framework. But were they *really* required knowledge to put the framework into practice?

In Chapter 2, I walked through how these theories helped me construct the framework. But now that it is operational, the foundational pillars it rests on matter less. The working framework I detail in this and following chapters encourages the forecaster to maintain discipline; to focus on the observable, material phenomena; and to focus on constraints rather than preferences. Individual preferences are the unreliable narrators of forecasting: misleading and unpredictable. Because they are not observable, they can only be inferred from behavior. And even then,

---

[3] Tetlock, *Expert Political Judgment,* 73.
[4] Ibid.

analysts are liable to make the fundamental attribution error and mistake constraint-led behavior for a preference realized.[5]

As I describe the constraint categories, Tetlock would – I hope – be proud of me. The next five chapters are eclectic in their approach. I favor no single theory or discipline. My "bag of tricks" is very large and holds a variety of social science disciplines.

I first apply Tetlock's suggested "ad hocery" to political constraints. Not all constraints are created equal, and power is the most important constraint – a lesson learned from years of applying the framework. Power is more important than wealth, the economy, markets, geopolitics, demographics, etc. It also dominates individual policymaker preferences, particularly as they cannot pursue their intentions without political capital.

"You May Have All the Money, Raymond … "

One of the best scenes in *House of Cards* takes place when Frank Underwood, the fictional vice president of the United States, squares off against billionaire tycoon Raymond Tusk. Frank wins, Tusk loses. But as they sit across from one another, Frank utters a gutting takedown:

> "You may have all the money, Raymond … *but I have all the men with guns.*"

Politics is the study of power: a force that compels others to do something they would *prefer* not to do. Yes, money is an important factor in power, but it is not the only one. The Soviet Union did not need wealth to threaten the US with nuclear annihilation. Power, or political capital, is not just about economics.

---

[5] Chapter 2 memory refresh: the fundamental attribution error is "a mistake analysts make when they attribute real-world outcomes to characteristics, personality, and moods of individual actors."

Political power is difficult to quantify or – most relevant for investors – compare across economies. It is simpler to compare countries' *material* power.[6] Ambiguity in political capital makes it more difficult to assess, for example, who has greater ability to enact policies: President Trump or President Macron.

For investors, this hard-to-quantify factor matters. Policymakers with ample political capital can expend it on unpopular policies, such as structural reforms. Though painful, these policies tend to have a positive impact on the economy, domestic assets, and the country's currency over the long run. China's one-party system affords it an abundance of such capital, which I examine later in the chapter.

A currency trader in emerging markets needs to be sensitive to such power flexes, as one of few indicators of long-term currency performance is comparative productivity levels. A key factor influencing those levels is whether policymakers pursue productivity-enhancing policies.

It helps to think of structural reforms – or any controversial or unpopular policy – in terms of a "J curve" (Figure 4.1). Whenever

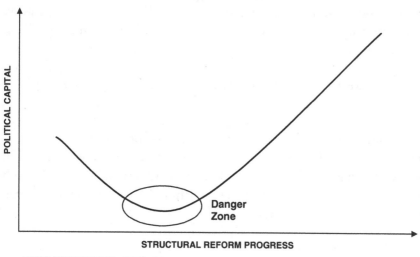

Figure 4.1   The J curve of structural reform.

---

[6] In Chapter 9, I elaborate on why such a one-dimensional comparison is dangerous.

politicians pursue such policies, they drain their political capital, writ large. In doing so, they enter the "danger zone": a moment of truth when the populace may reject the policy. A good example is the 2019 Argentinian election. President Macri thought he had enough political capital to pursue painful reforms, but he could not get out of the danger zone and failed to get reelected.

If investors could gauge the stock of political capital – predict not just when policymakers will wield it but how well-received those decisions will be – they could make actionable calls on where to invest or do business. Can President Macron overcome protests in France in 2020 the way that President Jacques Chirac could not in 1995?[7]

There is no widely accepted way to measure political capital. Some political scientists have tried to construct a leadership capital index, but it is difficult to operationalize, back test, and apply to market-relevant policies.[8]

A parsimonious political capital index would have to work across time, place, and political system. Absent this magical one-stop-shop indicator, I use an *ad-hoc* approach that works just fine. Multiple factors help me gauge political capital:

- **Popularity:** Policymakers who enjoy public support have political capital in the bank. Even authoritarian and semiauthoritarian states care about popularity: Saudi Arabia – with 50% of the population under 30 – and China – with over 50% of the population in the middle-class income group – are trying to reform. For those regimes, public support is all the more important because a loss of credibility can result in direr consequences than a lost election or lucrative retirement on the speaking circuit.[9] President Vladimir Putin made a huge effort to regain political capital in 2014, when the tensions in Ukraine led to a surge in support for his government

---

[7] Yes.

[8] Mark Bennister et al., "Leadership Capital: Measuring the Dynamics of Leadership," *SSRN Electric Journal,* December 15, 2013, https://papers.ssrn.com/sol3/papers.cfm?abstract_id=2510241.

[9] One advantage democracy has over more centralized governments is its tendency toward bloodless transitions of power.

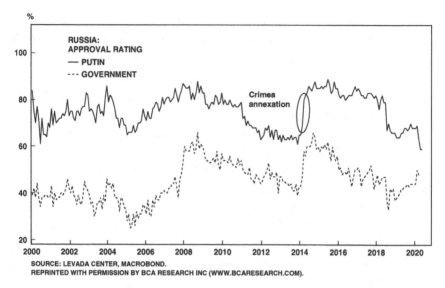

Figure 4.2 President Putin's political capital surged after Crimean annexation.

(Figure 4.2). His 2014 campaign was a (successful) attempt to correct his decades-low popularity.

- **Time in power:** If leaders are not vigilant, their time spent in power can drag down their popularity. The longer they are the ones to beat, the more opportunity for the public to beat them with social media, votes, protests, or more physical means. Those in it for the long haul can lose credibility and thus political capital. Accordingly, they become risk averse as elections near and as their "mileage" stacks up. In contrast, leaders who have just ascended to power – democratically or otherwise – have the most capital to burn thanks to the "honeymoon period." This fleeting moment of wedded bliss is the time to pursue unpalatable policies.[10] The duration, timing, and power of the honeymoon

---

[10] A 2019 IMF study showed that "reforms undertaken earlier in an incumbent's term do not affect election prospects." Gabriele Ciminelli et al., *The Political Costs of Reforms: Fear or Reality?* (Washington, DC: International Monetary Fund, 2019).

period vary depending on a government's leadership structure. In a presidential system, where contradictory voices may have equal sway, the president's starter capital depends on legislative math. In a parliamentary system, the head of government often commands the majority in a legislature. For a leader who ascends to power in a *coup d'état,* the best time to strike is while the opposition is cowed.[11]

- **Legislative math:** In democracies, room to maneuver depends on the legislative math. If the head of government does not command a legislative majority, to pass laws at all, she must curry favor with coalition partners and (in a minority government) the opposition.
- **Economic context:** A good economic crisis may help spur reforms, but it is difficult to see the incumbent ever benefiting.[12] In the Argentina example of Chapter 3, the incumbent, President Macri, did not benefit from the economic crisis in Argentina. However, the newly elected President Jair Bolsonaro in neighboring Brazil managed to push through pension reform, in part thanks to the deep recession that began under his discredited predecessors. Similarly, Spanish Prime Minister Mariano Rajoy pushed through aggressive supply-side reforms in the early 2010s thanks to the economic crisis that preceded his election in late 2011. Strong economic tailwinds are beneficial for incumbent political capital, but a crisis can also be positive for new leadership that steps in. When it comes to the economy, the public is a fair-weather friend to whomever is in office at the time.
- **Special interest group support:** In wielding political capital, powerful special interest groups have a collective action advantage over the broader population. They can eliminate the free-rider problem and bring greater resources to bear.[13] As a result, they

---

[11] And in jail … or worse.

[12] "Making Reform Happen: Structural Priorities in Times of Crisis," *OECD*, May 2010, https://community.oecd.org/docs/DOC-18533.

[13] Mancur Olson, *The Logic of Collective Action: Public Goods and the Theory of Groups* (Cambridge, MA: Harvard University Press, 1965).

make for costly opponents of policies *not* in their best interest. Policymakers who take on difficult reforms or policy need to expend ample political capital to defeat any opposing interest groups.

- **Global momentum**: Political movements often spread through osmosis, or a "regional contingency factor."[14] During the Third Wave of democratization in the late twentieth century, many countries became democracies. In Latin America, there was a regional pattern to its spread. The reality of global momentum means leaders who pursue globally trending policies will have an easier battle to wage.

... But Boris Has All the Rhetoric

Boris Johnson's conundrum from Chapter 3 reveals some of these political constraints in action. Johnson became the UK prime minister on July 24, 2019. He inherited a shaky coalition with the DUP and a withdrawal agreement that twisted London into a logistical pretzel – urban gymnastics carried out so the coalition could accommodate the small Northern Ireland party. Johnson also faced a surging Brexit Party, which threatened to scuttle the Tories' hold on the center-right electorate.

Johnson's use of tough rhetoric solved the challenge on his right flank. It signaled to hard-core Brexit supporters that he was the right man for the job, and eventually brought them back into the Conservative Party fold. Nonetheless, forecasters only accounted for the first move in the domino effect: Johnson's "I'd rather die in a ditch" rhetoric. As a result of their poorly researched predictions, odds of a no-deal Brexit rose drastically in the betting markets.

How should forecasters have reacted to the 10 Downing Street rhetoric?

---

[14] Samuel P. Huntington, *The Third Wave: Democratization in the Late Twentieth Century* (Norman: University of Oklahoma Press, 1991).

An analysis that factored in political constraints would have urged the analyst to ignore Johnson's rhetoric when determining the likelihood of a no-deal Brexit. He could not accomplish his stated preferred outcome due to multiple political constraints:

- **Popularity:** The public did not support a no-deal Brexit outcome. In fact, some polls suggested that "Bregret" was setting in, with a rising share of the electorate opposing Brexit altogether (Figure 4.3). In August 2019, only 38% of the public saw the no-deal Brexit outcome as "good" or "acceptable."[15]
- **Time in power:** For a caretaker prime minister, it would have been folly to immediately force an unpopular large-scale policy.

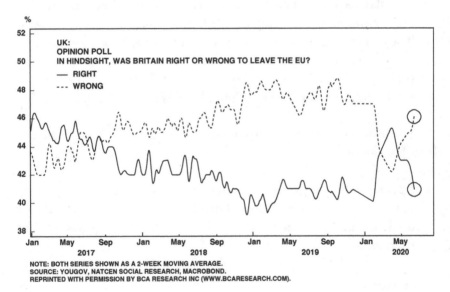

Figure 4.3   "Bregret" was a constraint.

---

[15] Matthew Smith, "By 48% to 35% Britons Would Rather Have No Deal and No Corbyn," *YouGov,* August 17, 2019, https://yougov.co.uk/topics/politics/articles-reports/2019/08/17/48-35-britons-would-rather-have-no-deal-and-no-cor.

Tory voters elected Johnson out of a pool of 160,000 members of the Conservative Party – median age: 120 years young.[16] His party did not want to move anything too quickly, let alone policy. Unlike a head of government with a fresh mandate, Johnson inherited an already shaky one from Theresa May. As a result, he inherited the time disadvantage of a party that has held power for a while and a disadvantage of a shaky coalition.

- **Economic context:** While the economy itself was stable in mid-2019, the British pound had been trading in concert with Brexit negotiations all year. The public had become receptive to the government's own fearmongering related to a no-deal Brexit contingency. The frustrated public would have blamed any negative economic impact squarely on the rookie Johnson administration.

- **Legislative math:** Legislative majority was the "clincher," the fulcrum constraint.[17] By August 2019, Tories had lost their majority. They were running the country with a minority coalition government – the weakest option in a parliamentary democracy. Out of a peak majority of 327 MPs following the 2017 election (317 Tory, 10 DUP), Johnson was down to just 298 MPs in a 650-seat house.[18]

Fortunately for Johnson, two political constraints most likely did not limit his actions:

- **Special interest group support:** Businesses had been vociferous opponents of a no-deal Brexit. Then again, they had opposed Brexit itself, and thus it is not clear to what extent this leaning was relevant to Johnson.

---

[16] Approximately.

[17] When a constraint is so powerful that it bends all other factors to it, I refer to it as a "fulcrum." It is the one constraint that forecasters should keep an eye on because if it changes at all, the entire analysis may have to pivot. It is, in Heuer's terminology, the most diagnostic of all variables.

[18] The Tory majority collapsed because Johnson himself moved to "remove the whip" – essentially expel – 21 "rebel" Tories for voting in favor of a bill that sought further delay to the then–Article 50 deadline.

- **Global momentum:** To the surprise of the British press, no other EU country seriously contemplated exit following the 2016 referendum. Only across the Atlantic pond did it find support in the Trump administration. Would the Trump administration have supported a no-deal Brexit? Probably. Overall, it is not clear whether global momentum had any impact on domestic politics. This factor was a wash.

Johnson faced four main constraints to a no-deal Brexit, some that he himself created by expelling Tory rebels from the party. His no-deal rhetoric therefore makes the most sense in the context of Tory party politics because it presents a plausible rationale for why Johnson might say one thing (no-deal) and do another (soft diplomacy). Political constraints to no-deal Brexit were overwhelming, no matter the preference of Johnson's administration.

Investors should have gone long the pound in the summer of 2019. The return from August 1 to the end of the year was 9%, a significant move for a liquid currency market. Constraints were overwhelming, material, and persistent. No-deal probability was under 10%, most likely much lower.

The *ad-hoc* method I applied to the Johnson scenario measures political capital in the short term and allows investors to forecast policies over the course of a policymaker's term but not beyond.

There is also a way to measure political constraints in a longer time frame, and it relies on the median voter theorem.

Introducing the Median Voter Theorem

In late 2015, I encountered cognitive dissonance in the financial industry. The Brexit referendum was around the corner, and then-candidate Donald Trump led the polls in the Republican Party primary race. But most of my clients wanted to talk about the 2017 French and Dutch elections. In London, one hedge fund manager flipped through my chart pack and tossed it aside. It was filled with data suggesting that Brexit and Trump odds were higher than the consensus. The manager said,

"We have telephone polls that suggest Brexit is highly unlikely. What else ya got?"[19]

By the end of 2015, Clinton's initial gargantuan polling advantage over Trump had shrunk to the "margin of error," as had the "Remain" lead over the "Leave" vote for the referendum. Still, investors were too complacent about the two upcoming plebiscites in the US and UK.[20]

Investors were "traveling with events." News coverage directed their journey, and it kept up a barrage of the outdated Eurosceptic narrative – while ignoring the populist revolt brewing in the two English-speaking countries.

My alarmist view instead relied on the median voter theorem (MVT).

Developed in the 1950s, MVT is one of the few codified theories of political science.[21] It posits that to win an election or stay in power, parties and politicians approximate the policy choices of the median voter. Empirical work since the 1950s has both confirmed and

---

[19] Full disclosure: I did not correctly forecast either Brexit or Trump. However, I assigned both events higher-than-consensus probabilities, which is all investors need to know to generate geopolitical *alpha*. In a November 1, 2016 analysis for BCA Research (available upon request) I assigned Donald Trump ~40% odds of winning the election. This was higher than 29% that Nate Silver's (excellent) *FiveThirtyEight* gave Trump, 15% that the *New York Time*'s Upshot assigned, 7% of the Princeton Election Consortium, or – wait for it – 2% that the HuffPost thought were Trump's odds. See Chapter 11 for more on the crucial concept of geopolitical *alpha* that gives this book its title.

[20] Granted, investors had good reason to direct their attention toward the Netherlands – not so much France. The populist Party for Freedom (PVV) in the Dutch election had a large lead, but the election was over a year away, and the European migration crisis was unsustainable. Ultimately, the theory that the migration crisis was giving the PVV strong tailwinds proved correct. Once the migration crisis abated, so did PVV support. Further south, French populist Marine Le Pen was polling terribly. Forecasts massively overstated her election odds. The call to go long euro ahead of the 2017 French election was one of the most fitting examples of geopolitical *alpha* I've ever experienced in my career. It is described in detail in Chapter 11.

[21] Don't tell any poli-sci friends, but it was actually economist Harold Hotelling who first posited the MVT in his 1929 article "Stability in Competition." His passing comment in an article otherwise focused on business decision-making remains prescient almost a century later. Harold Hotelling, "Stability in Competition," *Economic Journal* 39 (1929): 41–57. For an account of subsequent treatments of the concept in political science, see Duncan Black, "On the Rationale of Group Decision-making," *Journal of Political Economy* 56 (1948): 23–34; and Anthony Downs, *An Economic Theory of Democracy* (New York: Harper Collins, 1957).

challenged the theory. As such, its proponents in academia have fallen off. But for investing, I find it extremely useful as an approximation of the harder-to-quantify political capital and thus political constraints. Or, at the very least, it puts me on the right path to finding it.

Analysis using MVT requires three main assumptions:

- Voters' preferences are "single-peaked," meaning voters prefer one policy outcome over all other potential outcomes. This is a tough one. It is not clear that this is true at all.
- Preferences are considered over a single policy dimension. For example, a voter either supports gun legislation or not, or wants a greater or smaller role for the state in the economy. And in each election, the median voter makes a decision on this single policy dimension. It is also difficult to ascertain the validity of this assumption.
- Politicians want to attain, or retain, political capital above everything else, including consistent policy and positive societal outcomes – perhaps the toughest assumption to make of all three.[22]

As with any theory, the danger of MVT lies in how its application may simplify reality beyond recognition. It posits that, to win and maintain power, policymakers should follow a three-step process:

1. Identify the central issue of the day.
2. Ascertain the median voter's position on that issue.
3. Asymptotically approach the median voter's position, outflanking opponents in the process.

President Trump successfully identified the central issue of the 2016 election: globalization versus economic nationalism. He next ascertained where the American voter stood between those extremes. To the shock of most pundits, the American median voter was far less supportive of globalization (free trade and immigration) than assumed.[23] Finally,

---

[22] Just kidding!

[23] The Leave campaign in the UK confirmed the same realization: at the time of the referendum, the median voter was far less supportive of EU membership than previously thought.

Trump catered correctly to the median voter's position and won as a result.

Trump's campaign rhetoric against globalization was largely in line with Pat Buchanan's, who challenged the incumbent, George H.W. Bush, in the 1992 Republican primary. Buchanan's loss indicates that the US median voter was shifting toward globalization in 1992. Bill Clinton won the election as a pro-globalization Democrat (albeit with his own brand of populism). Another way to think of the median voter is as the political *zeitgeist* of the nation. The mild-mannered Buchanan had no chance in 1992, but 24 years later, the uncouth gameshow host did.

Median voter theory is such a powerful tool for predicting outcomes because it forces *all* policymakers to shift to the median position, lest they become irrelevant political outliers.

Figure 4.4 illustrates the concept. The first panel depicts the precept of the MVT, using the left-right economic dimension as the most salient

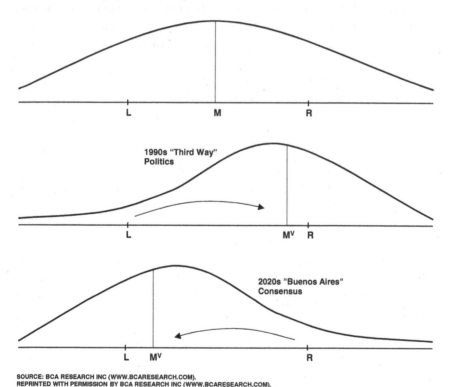

Figure 4.4 Median voter theorem in action.

topic of a particular election (the assumed single dimension). Candidates from the left and the right move to the middle to capture the median voter in a scenario where the median voter is a centrist. In this scenario, the median voter supports a perfect balance between *laissez-faire* and *dirigiste* economic models.

The second panel shows what likely enabled supply-side policies in the 1990s: the median voter moved right.

Across the political spectrum, left-leaning parties adopted center-right economic policies throughout the late 1980s and 1990s: Bill Clinton's US Democratic Party, Tony Blair's UK Labour Party, Gerhard Schröder's German Social Democratic Party, Paul Keating's Australian Labor Party, Jean Chrétien's Canadian Liberal Party, and Romano Prodi's Italian Democratic Party all traveled right, adopting a more *laissez-faire* economic outlook. This was referred to as "Third Way" politics.

Even in the emerging markets, a move toward *laissez-faire* economics and orthodox fiscal and monetary policy followed the ideological consensus of the 1990s; India's economy liberalized in 1991, and Deng Xiaoping's 1992 "Southern Tour" solidified China's pro-market reforms.

The median voter, and policymakers' appeals to her, played a role in the changes listed above. The median voter is a more powerful indicator of market behavior than the individual policymaker's preference. So to forecast policy, focus on the median voter, not the policymaker. If the median voter is shifting her preferences, it means that *all* parties, not just those in power, will respond and shift toward the median voter.

In 2015, I cautioned my clients that the most radical adherents to the *laissez-faire* economic model – the US and the UK – were the most at risk of a populist takeover. The US and UK median voter had moved away from *laissez-faire* capitalism toward something else. In Europe, the median voter was static, if not moving marginally *toward* the *laissez-faire* model. Unlike my peers in the financial industry, I did not fret about the French and Dutch elections. But my MVT-grounded analysis predicted that Brexit and the US election were much more likely to be market catalysts.

Predicting the Long-term: Welcome to the Buenos Aires Consensus!

In the 2020 global context of low growth and deflation – and a severe recession thanks to the COVID-19 pandemic – the pendulum of economic policy is swinging to the left. It is surprising to some that the US and the UK have been on the forefront of this global momentum. The deterioration of the middle class combined with the end of the Debt Supercycle has shifted voters to the left in both economies.[24] And wherever the voters go, policymakers soon follow.

Even the ostensibly "right-wing" Donald Trump and Boris Johnson.

What tenets of *laissez-faire* does Donald Trump practice? Fiscal prudence? Free trade? Noninterference in free markets? An independent central bank? I can ask the same questions of the post–David Cameron Tories and receive similarly negative answers, though to a lesser extent.

Policymakers' divergence from traditional conservative party rhetoric suggested that a paradigm shift was afoot, and the fulcrum constraint of the median voter was steering it.[25]

Another sign of the median voter's leftward influence is the opposition's behavior; the left-wing parties in both countries are not moving to the *center* to outflank Trump and Johnson. They are betting that the 2020 median voter is much more left of center. They are predicting that the median voter is amenable to experimentation with long-lost demand-driven policies. Enter Bernie Sanders, Elizabeth Warren, and Jeremy Corbyn … from stage left.

Even Joe Biden, who presents himself as a centrist on the campaign trail, is only centrist relative to self-described socialists. But he is running on a tax increase for high-income households and for businesses and on

---

[24] For decades, the Debt Supercycle allowed households to supplement their stagnant real incomes with credit until its end in 2010.

[25] As to why the median voter moved away from traditional right-wing policy: perhaps *laissez-faire* policies are not optimal in this brave new world of secular stagnation, deflation, and a COVID-19-induced recession. Although, I think that the shift in the median voter preferences is at heart a generational conflict. In 2020, the median voter is, for the first time in US history, a Millennial. From here on out, the median voter is only going to get more left-leaning on economic policy given the painful economic context that has defined Millennial, and especially Gen-Z, adult experiences.

capital gains and dividends. He has also proposed a plan to encourage unionization of the labor force and to include labor protections and environmental standards into all new trade deals (basically a politically correct version of Trump's nationalist protectionism). It is not exactly "democratic socialism," but it's a bold campaign strategy of tax raises and proworker policies. Eight years ago, pundits would have called it socialism.

The American and British median voter spoke loudly in 2016. As of 2020 in these countries, populist economic policies that diverge from *laissez-faire* orthodoxy are the median voter's preferred policy setting.[26] Pro-market policies are therefore unlikely to emerge from either country. To put it into terms most investors will understand: I am not holding my breath for Paul Ryan to return to politics.[27]

When historians canonize 2020 decades later, I predict they will blame the erosion of *laissez-faire* on COVID-19. But by the time the COVID-19 crisis hit, the *zeitgeist* had already turned. Policymakers and voters were already primed for unorthodoxy. The legislative efficiency of the US fiscal and monetary responses to the pandemic only surprised those without a framework to describe the median voter's economic policy position.

The monetary and fiscal response is diametrically different from the 2008–2009 experience.

In 2009, American legislators took nearly five months to pass fiscal stimulus. The size of the American Recovery and Reinvestment Act (ARRA) was 5.4% of the 2009 GDP. It passed the Senate with only three votes by the opposition party – the Republicans. In the House, not a single Republican voted for the bill. In total, 214 Republicans in Congress voted against the bill.

---

[26] For those still skeptical that these parties' policies diverge from *laissez-faire* economics, consider a traditional conservative's lament of Trump's ascendance: "When your *raison d'être* stops being *How can we hold to the principles of limited government and economic freedom?* and becomes *How can we hold on to this majority for one more cycle?* then you've become the very last thing that you're supposed to be against." Jeff Flake, *Conscience of a Conservative: A Rejection of Destructive Politics and a Return to Principle* (Random House, 2017), 13.

[27] Ryan is the architect of Trump's corporate tax cuts and the former Speaker of the House of Representatives. My unsolicited advice to Speaker Ryan would be to wait for the demand-driven policies to overshoot their mark – as all pendulum swings eventually do – and then come in as the savior. It will take 10 to 15 years, but it is the only way.

Lack of bipartisanship in 2009 is not merely a piece of political trivia. If you were an investor following the policy response in 2009, the strict party-line vote on ARRA was a crucial piece of information. It suggested that no future stimulus bills would be forthcoming, given the level of rancor that ARRA produced.

Eleven years later, with the median American now openly contemplating policies that would have been deemed "socialist" in the past, the *zeitgeist* is dramatically different. The Coronavirus Aid, Relief, and Economic Security Act (CARES Act) started off as a $1 trillion Republican proposal on March 18 and doubled in size a week later. It was conceived, passed, and doubled in size faster than anyone thought possible.

Not only is the size of CARES more than double that of ARRA – 11.2% of 2019 GDP – but it was passed with *no votes* in opposition. The Senate passed the bill with a 96–0 majority. The House passed it with a *voice vote;* in the process, the sole dissenter – Representative Thomas Massie of Kentucky – endured a modern version of tar-and-feathering from all corners, including President Trump.

In the short-term, confounding policy variables obscure voter median preferences. Governing coalitions, gerrymandered electoral results, and policy prerogatives of individual parties all mask the long-term influence of the median voter. President Trump, for example, won his election by appealing to the long-term median voter preference. He ran on an anti-trade, anti-establishment platform. However, his only substantive legislative accomplishment by February 2020 was a pro-corporate, conservative tax cut. And the cut did not align with median voter preferences.

The tax cut, passed in December 2017, proved to be a disastrous electoral pitch for the GOP in the November 2018 midterm elections, just as MVT would have predicted. Republican congressional candidates running for re-election ditched the tax cut talking point in 2018 as they faced angry constituents across the country. The aforementioned Paul Ryan saw the writing on the wall and quit while he was ahead.

The episode illustrates how MVT allows for policy to deviate from the median voter in the short term, but not in the long term. The American voter is on a journey of a major ideological pendulum swing. But it is unclear whether this switch will spur global momentum in the same direction. The US continues to stand out negatively on measures of income inequality and social mobility (Figure 4.5) as well as on measures of "middle class as percent of population" (Figure 4.6).

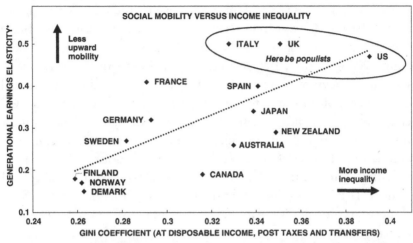

*GENERATIONAL EARNINGS ELASTICITY REFERS TO THE ELASTICITY OF THE CHILD'S EARNINGS WITH RESPECT TO THE PARENT'S. HIGHER ELASTICITY MEANS THAT THE CHILD'S EARNINGS ARE HIGHLY DEPENDENT ON THE PARENT'S, IMPLYING LOW SOCIAL MOBILITY.
SOURCE: CORAK (2011) AND OECD.
REPRINTED WITH PERMISSION BY BCA RESEARCH INC (WWW.BCARESEARCH.COM).

Figure 4.5   The US is an outlier in measures of inequality and social mobility.

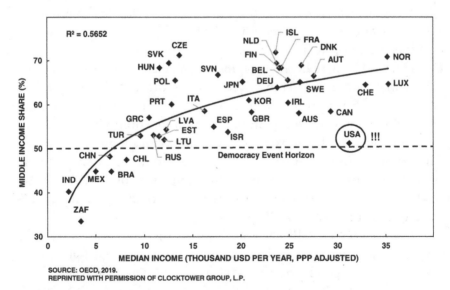

SOURCE: OECD, 2019.
REPRINTED WITH PERMISSION OF CLOCKTOWER GROUP, L.P.

Figure 4.6   The US is an outlier in measures of the middle class.

For investors, these metrics mean that even if the US sees a return of President Trump for a second term, the era when Americans embrace *laissez-faire* policies relative to the rest of the world is over. President Trump's 2016 election, Bernie Sanders' and Elizabeth Warren's candidacies, and a bevy of policies pursued by the Trump administration all indicate that policymakers respond to the median voter. And the US median voter demands *dirigiste*, left-leaning, demand-driven policies across the ideological divide. Sure, Republicans and Democrats will continue to fight over noneconomic, deliberately polarized issues such as abortion, gun control, climate change, Russia, racial inequality, and President Trump's conduct. But their adoption of unorthodox fiscal and monetary policies is bipartisan, as their response to the COVID-19 calamity attests.

As I write in Q1 2020, there is also the question of how policymakers will respond to the COVID-19-induced recession. I predict the left-moving median voter will be the fulcrum constraint limiting policymakers' response options. Even with nearly 15% of GDP committed to various stimulative measures, I believe that investors should err on the side of expecting greater government intervention in the economy, broadly defined – not just regarding the COVID-19 pandemic, but also in other future contexts.

(And as I sit here in late June, making final edits to this manuscript, the markets are again fretting over whether the CARES Act will be extended with new stimulus. It shows me that investors have still not realized the dramatic change in the reaction function of policymakers. The median voter has spoken. There is no political opposition to further stimulus. As such, I would expect an additional $1.5-$3 trillion in stimulus – both replenishing the expiring provisions of the CARES Act and a potential infrastructure bill – by the end of 2020, taking the US budget deficit to as high as 30% of GDP.)

Even if the COVID-19 recession is sharp but brief, as I have expected it to be from its beginning, policymakers will fight to the last man and respond like it is 2008. President Trump was elected in 2016 with unemployment at 4.7%, a fairly low figure, and American voters chose a TV gameshow host as a president because they were still angry about income inequality, globalization, and an anemic economic recovery. Neither Trump nor his opponents will wait around to see who the American public elects in 2024. Instead, they will try to get ahead by introducing a steady stream of ever more unorthodox policies to stimulate the economy.

I have dubbed this move away from *laissez-faire* policies of the Washington Consensus the Buenos Aires Consensus. The Washington Consensus is merely a catchall term for the policies that have defined the 1980-2010s era. The "Washington" in the term stands for Washington DC, the city where the two institutions most responsible for propagating its policy recommendations – the World Bank and the IMF – are headquartered. The consensus was defined by a set of policies that sought to remove democracy from economic policy. Independent central banking, counter-cyclical fiscal policy, *laissez-faire* regulatory framework ... all of these policies have a singular point in common: they remove the role of elected officials from economic policy.

Now, don't take me wrong. I say this in as normatively neutral way as I can. You wouldn't fly an airplane *democratically*, so why would you operate a central bank or fiscal policy with input from voters? Nonetheless, in the most enthusiastic adherents to the Washington Consensus – the US and the UK – the political pendulum is swinging back toward populism. Democracy is finding its way *back* into economic policy.

So why Buenos Aires? What does Argentina have to do with this populist backlash? Nothing other than that it has been beset with decades of populist policymaking. And after its latest plunge back into populism following the 2019 election, what better city to replace Washington for our new catchall term than Buenos Aires?

The downside of the populist "growth above all else" mentality that the Buenos Aires Consensus represents is that the US is likely to move further to the left on almost all economic dimensions. The net actions of American policymakers reflect the economic preference of the American median voter. If post-2016 policy shifts continue into 2020 and beyond, the US could be the first mover to spur global momentum away from

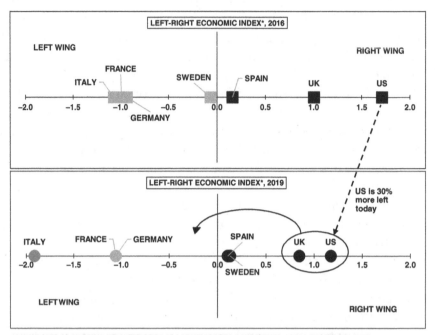

*CALCULATED AS AN EQUAL-WEIGHTED INDEX OF 5 STANDARDIZED COMPONENTS: LABOR PROTECTION INDEX,
GOVERNMENT REVENUE AS A PERCENT OF GDP, ALL-IN AVERAGE INCOME TAX RATE AT AVERAGE WAGE, REDISTRIBUTION
EFFECT ON GINI COEFFICIENT, AND EASE OF DOING BUSINESS RANKING.
SOURCE: OECD, WORLD BANK, BCA RESEARCH INC (WWW.BCARESEARCH.COM), CLOCKTOWER CALCULATIONS.
REPRINTED WITH PERMISSION OF CLOCKTOWER GROUP, L.P.

Figure 4.7   The coming Buenos Aires Consensus.

laissez-faire policies (Figure 4.7) — a transition away from the Washington
Consensus toward a Buenos Aires Consensus. Such a shift would impact
a wide swath of policies.

Over the next decade, I would expect more unorthodox fiscal and
monetary policy, an increase in antitrust cases, further fiscal easing, selective regulatory pressures, and higher taxes on both capital gains and
high-income taxpayers. If you're fretting about the extraordinary fiscal
cliff coming up in 2021, don't. Policymakers will assuage it with even
more fiscal stimulus.

The transition from the Washington to Buenos Aires Consensus will
dominate markets over the next decade. This transition is more relevant
than the US-China geopolitical rivalry, risks to European integration,

and technological change. All assets will be influenced by the deluge of fiscal and monetary policy.

Such a leftward move will sound the death knell for the US equity market's cyclical outperformance relative to the rest of the world. With US profit margins and valuations at historical highs, long-term investors should probably begin underweighting US assets on a multiyear horizon. The dollar has probably peaked in 2020 with a long-term decline ahead. This will especially be the case if the COVID-19 recession ends up being brutal but brief, as investors are starting to realize is the case. Once the recession is over, the immense amount of stimulus sloshing around the US economy will likely flee to other equity markets as investors seek returns in economies that are not printing their way to growth. While I would remain bullish on US equities in absolute terms, I'd use the "churn" of 2020 to reposition to European, Japanese, and EM equities on a decade-long strategic asset allocation.

The above paragraph would be my forecast and advice to investors no matter who wins the 2020 election. The median voter is the price maker in the political marketplace; in the long-term, politicians are mere price takers.

MVT in a Vote-less Nation: Does China Have a Median Voter?

The MVT is a great framework with which to gauge the long-term trajectory of policies. But is it limited to democracies?

It depends. In assessing the policies of North Korean ruler Kim Jong-un, MVT is useless. However, it makes strange sense for a non-democratically elected leader to pay attention to the preference of his median … citizen.

The collapse of the Soviet Union in 1991 jarred Chinese policymakers; if the Soviet Union could fall apart, so could China. And officials knew if this thought had occurred to them, it had also occurred to the Chinese median citizen.

China circa 1991 had only partly adopted pro-market reforms and opening up – it withdrew back into its communist shell after Tiananmen

Square. The precarious situation drove the Chinese Communist Party (CCP) to rethink its approach to domestic governance, ideology, economic development, and foreign policy. While there were initially many different voices within the party, the neoconservative faction eventually won out.

Party members published their views in the *China Youth Daily*, a newspaper associated with the China Communist Youth League – a CCP ruling faction. Titled "Strategic Choices and Practical Responses After the Collapse of the Soviet Union," the manifesto identified the party's biggest threat as its own self-ignorance.[28] The paper argued that the CCP's failure to properly transform from a revolutionary party to a ruling one led to such disasters as the Great Leap Forward and the Cultural Revolution. In light of the disintegration of the USSR, the most urgent task was to carry out gradual, constructive reforms to ensure social stability and higher economic productivity.

Several years later, the CCP General Secretary Jiang Zemin summarized the party's secondhand historical experience with his theory of "the Three Represents:"

- The party should represent the advanced productive forces in society.
- The party should represent advanced modern culture.
- The party should *represent the interests of the vast majority of the people* [emphasis added].[29]

The Three Represents are an attempt to asymptotically approach the position of the Chinese median citizen with the intention of avoiding the fate of the Soviet Union.

As Figure 4.8 depicts, China's 2018 GDP growth relative to its level of wealth leaves it vulnerable to falling into the dreaded middle-income

---

[28] Department of Thought and Theory, "China's Realistic Response and Strategic Choices after the Great Changes of the Soviet Union," *China Youth Daily*, July 31, 2006, http://m .wyzxwk.com/content.php?classid=13™id=7392.

[29] Jason Buhi, "Foreign Policy and the Chinese Constitutions During the Hu Jintao Administration," *Boston College International and Comparative Law Review* 37, no. 2 (Spring 2014): 253, http://ezproxy.lapl.org/login?url=https://search-proquest-com.ezproxy.lapl .org/docview/1663666068?accountid=6749.

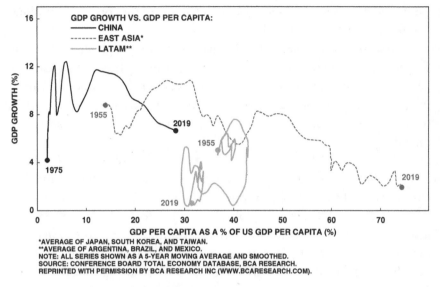

Figure 4.8   The dreaded middle-income trap.

trap.[30] Most Latin American countries whose growth rates slowed in the 1970s did not last as authoritarian regimes. Neither did the Soviet Union, whose GDP-*per-capita* growth stalled in the 1970s. Informed by the history of these countries and their experiences, CCP leadership understands that if China falls into the middle-income trap, it will likely meet the same fate. So officials are executing preventative measures.

Since 2017, Chinese policymakers have undertaken a set of painful structural reforms. At a time when the developed world is moving toward the Buenos Aires Consensus – a fancy way of saying populism – Beijing has enacted financial and macroprudential reforms that constrain growth. It is cracking down on both provinces' ability to raise independent sources of revenue and shadow banking, which greased the wheels of profligacy. Even China's response to the COVID-19

---

[30] Development Research Center of the State Council, the People's Republic of China, *China 2030: Building a Modern, Harmonious, and Creative Society* (Washington, DC: World Bank, 2013), https://www.worldbank.org/content/dam/Worldbank/document/China-2030-complete.pdf

pandemic has been conservative compared to the orgy of stimulus coming out of Europe and the US.

These reforms suggest that China's policymakers believe the best way to safeguard continued growth – especially in the face of China's demographic disadvantages – is to boost productivity. To do so, China streamlined capital allocation, ensuring that private enterprises take priority over unproductive state-owned enterprises in terms of access to capital.

Whether this effort survives beyond 2020 is a litmus test of policymakers' understanding of their constraints – that the Chinese median citizen can hold their political capital hostage and would prefer not to be hung out to dry during a global recession. To retain power, policymakers will eventually have to abandon painful reforms to stimulate in the face of the COVID-19 pandemic. However, at the time of writing, they have remained stubbornly committed to ensuring that real estate prices do not rise.

Why? Beijing is once again taking advantage of its abundance of short-term political capital for long-term gain. Although real estate stimulus is the most efficient way to jumpstart the economy, if Xi Jinping permitted real estate prices to rise in middle-class-laden coastal cities, it would create a longer-term political risk. The prices could lead a large, vocal populace to form opposition against the one-party government. The entire scenario may devolve into protests akin to those in Hong Kong.[31] Policymakers in China continue to emphasize Xi's mantra that "housing is for living, not speculation," potentially to the detriment of a fast recovery.

Concern over the median citizen's view also drove the Xi administration to enact sweeping anticorruption policies, curb pollution with

---

[31] The high real estate prices priced out Millennials and Gen Z Hong Kongers from home ownership, fueling protesters' anger and unrest. Alexandra Stevenson and Jin Wu, "Tiny Apartments and Punishing Work Hours: The Economic Roots of Hong Kong's Protests," *New York Times*, July 22, 2019, https://www.nytimes.com/interactive/2019/07/22/world/asia/hong-kong-housing-inequality.html.

draconian measures, and change the one-child policy and Hukou residency registration system.[32]

These measures indicate that Chinese leaders understand China's precarious position. The Chinese middle class makes up such a large portion of the population, and it is only growing. As of 2017, the middle class made up over 50% of the population (Figure 4.9), with wealth levels already above those of South Korea and Taiwan when they transitioned away from authoritarian rule (Figure 4.10). Because votes and polling are not options, the closest representation of the Chinese median citizen is popular middle-class support.

This popular support is a reliable predictor of China's future policies, so forecasters can treat it as a key constraint when forecasting Chinese government behavior. If policymakers were completely unconstrained

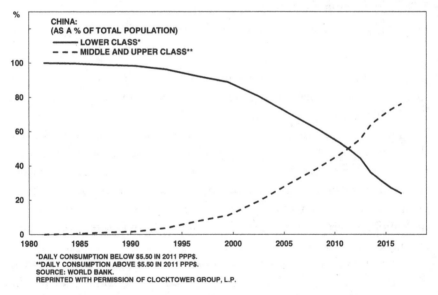

Figure 4.9   China is at a critical middle-class threshold.

---

[32] To reduce pollution, policymakers shut down entire factories in the worst-affected cities. Such drastic measures may appeal to the median citizen, but their mercilessness on newly jobless individuals means these types of actions are only possible in a one-party system.

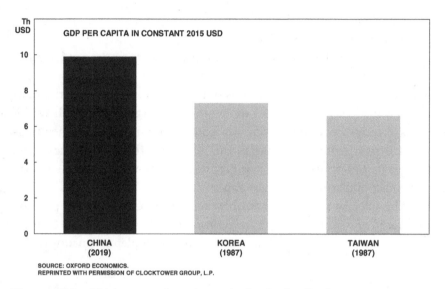

Figure 4.10   Chinese coastal provinces are already ripe for democracy.

by the middle class, they would simply stimulate the economy at every turn. They would have had little motivation or pressure to enact the 2017–2020 self-imposed slowdown.

There is one tenet of the MVT that does not apply to China: short-term competition. It is a good self-preservation measure for Chinese policymakers to respond to their "voters," but they need not worry that an opposing party will outmaneuver them. Beijing has to satisfy its citizens' demands for clean air and honest officials, but there is no political alternative waiting in the wings who will offer even cleaner air and even more honesty.

The absence of short-term competition provides Chinese leaders with the luxury of time to enact policies that are sometimes painful at first but that have long-term rewards; they are less subject to the "time-in-power" constraint.

But China's resilience only lasts up to a point. If the entire system collapses, all bets are off. As long as the CCP is in charge, it can tinker with painful policies more easily than an ineffective democracy can – though its path to policy reform is much more difficult than that of an effective democracy.

Wealth levels matter in the creation of an effective democracy. If I measure the effectiveness of democracy using Freedom House scores, where 1 represents the most effective democracy and 7 the least, there is a noticeable relationship between wealth levels and the quality of democracy (Figure 4.11).

But Figure 4.11 is not a positive for China. The chart does not presume causality. With a GDP *per capita* of just under $10,000 – and with many of its large, coastal provinces well beyond that – China appears to be right below the level where most effective democracies find themselves. This suggests that there are soon to be bottom-up pressures for greater political representation, particularly if policymakers lose credibility due to an economic, financial, or pandemic crisis.

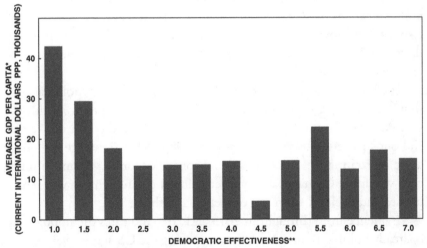

*SOURCE: IMF WEO, APRIL 2019.
**SOURCE: FREEDOM HOUSE (2019), DEMOCRATIC EFFECTIVENESS IS AN EQUALLY-WEIGHTED AVERAGE OF MEASURES OF POLITICAL RIGHTS AND CIVIL LIBERTIES, WITH 1 REPRESENTING THE FREEST COUNTRY, AND 7 REPRESENTING THE LEAST FREE.
REPRINTED WITH PERMISSION BY BCA RESEARCH INC (WWW.BCARESEARCH.COM).

Figure 4.11   Wealth supports effective democracy.

For Chinese policymakers, the 2020s are critical. China is undergoing structural reforms to further liberalize its economy. But it is, at the same time, consolidating more power in Beijing at the expense of the provinces. While to the global West, political centralization and economic liberalization are unpalatable – and even illogical – this combination is familiar to academia. Samuel Huntington's 1968 *Political Order in Changing Societies* warns against too-rapid political liberalization amid economic and social modernity because it could lead to collapse.

Given their nondemocratic structure, Chinese policymakers have more leeway when it comes to the political constraints of popularity and time in power, but not much. The days of the Cultural Revolution and the Great Leap Forward are gone. The rhetoric remains, but CCP leadership is far more wedded to the demands of its citizenry than Western commentators depict.

The greatest threat to Beijing's continued rule is that the more it centralizes power, the more it will lose a convenient scapegoat for policy mistakes: the provinces. The central government has blamed economic mismanagement, corruption, pollution, and even the COVID-19 response on provincial officials. As the central government increases its share of Chinese power, it will no longer be able to "pass the buck" to provincial officials.

If China's burgeoning and demanding middle class is a political constraint as of 2020, how will Beijing prioritize its competition with the US? An analysis using the constraint framework predicts an unexciting and out-of-consensus view. Just as post-1980s NBA fights are no longer quite as exciting ... because they no longer occur ... China's middle class will force China away from geopolitical excitement. It will retreat inward and back off from its competition with the US.

Evidence from throughout 2019 and 2020 indicates the middle class is already holding Beijing back from engaging the US aggressively. China stayed its hand during the Hong Kong protests, refusing to crack down harshly on the student protests. Beijing nominally kept its hands clean by allowing local law enforcement to deal with the unrest. Abroad, Beijing signaled a retreat from competition with the US when it agreed to the Phase One deal – a capitulation, considering the terms allow the White House to keep most of the tariffs on Chinese exports. Since President

Trump came to power, China has also avoided confrontations with the US military in the South China Sea. Incidents continued to happen, but on the margin and with lower frequency than under President Obama.

China's actions suggest President Trump hit China where it hurts: wealth generation, particularly among the middle class. And Beijing relented because keeping its middle class happy takes precedence over world domination. The Three Represents are still in place, but none have anything to do with Maoism or making China a global hegemon.

Of course, China wants to dominate East Asia and expand its global influence. But delivering economic growth to its middle class is the main priority because it is Beijing's constraint to action on any scale. Anything that impedes Beijing's ability to provide for the middle class – including a bid to challenge the US as a global hegemon – comes second.

The constraints that the Chinese median citizen places on policy-maker actions means there is a limit to how far China will push against the US. As long as economic growth, productivity growth, and escaping the middle-income trap remain the central goals in Beijing, there will be limits to Chinese expansionism.

Ironically, that also means that the greatest risk to global order and peace is American miscalculation of Chinese intentions, not actual Chinese aggression. My constraint-based framework suggests that Beijing is far more constrained than US policymakers seem to think. Chinese leaders are worried about their growth trajectory and the sustainability of a move up the value curve. If the US pushes Beijing too hard on trade and the economy, it will threaten the primary directive for China: escaping the middle-income trap. And *that* is when Beijing would have to respond with aggression.

Political Constraints: Takeaway

Political constraints are correlated with who has the most power, so they are *the* starting point for geopolitical forecasting. It is the least glamorous but also the most restrictive – and hence telling – constraint. To determine a situation's political constraints, a forecaster need not analyze bond yields and credit default swap (CDS) prices, make an order-of-battle comparison of two hostile militaries, or study history and geopolitics. It is domestic politics that determines the policymakers' maneuvering room, whether in an international or interparty conflict.

The concepts of political capital and the median voter help extract the motivating political constraints behind domestic policies. Political capital is difficult to measure, as it relies on an *ad-hoc* approach. Rather than a grand theory, it is contextual, and the careful forecaster applies it case by case. Its lack of uniformity in measure means it falls short in comparative study – for the time being. I hope in the near future, someone can offer a back-tested, actionable, political capital index that works across time and space.

In contrast to political capital, the MVT is more quantifiable, and therefore a more comfortable concept for those in finance to work with. In many contexts, the median voter's preference serves as a useful, more manageable proxy for political capital. It tells analysts to focus on the median voter when contemplating long-term policy trajectories of a country.

The median voter is the price maker in the political marketplace. Politicians are price takers.

Chapter 5

The Economy and the Market

"I used to think if there was reincarnation, I wanted to come back as the president or the pope or a .400 baseball hitter. But now, I want to come back as the bond market. You can intimidate everybody."
— James Carville, Clinton campaign strategist, 1993, as told
to the *Wall Street Journal*

M y first experience of macroeconomic and market constraints came early, at seven years old. It was 1989, and Yugoslavia's last prime minister, Ante Marković, was trying his best to hold the country together. He was dealing with more than the rising nationalism in the constitutive republics of the country: Marković was at the center of a classic EM balance-of-payments crisis.

In Chapter 1, I explained how Yugoslavia was a Cold War knight navigating the chess game of capitalism versus communism: it was an entire country levered to geopolitics. Belgrade managed its promiscuous foreign policy while sitting astride the NATO–Warsaw Pact rift. Not only did Yugoslavia make friends in the East and the West, but it also provided the Global South with engineering knowhow, which Yugoslavia exported for lucrative foreign currency contracts.[1]

Unfortunately for Yugoslavia's balancing act, a succession of external shocks destabilized the economy. The oil crisis of the 1970s hit Yugoslavia, an oil importer. Then came the 1980s, when competition from South Korea bit into the profit margins of its engineering outsourcing business. Finally, the textile industry faced competition from emerging Asian markets.

Yugoslavia dealt with these shocks by knocking on capitalism's door and asking to borrow a cup of sugar. It did not adjust its imports and investments to fit the new reality. It did not adopt austerity, cracking down on the twin ills of currency depreciation and inflation with hawkish monetary policy (i.e., raising interest rates). Instead, Yugoslavia borrowed from its friends in the West. Unlike its communist peers stuck behind the Iron Curtain, Yugoslavia accumulated a significant foreign debt that allowed citizens to live beyond their means.

In the late 1980s, the gravy train stopped. The international community became unwilling to lend to an irresponsible debtor. Yugoslavia's geopolitical worth waned as the Cold War wound down amid Gorbachev's reforms, and it could not guarantee its capitalist friends that it would be able to implement austerity. In 1988, facing rising prices and a falling dinar, the government relaxed income controls. Nominal wages rose by 5% per month in the last quarter of 1988. By September 1989, real wages had increased by 20% in eight months. The annual rate of consumer price inflation reached 13,000% in the fourth quarter of 1989.[2] Yugoslavia entered the dreaded wage–price spiral.

At the end of 1989, Prime Minister Marković tried to end the crisis. On New Year's Eve, he introduced a new currency pegged to the deutschmark, austerity, privatization of businesses, and wage freezes. He also instructed the National Bank of Yugoslavia to stop printing money.

---

[1] "The Global South" refers to the Non-aligned Movement – which Yugoslavia helped start – and to the Middle Eastern petrostates.

[2] *OECD Economic Surveys: Yugoslavia 1989–1990* (Paris: OECD Publishing, 1990), https://read.oecd-ilibrary.org/economics/oecd-economic-surveys-yugoslavia-1990_eco_surveys-yucs-1990-en#page3.

Inflation was stopped in its tracks in 1990, falling to *zero*. Marković's austerity gambit worked!

It was a pyrrhic victory. The austerity led to a collapse in economic output. The collapse in turn primed the battleground for populists running the constitutive republics to sow separatism and ethnic conflict. Serbia's Slobodan Milošević soon instructed the central bank to ignore the federal government and print money so he could fund his election campaign. When inflation returned, the median voter preference was to blame the technocrat in charge: Marković.

I remember this period vividly, even at seven years old. I learned what inflation was before my baby teeth fell out. The consensus view in the West is that Yugoslavia fell apart because of ethnic hatred. Yes, there was a lot of that. But for many, their ethnicity was not a huge aspect of their identity. At the very least, ethnicity was insignificant enough that children didn't pick up on the identity battle lines. My father had to sit me down and explain what it meant to be a Serb, as opposed to a Yugoslav. Some of my generational peers have similar stories, whether Croat, Slovene, or Bosniak.

Since leaving Yugoslavia, I have lived, studied, and worked in a number of places with an underlying thread of ethnic and sectarian tensions. And yet none of them resorted to the type of bloodletting that occurred in the country of my birth. Why?

The 1989/1990 Organization for Economic Cooperation and Development (OECD)'s economic survey of Yugoslavia is a heavy read.[3] The authors do not mention the bubbling nationalism and ethnic tensions, but their clinical dissection of the spiraling economic crisis is wreathed in foreboding. Yugoslavia had many problems – and yes, ethnic tension was one of them – but the macroeconomic environment limited how much political capital was available for the federal government to solve these problems. Had Yugoslavia enjoyed a different set of macroeconomic and market constraints, perhaps its story would

---

[3] A big shout-out to the OECD and its research staff! Their economic surveys are some of the best sources of information for anyone looking to get brought up to speed quickly on a particular country. The fact that their archive has old surveys available is also indispensable to any student of historical economic and financial crises.

not have ended in 1991.[4] Reformers like Marković may have had more maneuvering room to buy the loyalty of federal armed forces and move against the nationalists with force. Alas, we will never know.

Between a Rock and a Hard Place

One of the greatest challenges of geopolitical analysis is that forecasters are often not well-versed in economics and finance. Or even worse: they know just enough to wield the tools but do not have the expertise to do so safely. And by "safely," I mean without anything going so awry that crises and predictions blow up in their faces.

The Euro Area crisis demonstrates the consequences of forecasters' incomplete knowledge. Throughout the sovereign debt crisis (2010–2015), financial media breathlessly reported on the rising debt levels, deficits, and bond yields of the peripheral economies (Ireland, Italy, Greece, Spain, and Portugal). But these reports failed to factor in the symbiotic relationship between that profligate "periphery" and the "core" export-oriented economies: the supposedly austere Northern European economies that would refuse to rescue the common currency.

The doom-and-gloom prognosticators did not account for constraints on the breakup of the European monetary union. They focused on the preferences: on policymakers' supposedly pragmatic desire to either exit the Euro Area or kick another member out.

The deep geopolitical logic behind the union remained, regardless of peripheral economic struggles. Rather than creating centrifugal forces sufficient to send each country in a different direction, economics and finance actually played a centripetal force, playing a key role in the Euro Area's perseverance.

In this chapter, I deal with two constraints: macroeconomics and finance, or the market. The two exist in what George Soros calls a reflexive relationship, where investor perceptions can alter the economic

---

[4] And perhaps its basketball team would have given the 1992 Dream Team a run for its money! A worthy subject for another book ...

fundamentals.[5] Though they affect each other, the two constraints are distinct.

- **Macroeconomic Constraints:** To identify macroeconomic constraints, I rely on economic fundamentals: What are the main drivers of growth? Is productivity high, or is most growth a function of labor force growth? Are there structural imbalances in the economy – long-term unemployment and underemployment, over-regulation, protectionism of domestic industries, wealth inequality? Is the current account balanced or unbalanced? If the latter, does the imbalance stem from export dependency (like a commodity exporter) or too much imported goods and capital? To what extent does domestic macroeconomic policy encourage creative destruction and competition?

  These are the types of questions that ECON 102 students learn to ask and answer. I use macroeconomic fundamentals like a doctor uses the indicators of health (blood work, resting heart rate, etc.). A single red flag – high cholesterol – is easy enough to deal with in isolation. The doctor's orders: hit the treadmill and stop eating saturated fats. But if there are multiple markers off course, the doctor orders more work done. Like the doctor, if I find enough surprising answers to diagnostic questions, I investigate more thoroughly to find the root cause (my net assessment of India in Chapter 9 is a good example of this process).

- **Finance Constraints:** A country can have poor macro fundamentals for a very long time, but investor enthusiasm can keep the economy going. While they are in place, investor inflows mask the underlying imbalances – like ibuprofen masking a fever.

  Greece did not become an unproductive, overindebted, low-growth economy overnight in 2010. The roots of its structural decline stretch back to the 1990s. However, investors ignored the

---

[5] George Soros, *The Alchemy of Finance* (New Jersey: Wiley, 1987). A good example of reflexivity is the relationship between currencies and interest rates. A rally in a country's currency, even if initiated by speculative and short-term inflows, allows the central bank to lower interest rates. The reflexivity continues as the lower rates create a virtuous cycle that helps the economy grow and, in turn, appreciate the currency further.

fundamentals and plowed into its assets — particularly the bond market — regardless. Investor enthusiasm allowed policymakers to grow complacent.

The role of a functional market is therefore to discipline and constrain policymakers, but investors do not always foster such an environment. Markets are also not rational, but rather driven by narratives.[6] These narratives can make a downturn worse by exacerbating a panic, but they can also amplify a mania.

In the case of Mediterranean Europe in the 2000s, investors cheered the advent of the European monetary union, plowing into the bond markets of each member state. The yield convergence that this process initiated rewarded policymakers through no effort of their own (Figure 5.1). The market failed in its job. When the market finally woke up, it did so with a scream. Bond yields can be more powerful than missiles.

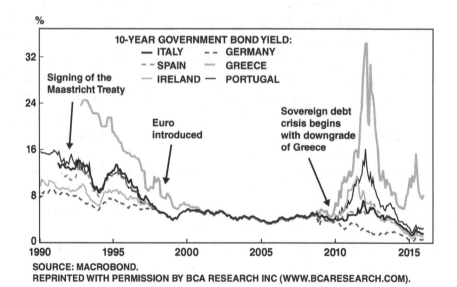

SOURCE: MACROBOND.
REPRINTED WITH PERMISSION BY BCA RESEARCH INC (WWW.BCARESEARCH.COM).

Figure 5.1 The market asleep.

---

[6] Robert J. Shiller, *Narrative Economics: How Stories Go Viral & Drive Major Economic Events* (Princeton, NJ: Princeton University Press, 2019).

In the rest of this chapter, I survey macro and market constraints by applying each to the Euro Area crisis. I illustrate why macroeconomic fundamentals and market forces acted as constraints to any country's preference to exit – even though the contemporary consensus was that such factors *encouraged* countries to exit the EU. Most investors and financial journalists thought the market was acting as a centrifugal force that would eventually send each country in Europe off on its own tangent. They reached that conclusion because they overstated policymaker preferences for exit, especially in Greece's case.

Fundamentals at Work: The German Question

The economy is a direct constraint to policymakers. High inflation and unemployment can combine to produce an elevated Misery Index, as occurred in Argentina.[7] However, forecasters need to look beyond the direct causal links and consider the subtler implications. One of the gravest errors Euro Area analysts committed was misunderstanding the power dynamic between Germany and the Mediterranean economies.

"The German Question" has been Europe's central geopolitical dilemma since the defeat of Napoleon. In the aftermath of the 1789 French revolution, Paris's new elite faced a dilemma: they needed to develop a system to control a heterogenous country no longer united by the monarchy.[8] The answer was a new governance model: nationalism. For the next hundred years, the state bureaucracy focused on turning "peasants into Frenchmen," in the words of historian Eugen Weber.[9]

---

[7] See Chapter 3.

[8] During this period, only 12–13% of the public within France's borders spoke *Île-de-France* French. Eric Hobsbawm, *Nations and Nationalism Since 1780,* 2nd ed. (Cambridge: Cambridge University Press, 1997).

[9] Eugen Weber, *Peasants into Frenchmen: The Modernization of Rural France (1870–1914)* (Stanford, CA: Stanford University Press, 1976).

Unfortunately for the Parisian elites, the advent of the nation-state in France was always going to end in the creation of Germany. Just as nationalism encouraged French peasants to become Frenchmen, it encouraged the German peasants, strewn across central Europe in three dozen sovereign states, to eventually become Germans.

German unification in 1871 created an economic and demographic superpower in the geographical heart of Europe. Due to its size and potential, from day one Germany elicited suspicion and fear in its comparatively diminutive neighbors. Aware of the target on their backs, German leaders sought to balance against the continent's other powers to prevent an anti-German bloc from forming – especially one led by France.

Twice, Germany chose to answer its own question through the application of force. Both times it failed, and the second time nearly wiped the nation out altogether. While Germany is a formidable country, it is no match for the rest of the continent united against it.

For Germany, unification with would-be opponents – the EU and the European monetary union – is an alternative path to resolving the German Question.

Contrary to popular belief, Germans did not create the euro as a ploy to undermine the economies of its European peers. Pundits point out that the European Central Bank (ECB) is headquartered in Frankfurt as proof of some Teuton conspiracy. It is not. Germany demanded that the ECB be housed in Frankfurt as a consolation for losing its currency.

The European monetary union exists so that the EU can function. A common market with no barriers to trade cannot exist without a common currency. Why? Because the temptation to depreciate one's currency – and gain competitiveness – is too great. If Italy were allowed to depreciate the lira by 15% every time its economy slowed, its trading partners would eventually balk and put up tariffs, and the European integrationist project would be over.

To prevent European countries from depreciating their currency for competitive advantage, members of the European Economic

Community (EEC) did not turn to the common currency solution immediately. Initially, the EEC created a convoluted dollar peg (referred to as the "snake in the tunnel"). When that did not work out, it pegged all European currency to the deutschmark. But that solution gave the Bundesbank too much power over European monetary policy.

These first attempts to stabilize the EU economy demonstrate that the goal of the third attempted solution – the euro – was not to benefit Germany but to constrain its power over European monetary policy.

Germany benefited anyway.

By pegging its currency to the other Euro Area currencies, the deutschmark was devalued by roughly 20% *vis-à-vis* its competitors (Figure 5.2). Think of the euro as a currency smoothie. Germany diluted the chalky protein-powder taste of its deutschmark by blending it with the sweet banana currencies of Italy, France, and Spain. Take the deutschmark out of the smoothie, and German goods suddenly appreciate by anywhere from 20% to God-knows-how-much percent.

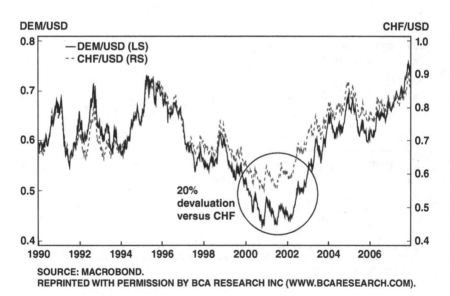

Figure 5.2   Germany diluted the deutschmark.

The German economy was also in dire need of reform in the 1990s. By the early 2000s, an over-regulated labor market and EU accession by Eastern European neighbors spurred Berlin to negotiate a reform package with its unions known as the Hartz IV reforms. These reforms caused a significant downtrend in the German unemployment rate and stabilization of its GDP growth (Figure 5.3).

Unlike the rest of Europe, Germany did not waste the early part of the twenty-first century. It rolled up its sleeves and undertook painful reforms. It cut long-term unemployment benefits and introduced short shift work. The long-term impact of the Hartz reforms was a dramatic decline in the unemployment rate, from a *peak* of 11.5% in January 2002 to 4.9% at the end of the current cycle. Reforms have also encouraged a steady increase in wage growth – albeit at a lower pace than productivity growth – despite the conventional view that they would have the opposite effect.

By the start of the Euro Area crisis in 2010, Germany had no choice but to bail out the Mediterranean countries. Berlin had spent two

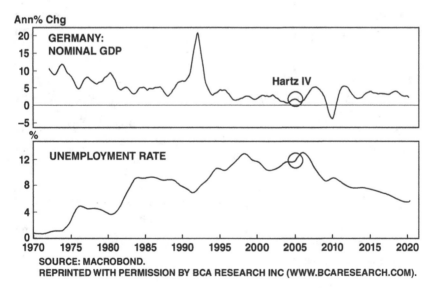

Figure 5.3   Germany got ready for the Euro Area.

decades preparing for the monetary union, tooling its export-oriented economy to be successful. And according to plan, the German economy was extremely export-dependent. A whopping 55% of German exports were bound for the EU in 2010. While exports to emerging markets, like China, had been growing, they still only accounted for 28% total exports at the time (Figure 5.4). Germany's dependence on Euro Area countries – which comprised 42% of its total exports – constrained policymakers from exiting in 2010, regardless of their preference.

Economic dependence on EU countries is Germany's fulcrum constraint to leaving the union, and it is only growing. The German economy will not find a new customer base in its own demographics. With a fertility rate of just 1.46 births per woman and a generally anti-immigrant turn in its politics, Germany domestic demand is unlikely to skyrocket. The economy will be dependent on exports – mostly to Europe – for the foreseeable future. Rising trade protectionism in the US and China – as well as an increased growth slowdown in the latter induced by the reforms discussed in Chapter 4 – means

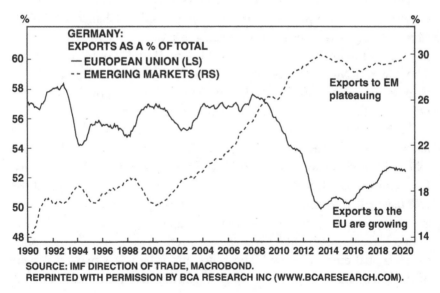

Figure 5.4   Germany needs Europe.

Germany is stuck with its EU peers and their common market. Germany is caught between a rock and a hard place: between EU customer dependence and no opportunity for customer acquisition elsewhere.

Throughout the 2010s, financial media ignored these fundamental macro constraints to a German exit from the Euro Area. Perhaps the media silence was a symptom of journalistic laziness, but the coverage was also biased toward Euroscepticism. The British press was especially slanted, projecting its own Euroscepticism onto the German public and policymakers. The phrase "rising German Euroscepticism" became shorthand for the (now woefully incorrect) reports filed by a slew of London-based publications.

To find a more accurate prediction of Germany's behavior, the pundits needed look no further than the polling. It did not take German median voters long to realize that their well-being was directly linked to that of the common currency union (Figure 5.5). Policymakers in Germany – even the Eurosceptic ones – soon followed and approved one bailout after another.

The extraordinary journey of the German median voter toward the most Europhile position has now culminated in Chancellor Angela Merkel's aggressive push for mutualization of debt across the union, once a Rubicon that most pundits thought Berlin would never cross. The Macron-Merkel proposal for a European Recovery Fund is likely to pass at some point in 2020, even if the "Frugal Four" – Austria, Denmark, the Netherlands, and Sweden – oppose it.

What Merkel has understood for some time is that Europe is on its own. Alternatives to integration do not exist in a multipolar world where European sovereign states face off against China, Russia, India, Iran, and yes, the US. And what Eurosceptic pundits in the US and the UK have failed to understand is that European policymakers and voters are not ... how to put this delicately ... stupid. A dissolution of the EU would leave countries like Sweden, the Netherlands, and Spain – once strong global empires, now living museums at best – as two-bit players of the Great Game in the twenty-first century. Even Germany, France,

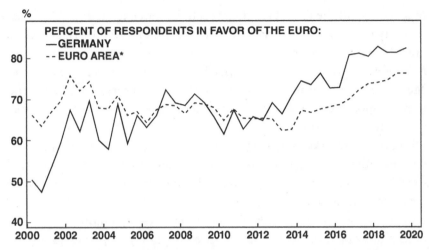

*AVERAGE OF GREECE, GERMANY, SPAIN, FRANCE, ITALY, PORTUGAL, BELGIUM, NETHERLANDS, AND AUSTRIA.
SOURCE: EUROBAROMETER, MACROBOND.
REPRINTED WITH PERMISSION BY BCA RESEARCH INC (WWW.BCARESEARCH.COM).

Figure 5.5 German support for the Euro Area is strong.

and Italy would struggle to pursue their national interests in an era of continental-sized powers.

While I suspect that Merkel took this geopolitical imperative into consideration from day one of the Euro Area crisis, it was the election of Donald Trump that spurred the famously cautious politician into dramatic action. In May 2017, Merkel met with President Trump at the G7 summit in Sicily. At that meeting, Trump blamed Germany for its massive trade surplus with the US and generally treated his German counterpart as a rival.

Following the summit, Merkel promptly flew back to Germany, straight into a Munich beer hall, and addressing a crowd of generally Eurosceptic members of the Christian Social Union (CSU) declared "The era in which we could fully rely on others is over … "[10] Her choice

[10] Matthey Karnitschnig, "What Angela Merkel meant at the Munich beer hall, *Politico*, May 28, 2017. https://www.politico.eu/article/what-angela-merkel-meant-at-the-munich-beer-hall/

of location and the crowd for the speech was notable. The CSU – a sister party of Merkel's Christian Democratic Union (CDU) – had taken a notably more Eurosceptic line throughout the Euro Area crisis, with its MPs often voting against the Chancellor on individual bailout decisions. Merkel's intention was to descend straight into conservative Bavaria and impress upon the most Eurosceptic of her allies that there were no alternatives to integration.

I do not see risks to European integration over the course of the next decade. Mini-crises may come and go – Italy always being a potential source of drama – but the geopolitical imperative is clear: integrate or perish into irrelevance. Europe is not integrating out of some misplaced utopian fantasy. And it is not seeking an ever-closer union for the sake of its bloody past. Its sovereign states are integrating – and yes, giving up sovereignty – out of weakness and fear. Unions out of weakness are often the most sustainable over the long term. After all, America's original 13 colonies integrated out of fear that the UK would eventually re-invade. And Swiss multi-ethnic cantons united because a failure to do so would have left them at the mercy of their powerful neighbors.

With European integration and unity a moot point, investors will profit by allocating to the continent over the next decade. Yes, Europe will also engage in Buenos Aires policies, but I doubt that the pendulum away from *laissez-faire* will swing as hard and fast as in the US.

Greece After the Euro: The Land of Milk and Honey?

The flip side of Germany's economic constraints is the story of Greece. Throughout the crisis, commentators argued that Greece should leave the Euro Area, devalue its currency, default on all its debt, and enjoy smooth sailing after the initial shock. Nobel Laureate Paul Krugman urged Athens to quit.[11] His fellow economist and

---

[11] Paul Krugman, "Ending Greece's Bleeding," *New York Times*, July 6, 2015, https://www.nytimes.com/2015/07/06/opinion/paul-krugman-ending-greeces-bleeding.html.

euro Curmudgeon-in-Chief Hans-Werner Sinn penned an op-ed in solidarity at the height of the 2015 Greek crisis.[12]

The Greeks paid no mind to the op-ed wizards. On the contrary, Greek support for Euro Area membership steadily increased as the crisis developed (Figure 5.6).

So, are Greeks stupid?

Absolutely not! Unlike the armchair pundits, the Greeks actually live in Greece. They know that without the membership in the EU, theirs is just another country in the Balkans.

The economists cheering "Greek exit" did so in a *ceteris paribus* world, which only exists in their social science laboratory. In this eerie

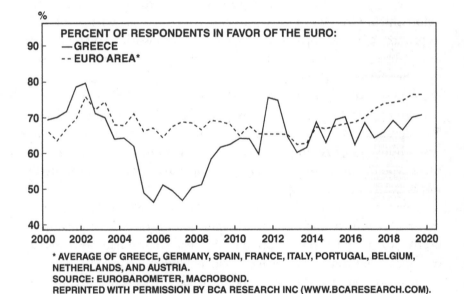

Figure 5.6   Silly Greeks, disagreeing with eminent economists.

---

[12] Hans-Werner Sinn, "Why Greece Should Leave the Eurozone," *New York Times*, July 24, 2015, https://www.nytimes.com/2015/07/25/opinion/why-greece-should-leave-the-eurozone.html.

environment, political risk to Greece neither precedes nor follows aban-
doning the currency union, and all policymakers managing Grexit have
PhDs in economics (and, presumably, op-ed columns in the *New York
Times*). But the argument was theoretical and as such is most effective
when executed in an Excel spreadsheet.

To blame Greece's currency for its uncompetitive economy is a
straw-man argument. The currency is the straw man, and structure
was Greece's real issue. Greece was in dire need of structural reforms
whether or not it remained in the Euro Area. To benefit from its
cheaper currency after "Grexit," Greece would have to receive direct
inflows of foreign investment. That was unlikely, given the subsequent
political instability that would have bracketed a Euro Area exit.

Greece also had little export revenue. Over the course of 15 years
before 2010, Greece lost nearly all export markets for what used to be
its primary exports: apparel articles, clothing accessories, and textiles. Its
export base became far less diversified, with petroleum refining essentially being the only one.

This specialization was not merely a function of its euro membership
but also of globalization and competition from Asian producers. Even a
50% devaluation of Greek products might not have overcome the labor
cost advantages of Asian producers. Asian economies monopolized the
exact type of cheap manufacturing products that used to constitute the
vast majority of Greek exports.

Manufacturing in 2015 accounted for only 28% of Greece's total
exports (of which roughly a third were mining-related), compared to
nearly 50% in 2001. The drop indicates that Greece had no manufacturing base left to take advantage of currency devaluation.

It is possible that the Greek policymakers who had just extricated
Greece from the EU would have implemented the pro-market structural
reforms necessary to attract foreign investors looking to capitalize on
currency devaluation. But then, had Greek policymakers been willing
to bear the pain of such a thorough policy change, they would have
focused on the reforms – not exiting the Euro Area.

Perhaps I have the advantage of hindsight, but back in 2015, pundits calling for a Greek exit from the Euro Area thought Argentina a good example of a successful separation. Hilarious in 2020, but let's take the argument seriously. Argentina was a poor example for Greece because in 2001, Buenos Aires benefited from a much more favorable global context than the Greece of 2015. Argentina, a commodity exporter, had the good luck to default and devalue in 2001, at the beginning of a commodity bull market unlike any in history.

The macro context for a Greek exit in 2015 was much worse. Global trade was, and continues to be, in a downtrend. Again, especially compared with Argentina's situation in 2001, Greek devaluation would not yield much bang for the euro. Or the drachma.

Greece was also unlike Argentina in that it remains completely dependent on imports for energy. In 2015, Greece imported roughly 64% of all its energy needs. Because of its reliance on energy imports, devaluation would have likely led to an immediate spike in prices of everything involving energy ... so, everything but the beach sand. Even food prices would rise due to the higher cost of transportation and production. Under the leadership of a steady government with strong support, the inflation spike would be short and vicious. But Greece's populist government would have likely panicked and printed money, moving the country toward the same hyperinflationary cycle that Yugoslavia experienced in 1989.

I assume the government in charge would panic and print its way out of the crisis because Greece has high levels of public employment and expenditure. The easiest way for the government to retain median voter support, and thus political capital, would be to print drachmas. To appease voters, the government would keep pensions and public wages in line with the higher cost of imports and skyrocketing prices. Over 50% of households depend on pensions for income. The median voter – who, as discussed in Chapter 4, dictates policy – would not take an inflationary shock lying down.

Inflation or no, tourism accounts for around 9% of Greek GDP and might improve on the back of a cheaper currency. But more tourism is not an optimal outcome for Greece. It is a low value-add and does not contribute much to a country's productivity growth. It also has a finite ability to absorb employment.

Ultimately, Greece did not leave the Euro Area. Its populist government, led by Alexis Tsipras, enacted the same painful structural reforms that pundits claimed would never happen. This is an extraordinary outcome given that Prime Minister Tsipras led the "Coalition of the Radical Left" (SYRIZA), which in 2015 was Eurosceptic. Yet he relented under the pressure of material constraints, tightened the country's belt, and bore the cross of reform and austerity. That cross has been passed to Prime Minister Kyriakos Mitsotakis, and he is maintaining its weight.

Since the reforms, Greek unit labor costs have fallen relative to the rest of the Euro Area. They are still high, but not egregiously so (Figure 5.7), eliminating a large part of the accumulated competitiveness

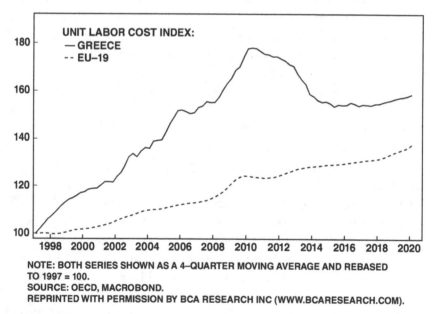

NOTE: BOTH SERIES SHOWN AS A 4–QUARTER MOVING AVERAGE AND REBASED
TO 1997 = 100.
SOURCE: OECD, MACROBOND.
REPRINTED WITH PERMISSION BY BCA RESEARCH INC (WWW.BCARESEARCH.COM).

Figure 5.7   Why leave when the hard work is done?

gap built up since 2000. Greece accomplished the painful budget consolidation that most commentators thought impossible. Its primary budget balance (excluding interest payments on debt) improved from a deficit of 10% in 2009 to a surplus of 4% in 2019 (Figure 5.8). Such a fiscal adjustment would have caused other countries to tear themselves apart. But Greece held together thanks to the strong economic constraints that prevented the "easy way out," a path that would have led – fittingly for the Greeks – to a pyrrhic victory. Because most of its debt is held by the official sector at negotiated rates, Greek interest payments account for only 3.5% of GDP – on par with the US and the wider Euro Area.

The pundits and economists cheering for Grexit knew less than the Greek median voter. Greek citizens and policymakers understood very well that they do not live in a *ceteris paribus* theoretical dreamland. They live in Greece.

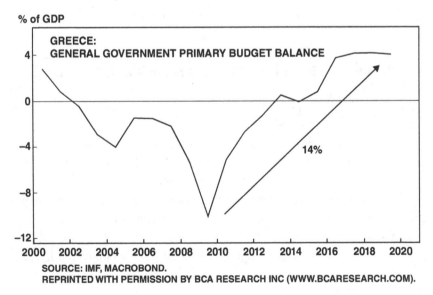

Figure 5.8   A herculean fiscal adjustment.

The Euro Area sovereign debt crisis illustrates how economic and market constraints interact to force policymakers onto paths that are difficult to forecast using preference-based analyses. Even the least likely of politicians – Trotskyite communists like Tsipras – turn into Thatcherite supply-side reformers when faced with constraints. Material constraints force policymakers down the path of least resistance.

Forecasters should keep in mind that this path is not always easy to see from the vantage point of an investor. In 2010, it was out of consensus that Berlin would allow the ECB to directly purchase government debt, let alone that – ten years later in 2020 – the Commission would issue mutualized debt obligations on behalf of the Mediterranean and Eastern European EU member states. In 2015, it was *definitely* out of consensus that Greece would successfully adjust its budget balance by an extra 5% of GDP. In both cases, the analysts driving public opinion did not account for economic and market constraints. And they have not yet adjusted their forecasting methods. As of 2020, pundits and armchair analysts still expect Italy to leave, Germany to fall prey to populists, and the TARGET2 mechanism to end all human existence.[13]

Geopolitics versus Economics: Is Trade War Sustainable?

Another dynamic where forecasters underestimate economic and market constraints is the US–China trade war.

There is a growing consensus that China and the US are destined to replicate the Cold War of the twentieth century. In this hypothesis, the trade dispute is the tip of the geopolitical iceberg.

I played some part in building this consensus – at least as far as the investment community is concerned – by publishing "Power and Politics in East Asia: Cold War 2.0?" in September 2012. For much of the past decade, *Geopolitical Strategy* – the investment strategy publication

---

[13] Never heard of the TARGET2 mechanism? Good. It will not collapse the Euro Area, and neither will any of the other scenarios I mention. In the last section of this chapter, I elaborate on precisely how not-dangerous TARGET2 is to the Euro Area.

I created in 2011 with BCA Research – operated according to the thesis that geopolitical risk was rotating out of the Middle East and into East Asia. The risk relevant to investors was shifting from an area where risk was fading to one where it would soon increase – a red flag for investors. And China fell right into the zone of rising geopolitical risk.

This thesis remains cogent, but a potential "Silicon Curtain" does not automatically equate to two bifurcated zones of capitalism. Trade, capital flows, and human exchanges between China and the US will continue and may even grow.

Certainly, policymaker preferences in both countries are turning more confrontational. Nationalist sentiment is on the rise in China, and Beijing may even stoke the sentiment to distract its burgeoning middle classes from other, domestic, ills. In the US, a new McCarthyism is looming, with China hawks looking for any reason to ban or limit even innocuous economic interactions with China.[14]

Despite these preference sets, macroeconomic constraints – boosted by the multipolarity of the global order – will prevent a total bifurcation of capitalism.

Power Dynamics and Ancient Greece: A Theory Interlude

Speaking in the Reichstag in 1897, German Foreign Secretary Bernhard von Bülow proclaimed it time for Germany to demand "its own place in

---

[14] Not all national security–motivated trade protectionism is an act of McCarthyism. There are plenty of reasons to ensure the security of supply chains of critical products. However, some US lobby groups are already using "national security" as a catchall term to get favorable legislation passed. My favorite example of US over-reaction to China is Congress's passage of a 2020 defense appropriations bill. One provision bans US municipalities from purchasing Chinese-built buses and rail cars. It had nothing to do with funding defense spending, but US lobbyists inserted it to protect domestic industry from Chinese-manufactured electric buses. Because Chinese military would be able to spy on US citizens via the buses ... if they made any in the first place. Buses are manufactured *in the US!* The Chinese company most affected by the provision, Build Your Dreams (BYD), has manufacturing plants in Illinois and California. In the event of a war, the US could simply nationalize the factories and capture Chinese know-how.

the sun."[15] The occasion was a debate on Germany's policy toward East Asia. Bülow soon ascended to the chancellorship under Kaiser Wilhelm II and oversaw the evolution of German foreign policy from *Realpolitik* to *Weltpolitik*. While Chancellor Otto von Bismarck cultivated *Realpolitik* as a cautious balancing of global powers, Bülow and Wilhelm II sought to use *Weltpolitik* to redraw the status quo through aggressive foreign and trade policy.

Imperial Germany joined a long list of antagonists, from Athens to 2020's People's Republic of China, in the tragic play of history dubbed the "Thucydides Trap."[16]

Students of world history know the underlying concept. Its name is derived from Greek historian Thucydides and his seminal *History of the Peloponnesian War*.[17] Thucydides explains why Sparta and Athens went to war but, unlike his contemporaries, he does not moralize or blame the gods. Instead, he stoically describes the cause: revisionist Athens and established Sparta had no recourse but war due to a cycle of mistrust.

Graham Allison, a scholar of international relations, argues that the interplay between a status quo power and a challenger almost always leads to conflict. In 12 out of the 16 cases he surveyed, military conflict broke out. Of the four cases where war did not develop, three involved transitions between countries that shared a deep cultural affinity and respect for the prevailing institutions.[18] In those cases, the transition involved new management running what is essentially the same world system. The final of the four non-war outcomes was the Cold War between the Soviet Union and the US.

What causes the Thucydides Trap to ensnare rivaling powers? The size of a status quo power's sphere of influence remains the same as when it stood at its zenith of power. Its inevitable decline relative to that zenith

---

[15] "Bernhard von Bülow on Germany's 'Place in the Sun,'" *German Historical Institute* 3 (1897): 1074–1083, http://germanhistorydocs.ghi-dc.org/pdf/eng/607_Buelow_Place%20in%20the%20Sun_111.pdf

[16] Graham Allison, *Destined for War: Can America and China Escape Thucydides's Trap?* (New York: Houghton Mifflin Harcourt, 2017).

[17] Thucydides, *History of the Peloponnesian War* (London: Penguin Classics, 1972).

[18] The three cases are Spain taking over from Portugal in the sixteenth century, the US taking over from the UK in the twentieth century, and Germany rising to regional hegemony in Europe in the twenty-first century.

leads to "imperial overstretch." To combat the problem, the hegemonic or imperial power erroneously doubles down on maintaining a status quo it can no longer afford.

To anyone who has played the board game Risk, this dynamic is well known. The status quo power is the player who already secured a continent. In Risk, controlling a continent comes with a bonus: extra troops every turn. The status quo power cannot allow anyone else to gain a foothold on a continent. It erodes their relative power. Regional hegemony is a perfect jumping-off point toward global hegemony. It gives the challenger power a home base it does not have to spend material resources defending (and the extra troops every turn to boot!).

The hegemon therefore feels threatened even if the challenger's intentions are limited and restrained (although they are often ambitious and overweening). The "tragedy of great power politics" is that the established power does not react to intentions, it reacts to capabilities. The intentions of the newcomer are immaterial – all that matters to the hegemon is that the challenger's capabilities are material and unchanging, whereas its intentions are perceived and ephemeral.[19]

Relative Gain: Why Trade Wars Fizzle in a Multipolar World

The challenging power always has an internal logic to justify its ambitions. As of 2020, in China's case, there is a zealous belief among the elite that the country is reverting back to the way things were for centuries. Whether 2020 China is a challenger or status quo power depends on historical perspective. Twenty-first-century China is a "challenger" power to the status quo of the past 300 years. But it is the "established" power of the past four millennia. The consensus in China is to take the long view. As such, it should not have to defer to the prevailing global status quo. After all, the contemporary context is the result of Western imperialist "challenges" to the established authoritarian Chinese order.

To further justify its ambitions for global influence, China cites that it is at least as relevant to the global economy as the US, and therefore

---

[19] John Mearsheimer, *The Tragedy of Great Power Politics* (New York: W.W. Norton & Company, 2001).

deserves a greater say in global governance. While the US still takes a larger share of the global economy as of 2020, China has contributed 23% to incremental global GDP growth over the past two decades, compared to 13% for the US. Over time, China's economic demand carries more weight.

Like China's claim to power, President Trump's aggressive trade policy also makes sense in a political theory context – to a point.

The political science theory of realism focuses on relative gains over absolute gains in all relationships, including trade. Trade leads to economic prosperity, prosperity to the accumulation of economic surplus, and economic surplus to military spending, research, and development. But two rival states that only care about relative gains produce a zero-sum game – along with zero room for cooperation. It is a "prisoner's dilemma" that can lead to suboptimal economic outcomes because both actors chose not to cooperate.

Figure 5.9 illustrates the effects of relative gain calculations on the trade behavior of states. In the absence of geopolitics, demand (Q_3) is satisfied via trade ($Q_3 - Q_0$) due to the inability of domestic production (Q_0) to meet it.[20]

However, a geopolitical externality – such as a rivalry with another state – raises the marginal social cost of imports. Trade allows the rival to gain more out of trade and "catch up" in terms of geopolitical capabilities. The trading state therefore eliminates such externalities with a tariff (t), raising domestic output to Q_1 while shrinking demand to Q_2. Imports fall to $Q_2 - Q_1$, a fraction of where they would be in a world absent geopolitics.

The result? In a bipolar world where two superpowers face off, relative trade gains dominate.

What about a unipolar world? In a unipolar moment, where a single hegemon is in charge, the hegemon relaxes its relative concerns as prospects of a rival dim. As political scientist Duncan Snidal argues in a 1991 paper,

> When the global system is first set up, the hegemon makes deals with smaller states. The hegemon is concerned more with absolute

---

[20] Figure 5.9 is adapted from Joanne Gowa and Edward D. Mansfield, "Power Politics and International Trade," *American Political Science Review* 87, no. 2 (June 1993): 409.

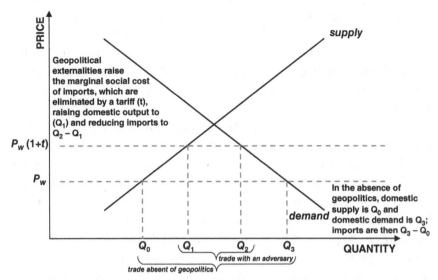

REPRINTED WITH PERMISSION OF CLOCKTOWER GROUP, L.P.

Figure 5.9   Trade war in a bipolar world.

gains, [but] smaller states are more concerned with relative, so they are tougher negotiators. Cooperative arrangements favoring smaller states contribute to relative hegemonic decline. As the unequal distribution of benefits in favor of smaller states helps them catch up to the hegemonic actor, it also lowers the relative gains weight they place on the hegemonic actor. At the same time, declining relative preponderance increases the hegemonic state's concern for relative gains with other states, especially any rising challengers. The net result is increasing pressure from the largest actor to change the prevailing system to gain a greater share of cooperative benefits.[21]

When a unipolar hegemon sets up the global system, small states are initially more concerned with relative gains because they are far more sensitive to national security than the hegemon. The hegemon has a preponderance of power, so it can afford to be more relaxed about its security needs. The states' different priorities explain why Presidents George Bush, Sr., Bill Clinton, and George Bush, Jr., all made "bad deals" with China.

---

[21] Duncan Snidal, "Relative Gains and the Pattern of International Cooperation," *American Political Science Review* 85, no. 3 (September 1991): 720.

Writing nearly 30 years ago, Snidal cogently described the current US–China trade war. He also predicted that the US would sour on the original arrangement as it became more aware of relative trade-offs. Snidal thought he was describing a coming decade of anarchy. But he and fellow political scientists writing in the early 1990s underestimated American power. The "unipolar moment" of American supremacy was not over; it was just beginning! As such, the dynamic Snidal described took 30 years to materialize.

When predicting what the transition away from US hegemony might look like, most investors latch onto the Cold War model, as it is the only period in the past 50 years that was not unipolar. Moreover, the Cold War provides a simple, bipolar distribution of power that is easy to model through game theory. The excerpt from Snidal's paper would be sufficient analysis – were a bipolar dynamic imminent. The US and China would divide the planet in two like the US and the Soviet Union. America would abandon globalization totally, impose a draconian Silicon Curtain around China, and coerce its allies to follow suit. Many policy-makers in both Beijing and Washington would likely prefer this outcome.

But most of human history has been defined by a *multipolar* distribution of power between states, not a bipolar one.

The US–Soviet Cold War is a poor analogy for the world of 2020. In a multipolar world, Snidal concludes, "States that do not cooperate fall behind other relative gains maximizers that cooperate among themselves. *This makes cooperation the best defense (as well as the best offense) when your rivals are cooperating in a multilateral relative gains world* [emphasis added]." Snidal shows via formal modeling that as the number of players increases from two, sensitivity to relative gains drops. With each new player, countries maximize their absolute gains to remain competitive among a larger set of actors.[22]

The US–China relationship does not occur in a vacuum. It is moderated by the global context, which in 2020 is one of multipolarity where the EU, Russia, India, Iran, Turkey, Mexico, and Brazil are all major

---

[22] Snidal, "Relative Gains and the Pattern of International Cooperation," 722. I do not review Snidal's excellent game theory or formal modeling, as it is complex and detailed. However, I encourage intrigued readers to pursue the study on their own.

economic and geopolitical players. In a multipolar world, economic constraints behave differently than they do in a bipolar or unipolar one.

"Multipolarity" refers to a distribution of geopolitical power in which one or two powerful players no longer hold the lion's share of it. The post-2010 world is moving in this more pluralistic direction. Europe and Japan have formidable economies and military capabilities. Russia remains a potent military power, even as India surpasses it in terms of overall geopolitical power. Iran, Turkey, Mexico, and Brazil are all also asserting their independence in an increasingly complicated and messy world.

A multipolar world is the least ordered and the most unstable of world systems for three reasons:

- **Math:** Multipolarity facilitates the creation of more potential "conflict dyads" that can lead to conflict. In a unipolar world, there is only one country that determines rules of behavior. Conflict is possible, but only if the hegemon allows it. In a bipolar world, conflict is possible, but it must align along the axis of the two dominant powers. In a multipolar world, alliances are constantly shifting and producing novel conflict dyads. Countries need no permission from global rule-setter(s) to engage in conflict.
- **Lack of coordination:** Global coordination suffers in periods of multipolarity as there are more "veto players," or actors with sufficient power to strike down a global initiative. Multipolarity suffers from the same disadvantage as a legislative democracy: there are more checks and balances than in a centralized power structure. Any of these could become a stumbling block to a single coordinated effort. During times of stress, such as when an aggressive revisionist power uses force or when the world is faced with an economic crisis or a pandemic, lack of global coordination is especially costly.
- **Mistakes:** In a unipolar and bipolar world, there are a very limited number of dice being rolled at once because fewer groups have the independent power to enforce their actionable decisions. As such, the odds of large-scale tragic mistakes are comparatively low, and complex formalized relationships with rules of engagement can mitigate the fallout. The US–Soviet mutually assured destruction, grounded in formal modeling of game theory, was one such

relationship. But in a multipolar world, something as random as an assassination of a dignitary can set a world war in motion.[23] The multipolar system is far more accident-prone and dynamic and thus unpredictable.

Figure 5.10 is modified for a multipolar world. Everything, except the highlighted trade lost to other great powers, is the same as in Figure 5.9. In a multipolar world, the state considering tariffs in an attempt to lower the marginal social cost of trading with a rival must account for this lost trade. In the context of the Trump-era trade war with China, this gap would encompass all European Airbuses and Brazilian soybeans sold to China in place of American exports. For China, it would encompass all of the machinery, electronics, and capital goods produced in the rest of Asia and shipped to the United States.

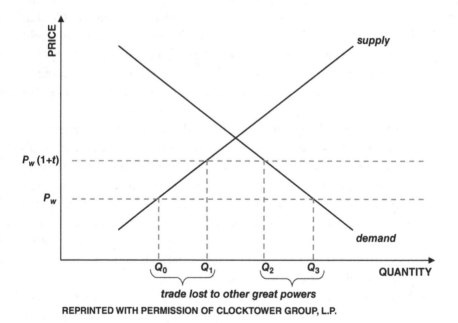

Figure 5.10 Trade war in a multipolar world.

---

[23] Shout out to my homeland of Serbia!

The US and China's lost trade in a multipolar world is the fulcrum constraint preventing both from an all-out trade war.

Washington, in the wake of its China tiff, could cajole its allies to take advantage of the resulting lucrative trade lost $(Q_3 - Q_0) - (Q_2 - Q_1)$. But empirical research suggests that US allies – Europe, Japan, South Korea, Taiwan, etc. – would ignore such pleas for unity. Alliances forged in a bipolar system produce a large, statistically significant impact on bilateral trade flows – a relationship that weakens in a multipolar context.[24]

Unless the US makes a wholehearted diplomatic effort to tighten up its alliances and enforce trade sanctions – unlikely under any second-term Trump administration – the self-interest of US allies will drive them to continue trading with China. The US will not be able to exclude China from the global system, nor will China be able to achieve Xi Jinping's vaunted "self-sufficiency."

Both World Wars I and II offer precedent for this view in the form of historical examples. They demonstrate that economic constraints can, and have, over-ruled geopolitical imperatives and policymaker preferences.

The World Wars: Economic Constraints in a Multipolar World

In 1896, a bestselling UK pamphlet, *Made in Germany*, painted an ominous picture: "A gigantic commercial State is arising to menace our prosperity, and contend with us for the trade of the world."[25] "Look around your own houses," author E.E. Williams urged his readers. "The toys, and the dolls, and the fairy books which your children maltreat in the nursery are made in Germany: nay, the material of your favorite (patriotic) newspaper had the same birthplace as like as not." Williams later wrote that tariffs were the answer and that they "would bring Germany to her knees, pleading for our clemency."[26]

---

[24] Gowa, "Power Politics," 409.

[25] Ernest Edwin Williams, *Made in Germany,* reprinted ed. (Ithaca: Cornell University Press, 1896), https://archive.org/details/cu31924031247830.

[26] Quoted in Margaret MacMillan, *The War That Ended Peace* (Toronto: Allen Lane, 2014).

By the late 1890s, the UK government knew that Germany was its greatest national security threat. The German Naval Laws of 1898 and 1900 launched a massive naval buildup with the singular objective of liberating the German Empire from the geographic constraints of the Jutland Peninsula. By 1902, the first lord of the Royal Navy noted that "the great new German navy is being carefully built up from the point of view of a war with us."[27]

To guard against the threat of Germany, London signed a set of agreements with France in April 1904 known as *Entente Cordiale*. Germany immediately tested the *entente* in the 1905 First Moroccan Crisis, which only galvanized the alliance. France and the UK brought Russia into the pact in 1907, creating the *Triple Entente*.

In hindsight, the alliance structure was an obvious solution to Germany's meteoric rise from unification in 1871. However, I do not underestimate the magnitude or ingenuity of these geopolitical events. For the UK and France to formalize the 1904 alliance, they had to overcome half a millennium of conflicts, many of them resolved in the past with blood. Their alliance signaled a tectonic shift — one that they undertook against the grain of history, entrenched enmity, and ideology.[28]

Political scientists and historians agree that geopolitical enmity rarely produces the bifurcated economic relations exhibited during the Cold War. Both empirical research and formal modeling show that trade occurs even among rivals and during wartime.[29]

---

[27] Peter Liberman, "Trading with the Enemy: Security and Relative Economic Gains," *International Security* 21, no. 1 (Summer 1996): 147–175.

[28] France and Russia overcame even greater bitterness due to the ideological differences between a republic founded on a violent uprising against its aristocracy – France – and an aristocratic authoritarian regime – Russia.

[29] James Morrow, "When Do 'Relative Gains' Impede Trade?" *The Journal of Conflict Resolution* 41 no. 1 (February 1997): 12–37; Jack S. Levy and Katherine Barbieri, "Trading with the Enemy during Wartime," *Security Studies* 13, no. 3 (December 2004): 1–47.

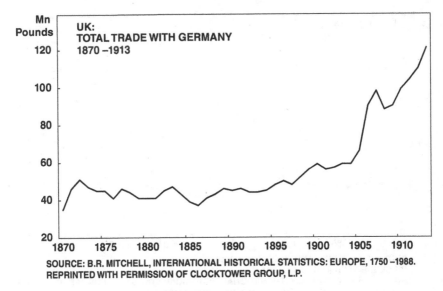

Figure 5.11   The Allies traded with Germany ...

Economic exchange certainly occurred between the UK and Germany, whose trade steadily increased right up until the outbreak of World War I (Figure 5.11). This behavior could be written off due to the UK's ideological commitment to *laissez-faire* economics. Or perhaps London feared for its lightly defended colonies (the least protected should the UK become protectionist).

These arguments suffice for the UK's behavior in isolation, but they do not explain why, during the same period, Russia and France both increased trade with the German Empire as well (Figure 5.12). Either naïve policymakers blind to the impending war led all three states into trading with the enemy – unlikely given the empirical record of war foreknowledge – or they could not afford to lose to *each other* the gains of trade with Germany. The allies were scared of losing absolute trade gains to *each other*. This fear kept them trading with the enemy.

A similar dynamic was afoot ahead of World War II. US–Japan relations soured in the 1930s when the Japanese invaded Manchuria in 1931. In 1934, Japan withdrew from the 1922 Washington Naval Treaty – the

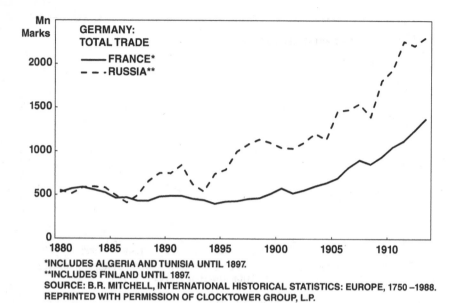

*INCLUDES ALGERIA AND TUNISIA UNTIL 1897.
**INCLUDES FINLAND UNTIL 1897.
SOURCE: B.R. MITCHELL, INTERNATIONAL HISTORICAL STATISTICS: EUROPE, 1750–1988.
REPRINTED WITH PERMISSION OF CLOCKTOWER GROUP, L.P.

Figure 5.12 ... Right up to World War I.

bedrock of the Pacific balance of power – and began a massive naval buildup. In 1937, Japan invaded China. Despite the clear and present danger these actions signified, the US continued to trade with Japan right up until July 26, 1941 – a few days after Japan completed the invasion of Indochina (Figure 5.13). On December 7, Japan attacked the US.

An analyst may attribute these trade patterns to policymakers' incompetence instead of deliberate intention, in which case, world leaders learned their lesson from these past events. Precisely because policymakers sleepwalked into the First and Second World Wars, they will not (or *should* not) make the same mistake in the new century.

But I am skeptical of the view that policymakers in the early and mid-twentieth century were somehow defective (as opposed to today's enlightened leaders). The constraint framework urges the analyst to seek systemic reasons for the behavior of leaders, as opposed to writing off unexpected behavior as outliers or preference.

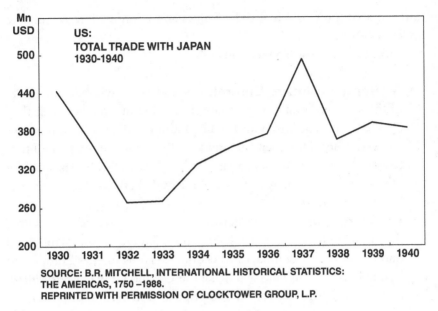

SOURCE: B.R. MITCHELL, INTERNATIONAL HISTORICAL STATISTICS:
THE AMERICAS, 1750 –1988.
REPRINTED WITH PERMISSION OF CLOCKTOWER GROUP, L.P.

Figure 5.13 Japan and the US kept trading right up to the war.

Political science theory explains why London and Washington continued to trade with the enemy despite the clarity of the threat. The systemic nature of the multipolar economic constraint means policymakers are less sensitive to relative economic gains. Multipolarity confronts states with a collective action problem thanks to changing alliances and the difficulty of disciplining allies' behavior.

In the case of the US and China, President Trump exacerbates this mandatory self-reliance because he tends to skirt multilateral diplomacy and focuses to the point of obsession on mercantilist measures of power (i.e., the US trade deficit). If the anti-China trade policy included a magnanimous approach to trade relations with allies, the measure could have produced a "coalition of the willing" against Beijing. But trade deficit concerns prevent the Trump administration from monetarily rewarding US allies. After two years of tariffs and threats against the EU, Japan, and Canada, the Trump administration has already signaled to the rest of the world that old alliances and coordination avenues are up for revision.

I foresee two possible scenarios:

- **Attempted Damage Control:** US leadership will become aware of the systemic multipolar economic constraints under which they operate, and trade with China will continue – albeit with limitations and variations. However, such trade will not reduce the geopolitical tensions, nor will it prevent a military conflict. In fact, the probability of military conflict may *increase* even as trade between China and the US remains steady.
- **Doubling Down:** US leadership will fail to correctly assess that they operate in a multipolar world and will give up the highlighted trade gains from Figure 5.10 to economic rivals such as Europe and Japan. This shift in trade will make the US and China, *ceteris paribus*, poorer, further reinforcing the multipolar distribution of power.

The constraint framework strongly favors the first scenario.

President Trump's Phase One deal is a giant concession to the multipolar nature of the world.[30] So is his tweet on February 18, 2020, blasting a proposal by his own government to curb US sales of jet engines and other aviation components to China. Trump's reasoning for railing against his own documented antitrade preference:

> We're not going to be sacrificing our companies ... by using a fake term of national security. It's got to be real national security. And I think people were getting carried away with it. I want our companies to be allowed to do business. I mean, things are put on my desk that have nothing to do with national security, including with chipmakers

---

[30] In the Phase One deal, President Trump agreed to ease up on existing tariffs and suspend planned tariffs on consumer goods. In return, China ensured that it would not shift trade to American allies.

and various others. So, we're going to give it up, and what will happen? They'll make those chips in a different country or they'll make them in China or someplace else.[31]

To paraphrase my favorite quote from one of my favorite movies: on a long enough time line, the ignorance rate for policymakers falls to zero. Material constraints – such as the risk of Boeing losing business to Airbus in China – are a disciplining mechanism that force policymakers back onto the path of least resistance. In a multipolar world, economic constraints to trade war are more restrictive than in any other system. As such, the trade war between China and the US is unsustainable. There are many things for investors to worry about in the 2020s, but the trade war is not one of them.

Economic and Market Constraints: Takeaway

Armchair forecasters and pundits often invoke economic and market constraints but rarely wield specific barriers in their analyses. Economics and finance require some level of expertise that these talking heads do not always possess.

These constraints operate according to the well-known Keynes adage: "If you owe your bank a hundred pounds, you have a problem. But if you owe a million, it has." *The Economist* later added a corollary: "If you owe your bank a billion pounds everybody has a problem."

In a multipolar world, if any one state fails in a spectacular, Greek-debt-crisis fashion, there are negative implications for every other power, big or small. It is not intuitively obvious why this is so. During the Euro Area crisis, reductive reasoning consistently got the complicated web of relationships wrong. A Greek exit could have unraveled the entire Euro Area, which would have imperiled Germany's

---

[31] Jeff Mason and Makini Brice, "Trump Blasts Proposed US Restrictions on Sale of Jet Parts to China," *Reuters*, February 18, 2020, https://www.reuters.com/article/us-usa-trade-china/trump-blasts-proposed-restrictions-on-china-trade-wants-china-to-buy-u-s-jet-engines-idUSKBN20C1ZV.

economic model. Fearing the impending domino effect, German policymakers would eventually do "whatever it takes" to ensure that their economy did not collapse.

As of 2020, forecasters still misuse macro and finance to predict geopolitical events. Experts often cite Euro Area TARGET2 imbalances as a sign that the monetary union is doomed.[32] In 2010, the TARGET2 banking imbalance stood at €0.3 trillion. In 2020, that number is close to €1.5 trillion.

In a reality that acknowledges the influence of market and economic constraints, the TARGET2 mechanism is not a divisive force. It is actually one of the sinews that binds European countries together.[33]

The growing imbalance means that Germany's exposure to "Italian euro" assets has surged via the ECB's massive purchases of Italian debt. At the same time, Italian investors have parked their cash in German banks, meaning they are owed "German euros." With such a TARGET2 imbalance, the lender – not the debtor – has the most to lose. The biggest casualty of the euro's disintegration would be Germany, as it would effectively mean Italy had declared bankruptcy and canceled its payment plan. This possibility gives Berlin yet another incentive to remain conciliatory and eventually concede to greater fiscal integration, which it did in summer of 2020.

Forecasters misuse economics and markets in their analyses for reasons aside from insufficient expertise:

- **Outdated Knowledge Base:** Time is money, and few besides academics have a surplus of it to debate the details of the TARGET2 mechanism. Wielding economics and finance for geopolitical forecasting requires not just some level of the discipline's know-how but also constant updating of that knowledge.
- **Assumed 1:1 Constraint–Policymaker Relationship:** Analysts also often linearly extrapolate policymaker behavior from a single

---

[32] TARGET2 is a real-time gross settlement system operated by the Euro Area. It settles payments related to the monetary union's monetary policy operations, as well as bank-to-bank and commercial transactions.

[33] My friend and former colleague Dhaval Joshi – BCA's chief European strategist – first made this argument.

economic or market constraint. As this chapter discusses, other policymakers, constraints, and market influencers guarantee that the relationship is rarely linear. Below are two examples of such simplified forecasting:

Example 1: In the face of a bond market riot caused by the Euro Area sovereign debt crisis, the German predilection for hawkish monetary policy will collapse the monetary union.

Example 2: President Trump's protectionism and an aggressive national security agenda toward China will cause US companies to lose an important export market.

Both forecasts were wrong because they misunderstood the interaction between policymakers and their constraints. Preferences were ultimately *bent* to constraints so that German policymakers accepted a dovish ECB monetary policy – and basically crossed every red line they ever set (Figure 5.14) that assuaged the bond market riot. President Trump negotiated a trade deal with China that saw Beijing commit to buying more

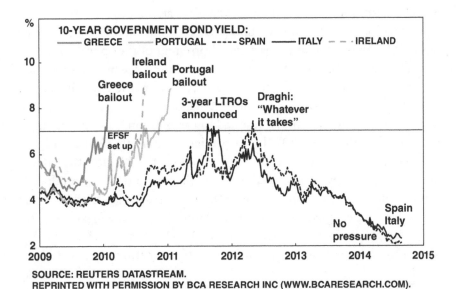

Figure 5.14 Never assume red lines when Euro Area death is on the line.

US products that could lead to an expansion – not the end – of US–China trade relationship.

- **No Perception of Subtlety:** Analysts often fail to consider the less flashy but discoverable aspects of a global crisis. During its debt crisis, pundits argued that Greece should exit because of variables that were easy to chart on a Bloomberg screen – such as bond yields, deficits, and debt redemption schedules. But Greece's problems were much deeper than what was flashing on the screen. They were structural and fundamental. Ultimately, the Greek people themselves understood this, which is why they did not choose the "easy way out" of leaving the Euro Area.

A final word of caution: the 2008 Great Recession introduced investors, journalists, and commentators to an alphabet soup of doom, from mortgage-backed securities (MBS) to collateralized debt obligations (CDOs). The COVID-19-induced recession has done the same, with the alphabet soup filling up our collective cognitive bowl faster than we can keep up. Still, everyone is on the lookout for the *next* complicated, technical acronym that ends the world.[34] Many of those searching for doom have little idea what they are looking for. But due to confirmation bias, they usually find it in economics and finance: a fertile ground for overly technical, jargon-y horsemen of the apocalypse.

This tendency toward doomsday predictions is why my two main case studies in this chapter – the Euro Area crisis and the US–China trade war – demonstrate how economic and market constraints strong-armed policymakers into action that resulted in crises ending, not deepening.

I believe that the COVID-19 pandemic is another such crisis. In Chapter 8, I posit that the costs of sustaining the "flatten the curve" mitigation strategy are so astronomical they would likely produce a depression. The costs will prove prohibitive, especially relative to the objective dangers posed by the virus, constraining policymakers to alter the strategy. Politicians' response to COVID-19 is therefore another example where economics and markets will constrain policy behavior.

---

[34] The aforementioned TARGET2 mechanism fits all of the above doomsday criteria, which is why it appears on a regular basis on the pages of the *"Apocalypse Now"* blog-that-shall-not-be-named (but rhymes with "gyro wedge").

Constraints do not guarantee that policymakers always do the right thing or that the path of least resistance always leads to bliss. A pernicious macroeconomic context often leads to ruin, which is why I began the chapter with the tragedy of Yugoslavia. The absence of constraint-sensitive market feedback can often delay the necessary corrective policies – a delay that only exacerbates future crises. Such a delay in the case of the COVID-19 pandemic will lead to an economic depression; for example, if I am wrong and lockdowns are reimposed. If it does, feel free to use the pages of this book for … well you know what.

Chapter 6

Geopolitics

"Who rules East Europe commands the Heartland;
Who rules the Heartland commands the World-Island;
Who rules the World-Island commands the world."

— Sir Halford John Mackinder

Yes, I buried the "geopolitics" lead – in a book about forecasting geopolitics – all the way in Chapter 6. Halfway through the book, you might be dismayed to still be wondering: what is "geopolitics" anyway? Even more bewildering: my choice puts it below politics, the economy, and finance in the constraints hierarchy.

Geopolitics is a nebulous discipline. Most use it as a catchall phrase for interstate relations in the international sphere. For investment professionals, geopolitics connotes the unknown, unstructured, uncomfortably qualitative variable that intrudes upon their numbers-obsessed profession.

Geopolitical analysts claim it is the ultimate arbiter of the future because it deals with immutable, universal variables (i.e., natural endowments, demographics, and geography). Analysts confidently forecast the future using the geopolitical crystal ball: a tactile relief map where the topography stands out in three dimensions. Their predictions rival the certainty and, in some cases, grimness, of the best psychics.

The future of Poland is dire, as it is destined to be filleted anew by its ravenous neighbors. Canada's grim weather report is to be torn asunder by its regionalism and high infrastructure costs. And the US will live happily ever after. It will remain an Empire forever, sheltered as it is between two oceans, blessed by navigable rivers, and endowed by a cornucopia of natural resources. Sounds familiar? This kind of determinism thrives among geopolitical thinkers.

My father introduced me to geopolitics through a mixture of politically incorrect Eastern European stereotyping – "Koreans go *hard,* Marko … *hard"* – and football (sports-related, but also politically incorrect stereotyping) – "Germans are disciplined, never tire, and press all night." He boiled every country's foreign policy (or football tactics) down to a set of immutable characteristics.

Italians played defensively – *catenaccio* – because, well, they couldn't attack to save their lives. The English tried to lob the midfield with long balls and target mammoth strikers. Americans played with a naïve earnestness that was only possible for a New World power, unafraid and unaware of their certain defeat. The Dutch *totaalvoetbal* was as rehearsed and clinical as their integration into the global supply chain. And Yugoslavia … we played with the creativity and passion of Brazil coupled with the tragicomedy of Argentina. Any day, *Plavi* could beat (or lose to …) anyone.

My passion for football eventually waned, but a top-down, geopolitical mentality stayed with me. Football, especially international football, is all about the system. A team can have multiple superstars on its roster, but if they do not mesh quickly enough for a tournament like the World Cup, even the most loaded team will embarrass itself. To fast-track the meshing process, national teams adopted a particular style that was easy to slot players into.

As a young kid, I remember watching my dad sit at the edge of a small coffee table, puff his cigarettes like a skyscraper on fire, and decree

(10 minutes in) which team would win, why, and by how much. I would protest, point out the quality of the players, the big names on the roster, and their stats in club football back in Spain, Italy, or England. None of it mattered to my dad. He had "read" the macro context and made his forecast. Much to my annoyance, he was correct on all counts more often than not.

My father's passion for top-down football handicapping got me hooked on the macro perspective, but working for George Friedman taught me how to apply it outside the football pitch. Friedman founded Stratfor, the geopolitical intelligence firm, in 1996.[1] It was the absolute worst time to start a geopolitical analysis firm. American power was at its zenith, globalization was in full swing, and few people cared about geopolitical risk. Nonetheless, visionaries such as Friedman and Ian Bremmer, who founded Eurasia Group in 1998, saw an inefficiency in the market and sought to fill it with rigorous analysis.

At Stratfor, I learned how to read the news, ignore the "quality of the players," and focus on the system. Working for George was even more annoying than watching football with my dad. He would stubbornly point out the systemic nature of a geopolitical relationship, ignore the messy details I had labored over for weeks, and conclude with a forecast. Again, more often than not, he proved to be correct.

Unlike my peers at the firm, I did not resist George's "breaking-in" process. Having completed my PhD coursework at the University of Texas in comparative politics, I was primed to accept a systemic world-view. And having grown up on football strategy, I was not afraid to ignore the individual playmakers and focus on the overarching strategy.[2]

Geopolitics is parsimonious and predictive because it posits that states are imprisoned, or blessed, by their geography. For academia,

---

[1] In 2015, George left Stratfor and founded Geopolitical Futures.

[2] I wonder if I would be the same kind of thinker had I grown up watching basketball, which has become my passion. Basketball is far more dominated by individual stars because the court is smaller and there are only five players per side, allowing for, in geopolitical terms, a more bi- or unipolar power dynamic. As such, a dominant player – say a Michael Jordan or Kobe Bryant – can control the game and will his team to victory. Since becoming a much bigger fan of basketball than football, I've found that while the team system may matter less, team *chemistry* may be even more important in basketball. Clearly a topic to expand on in the second book.

geopolitics is *too* parsimonious. And the professors are correct! Mountainous terrain combined with ethno-linguistic heterogeneity has consigned Afghanistan and Bosnia to centuries of conflict, but Switzerland, cursed with similar topography and heterogeneity, is doing just fine.

Geography is not destiny. And it is not immutable. *La Manche* was much harder to ford when the Spanish Armada sailed in 1588 than when the *Luftwaffe* flew over to drop bombs during the 1940–1941 Blitz. The US was not quite so navigable before the completion of the Erie canal in 1825. In the fourteenth century, Portugal was so impoverished by the black plague that its interior villages depopulated as the country desperately threw itself into the sea. Few would have predicted that in less than a century, the tiny Portugal – whose paltry agricultural output remained static and sparse – would launch the Age of Exploration and divide the planet with its much more fertile neighbor, Spain, in 1494.

So, as I advance through this chapter, remember that geopolitical analysis alone does not make an accurate forecast.

This book exists because I never grew out of being annoyed at the parsimony of my dad's and George's approaches to analysis. There are far more constraints to policymakers than just geography and Great Power geopolitics, a realization that dawned on me during the Euro Area crisis. To correctly forecast that crisis, I had to understand domestic politics, economics, and financial markets. The crisis saw a continent wreathed in geopolitical conflict for *millennia* brush it off, overcome it, and almost redraw the geography of Europe. With a tsunami of economic reform, it overcame its geography, demographics, and "navigable rivers" problem.[3]

Nonetheless, geopolitics *is* a crucial variable that investors sometimes ignore – and sometimes obsess over to the exclusivity of others. My goal in this chapter is to help investors locate that illusive, *alpha*-generating middle ground.

---

[3] Some think that Europe is doomed because its navigable rivers all drain into different seas. Please, light me on fire now.

Origins of Geopolitical Theory

The theoretical foundations of geopolitics are thin. There are only two notable "fathers" of geopolitics: Alfred Thayer Mahan and Halford Mackinder. They both dedicated their lives to elucidating the "Grand Strategy" for great powers: the implicit but influential geopolitical imperatives, rooted in geography, from which a country derives its day-to-day foreign policy.

Mahan was a US Navy admiral and lecturer at the Naval War College. For him, the US imperative, or grand strategy, was to build a navy to dominate the oceans – the global "commons." They are indispensable to modern trade and economy, and thus attainment of "hard power."[4] Hard power is the "power (of a nation state, alliance, etc.) characterized by a *coercive* approach to international relations, often involving military action [emphasis added]."[5]

A strong navy is the defining characteristic of a powerful state, as it gives military supremacy over vital trade routes and ensures that global commerce operates in its interest. If this sounds like the twenty-first-century US grand strategy, it is because Mahan influenced American policymakers in the early twentieth century. Theodore Roosevelt subscribed to Mahan's thinking, which included building the Panama Canal. Mahan's *The Influence of Sea Power upon History* and similar work by British strategists provided a historical and strategic framework for the UK–Germany naval race that helped cause World War I.[6]

Mackinder, a British geographer and academic, focused on the Eurasian landmass rather than the oceans.[7] In his view, Eurasia had

---

[4] Alfred Thayer Mahan, *The Interest of America in Sea Power: Present and Future* (Boston: Little, Brown and Company, 1918).

[5] The other approach to power is "soft" power, in which a nation relies on cultural or economic *persuasion* rather than military-backed coercion. *Oxford English Dictionary,* s.v. "hard power," accessed March 6, 2020, https://www-oed-com.ezproxy.lapl.org/view/Entry/84122?redirectedFrom=hard+power#eid69704699.

[6] Mahan, *The Influence of Sea Power upon History (1660–1783),* 15th ed. (Boston: Little, Brown and Company, 1949).

[7] Halford John Mackinder, *Democratic Ideals and Reality: A Study in the Politics of Reconstruction,* 15th ed. (Washington, DC: National Defense University Press, 1996).

enough natural resources (Russia), population (China), wealth (Europe), and geographic buffer from naval powers (surrounding seas) to become self-sufficient. Hence, any great power that managed to dominate Eurasia, or the "World Island" as Mackinder coined it, would have no need for a navy. It would become a superpower by default.

The political consulting community tends to overstate geopolitics as a primary causal mechanism in global events. The subject – by definition always writ large – enables a generalist to advise clients on Canadian politics on Monday, global energy on Tuesday, and Middle East intrigue on Wednesday. In forecasting, the far-reaching quality of geopolitics provides the most value for the least work put in. It is the generalist's shortcut.

For the generalist, political analysis (Chapter 4) is too contextual and requires a lot of work and knowledge. Sure, it is the most powerful – and therefore predictive – constraint, but it requires the analyst to understand the differences between Italian and Brazilian electoral systems.

Economics and finance (Chapter 5) require specialized knowledge that most analysts in the political consulting industry lack or wield awkwardly. It also requires the same expert-level comprehension not just of different economies, but also of asset classes, monetary policy, and banking systems.

In contrast, geopolitics can be a one-stop shop for making forecasts. It is analytical fast food – an intelligence-by-assembly-line approach to forecasting. My favorite of these happy-meal forecasts include the following: Polish policymakers will always approximate paranoia, given that they are located on the North European Plain; the US will forever remain a safe haven, thanks to its two oceans;[8] and China will never gain global influence because it is hemmed in by the Tibetan plateau on the west, the Gobi Desert in the north, and the "first island chain" in the east.

Relying on geopolitics in isolation is like driving a car with a rearview mirror, a GPS system, and a pitch-black windshield. The driver knows where he's been and the final destination, but he's completely blind to what is right in front of him.

Despite its limitations, geopolitics is a powerful constraint in the framework's structure and plays a role in most international events.

---

[8] Remember aviation is no match for salty water.

The previous chapters' assessments of the Brexit imbroglio, Chinese domestic politics, the Euro Area crisis, and the US–China trade war would have been incomplete without an understanding of geopolitics. But it is not clear whether, as its adherents might claim, geopolitics was policymakers' fulcrum constraint for each issue.

I now turn to two scenarios where an understanding of geopolitics remains critical for making a forecast. They are the following: US grand strategy and Russian military intervention abroad.

The Trump Doctrine

Every US president, knowingly or not, has tried to construct a foreign policy "doctrine" during his presidency. There is rarely a single document that elucidates it. Scholars and journalists weave the ideas together from speeches, policy decisions, the administration's resource allocation, and rhetoric.

In 2017, Trump was in his presidential infancy. However, his actions and statements gave political commentators a rough idea of where his doctrine was headed. There were three main lines of thought in President Trump's doctrine:

- **Transactionalism:** Long-term alliances and commitments abroad must have a clear, immediate, and calculable benefit for the US "bottom line." Therefore, Japan and South Korea should pay more for the benefits of US alliance, and NATO is a drain on American resources. All alliances and American commitments are therefore negotiable. You want protection? "Pay up."
- **Mercantilism:** The US has no permanent allies, only trade balances that *must* be positive. In the pursuit of this ideal, President Trump initiated a trade war with China; threatened Canada and Mexico with a protracted tariff war; and singled out Germany, South Korea, and Japan as potential candidates for trade action down the line. Any country that sports a significant trade surplus with the US is in Washington's crosshairs.
- **Nationalism:** In his inaugural address, President Trump said that "it is the right of all nations to put their own interests first" and

that America "[does] not seek to impose our way of life on any-one." This point is a stark departure from the ideologically driven foreign policies of both the Bush Jr. and the Obama administrations. There is a different ideology underpinning Trump's foreign policy: nationalism.

Under the tenets of this inchoate "Trump Doctrine," NATO and the EU are not just nuisances, but detrimental to US interests. If it became an active, consistent doctrine, its negative attitude toward Western nations and their global institutions would mark a profound shift in US foreign policy thinking. No wonder then that the Washington establishment revolted against the shift and launched a prolific op-ed writing campaign![9]

Both NATO and the EU obstruct Trump's ideological tenet of nationalism. They are international organizations that pool sovereignty for some predetermined common goal. Because the common goal has nothing to do with the immediate, domestic, and economic goals of the US, the two organizations threaten US interests.

NATO demands a US overseas commitment with little material gain in return. This imbalance is not a new bone of contention. President Obama complained about the failure of NATO member states to pay their fair share (2% of GDP on defense) for collective self-defense. Obama's strategy was to cajole European allies to boost defense spending; NATO's existence was never in question. But Trump does not see

---

[9] Constanze Stelzenmüller, "At Last: The Trump Doctrine, Revealed," *The Brookings Institution*, June 5, 2017, https://www.brookings.edu/blog/order-from-chaos/2017/06/05/at-last-the-trump-doctrine-revealed/; Amy Zegart, "The Self-inflicted Demise of American Power," *The Atlantic*, July 12, 2018, https://www.theatlantic.com/international/archive/2018/07/trump-nato-summit/565034/; Eliot A. Cohen, "America's Long Goodbye – The Real Crisis of the Trump Era," *Foreign Affairs*, January/February 2019, https://www.foreignaffairs.com/articles/united-states/long-term-disaster-trump-foreign-policy; Jeffrey Goldberg, "A Senior White House Official Defines the Trump Doctrine: 'We're America, Bitch'," *The Atlantic*, June 11, 2018, https://www.theatlantic.com/politics/archive/2018/06/a-senior-white-house-official-defines-the-trump-doctrine-were-america-bitch/562511/; and for a much more positive reaction to the doctrine: Michael Anton, "The Trump Doctrine," *Foreign Policy*, April 20, 2019, https://foreignpolicy.com/2019/04/20/the-trump-doctrine-big-think-america-first-nationalism

any benefit in America paying for Germany's defense, especially when Germany has a sizeable trade surplus with the US.

The EU runs a large current account surplus in general and a trade surplus with the US in particular. To the Trump administration, the EU is a *rival* – perhaps even more than Russia, which, when viewed through a purely mercantilist lens, may not be a friend, but is not a foe either.

Trump's foreign policy is based on an understanding that the world is multipolar and that the US is in a geopolitical decline. Data supports this assertion, and Trump's doctrine aligns with that of the Obama presidency in that sense. Both recognize that the US can no longer act unilaterally and that it must retrench from its global responsibilities. But while Obama sought to enhance US power by relying on allies and supranational organizations, Trump seeks to geopolitically deleverage. Such a deleveraging, when combined with mercantilism, may cause America's traditional allies to try harder for its approval, like Trump assumes. Or it may push America's traditional allies away from Washington's orbit.

If the new doctrine forces allies out of the transatlantic orbit that Washington has maintained since 1945, these countries will pursue alternative economic and security relationships to hedge against America's lack of commitment. They may resort to outright hostility. Japan and South Korea, to offset potential tariffs and a drop in US military support, will become friendlier with China to fulfill both their security and economic needs. Absent US support, Japan and South Korea need better China relations to avoid conflict and to access new consumer markets. The same goes for Europe, with Germany and others eager to step in for the US by selling more to China amid US–China trade conflicts, as I discussed in Chapter 5.

The Trump Doctrine, taken to its conclusion, results in an American foreign policy that pushes Eurasia toward the kind of integration – if not exactly alliance – that Mackinder feared. Since greater Eurasian coordination could eventually develop into a dynamic of its own, this process directly contravenes the central tenet of American grand strategy: *Prevent any one power from dominating Eurasia.*

Trump, his supporters, and his advisors may believe that the twentieth century is over and post–World War II American alliances have atrophied. They have. Russia is not the Soviet Union. It is no surprise that NATO is having an identity crisis when it no longer has a peer enemy to defend against.

But geography has not changed. The US is still far from Eurasia, and Eurasia is still the "World Island." The Trump Doctrine ignores the entire twentieth century, during which the US had to intervene in Europe *twice* and Asia *three times* – at a huge cost of blood and treasure – to prevent the continent from unifying under a single hegemon. The US set up international organizations after the Second World War to ensure that it would not have to intervene in Europe again to prevent World Island domination.[10] The security and commercial system in Asia Pacific serve a similar purpose.

These transoceanic alliances and organizations are not vestiges of a past that has vanished, but ongoing attempts to manage a continental geography that is immutable. The Trump Doctrine threatens to undermine an imperative of American hegemony. If carried out to the letter, it will end American dominance on the world stage.

There is a significant probability that President Trump will pursue his doctrine to its ultimate conclusion, especially if he wins a second term and thus becomes free of re-election-imposed median voter constraints. However, it is unlikely because geopolitical constraints on the doctrine are too vast. The Trump Doctrine raised a specter, however faint, that has not existed seen since the Molotov–Ribbentrop Pact between Russia and Germany in 1939: a united Eurasian continent marshalling all its human, natural, and technological resources against the US. The last time that happened, around 400,000 Americans lost their lives to preserve US security. Loss of America's Eurasian anchor – NATO and European alliances – would prove too great a shock to American hegemony. It would also spell the end of Western dominance over the world that has been a *fait accompli* of geopolitics since 1492.

This potential World Island forms the Trump Doctrine's fulcrum constraint to action. It explains why, despite his stated preference, Trump

---

[10] These organizations include NATO and the EU as well as the United Nations (UN), IMF, and others.

said he supported NATO's mutual defense pact, Article V.[11] The threat of
a World Island drove the December 2017 National Security Strategy to
take a more muted stance on the transatlantic rift than President Trump's
original statements indicated. The strategy refers to the NATO alliance
as "one of our great advantages over our competitors," and maintains
that "the United States remains committed to Article V of the Washington Treaty."[12] While the National Security Strategy's direction does
not guarantee that geopolitical constraints permanently anchor Trump's
foreign policy, it does indicate that the constraints influence policymaker
decisions.

Three years later, most of the authors of the December 2017
National Security Strategy have been ignominiously removed from the
White House. Nonetheless, the framework suggests that even if their
replacements are ideologues, the power of the geopolitical constraint
would again keep policymakers anchored to the main tenets of the
transatlantic grand strategy. Material constraint – geopolitics – will
ultimately win out over ideology – nationalism.

Russia's Constraints Abroad

The Crimean Peninsula was annexed by Russia in February–March
2014. It was the first annexation of territory in Europe by force since
the Second World War. The question on investors' minds was, "Where
will Russia stop?"

A month after annexation, the Donbas War began. Donbas is a
region of East Ukraine through which the Donets River flows. Ethnic
Russians form a large minority in the two main *oblasts* (states) that make

---

[11] Jacob Pramuk, "Trump Endorses NATO's Mutual Defense Pact in Poland, After Failing
to Do So on First Europe Trip," *CNBC*, July 6, 2017, https://www.cnbc.com/2017/07/
06/trump-us-stands-firmly-behind-nato-article-5.html.

[12] Donald J. Trump, *National Security Strategy of the United States of America*, December
2017, https://www.whitehouse.gov/wp-content/uploads/2017/12/NSS-Final-12-18-
2017-0905-2.pdf

up the district: Luhansk and Donetsk. A majority of the people in the region, including many ethnic Ukrainians, are Russophone.

It seems hypocritical for Moscow to attack Ukraine and support an insurgency in Donbas. But the moves were not irrational or inexplicable. Russia's intervention in Crimea was part and parcel of the same geopolitical constraints that motivate other powers to pursue spheres of influence. Geopolitical constraints also dictated its actions in Donbas. Russia's Crimea military intervention was symptomatic of its fulcrum geopolitical constraint: Moscow has very little to offer to the members of its sphere.

Moscow's primary geopolitical focus is the post-Soviet space, the crown jewel of which is Ukraine. As Russian exports are uncompetitive outside of the post-Soviet arena, Moscow created a customs union to protect this economic sphere – and it eventually became the more comprehensive Eurasian Union. The union's aim was to cement and institutionalize Russian influence. Without Ukraine, the Eurasian Union would shrink to Russia and a collection of Lilliputian economies from Central Asia and the Caucasus. To achieve its goal, Moscow needed Ukraine.

Ukraine is the backbone of Russia's Eurasian Union project for a few reasons. In 2014, it was one of the top destinations of Russia's nonenergy exports, as well as Russia's key market for financial and nonfinancial corporations. Its demographic is ethnically and linguistically similar to Russia's, allowing the bigger country to easily supplement its flatlining population. Ukraine is a geographic buffer between Russia and NATO member states. Crimea houses the headquarters of Russia's Black Sea Fleet and provides Moscow with a strategic anchor in the Black Sea (although that anchor's critical nature is often overstated given that the port of Novorossiysk on the eastern shores of the Black Sea exists).

Considering Ukraine's importance to Russia, Moscow's military intervention seemed rational.

But it did raise an important question regarding Moscow's shift in strategy. When the 2005 Orange Revolution put a pro-West government in power in Kiev, Moscow did not react militarily. Instead, it played the long game, patiently undermining the pro-West government with political and economic pressure until the 2010 election: the nominally pro-Russian Viktor Yanukovych was victorious. Moscow had (success-fully) meddled without military intervention. Why, then, did Moscow feel such an urgency to act militarily in 2014?

The answer to this question lies in the appeal – or lack thereof – of being inside Russia's sphere of influence. Russia offers the following three membership perks to states within its sphere:

- **Geography:** Russian client states lie along the borders of the for-mer Russian Empire/Soviet Union; historically, they are Moscow's security buffers. Geographically, this location situates them between a major mountain chain (the Caucasus, the Carpathian, or the Tien Shen Mountains) and Moscow. Due to the mountainous terrain on the non-Russian side of their border, the path of least resistance for trade leads through Moscow. This Russia-centered trade flow is especially true for commodity exporters such as Kazakhstan, Turk-menistan, Uzbekistan, and Azerbaijan, and far less for Ukraine.
- **Natural Resources:** For ex-Soviet states that are not commodity producers, Russia provides access to cheap energy, but it comes at a high political cost. The low prices require *quid pro quo* concessions.
- **Protection Racket:** Russia supplies former Soviet states with secu-rity from external threats, domestic threats, and even each other.[13] Viewed in this context, Russia's military intervention in Ukraine sig-naled to other client states that it would protect governing elites from domestic unrest. Yanukovych may have been deposed, but thanks to Russia he is alive and well.[14]

While the Crimea military strategy did reassure other Russian dependents, it led some Ukrainians to reject membership in Russia's sphere. Although the media presented Ukraine as evenly split between the East and the West, the reality is more nuanced. The 2010 election results did not represent an East/West split in voter preference. There were other reasons – confounding variables – influencing citizens who

---

[13] In the Armenia–Azerbaijan context, Russia is ostensibly protecting each client state from the other.

[14] Whether he still has access to a golden toilet is unclear.

voted for the "pro-Russian" candidate. As a result, there were far more pro-West citizens than a simplistic, single-dimension analysis of the polls would indicate.

Viktor Yanukovych did not win the 2010 elections because he was pro-Russian; he won because he campaigned on a pragmatic, pro-Ukrainian platform that prioritized EU integration and appealed to a broad coalition of voters.[15] Certainly, he won more votes in the eastern part of Ukraine, but he would not have beaten the pro-West candidate without softening his stance on EU accession.

From the Russian perspective, a client state's pro-West preference is worrying because Moscow cannot offer the scale of economic and social development that comes with EU accession. Ukraine had flirted with EU and NATO accession for over a decade, although the odds of NATO accession were never high.[16]

For all of its faults, the EU has a proven track record in wealth generation and governance improvement. Joining the EU is a difficult process that requires implementing painful structural reforms, but it also provides access to the EU's enormous market and invites Western investors to search for opportunities in the candidate country. Membership – even just candidate status – provides an important good-housekeeping seal of approval.

Russia has no equivalent offer. Membership in the Russian sphere confers no comparable benefits, as becomes apparent through Ukraine's experience relative to the economic performance of its two former communist peers: Poland and Romania (Figure 6.1). For Ukraine, the post-Soviet era has been a tragedy of "You could've been a contender" proportions.

Russia resorted to a military intervention in Ukraine because membership in the Russian sphere was inferior to membership in Europe's.

---

[15] After all, he had the services of an expert campaign strategist: Paul Manafort.

[16] Many Western Moscow apologists have laid the blame for Russia's aggression on the EU and US due to their apparent desire to fold Ukraine into NATO. This is incorrect. While the US did once entertain the idea seriously, it was vetoed by Germany at the 2008 Bucharest summit, six years before Crimean annexation. In other words, it did not matter what the Obama and Bush Jr. administrations wanted. Germany was adamantly opposed to a Ukraine accession to NATO. President Putin knew this and invaded Ukraine anyway. But Moscow has itself fanned this theory so as to justify the intervention.

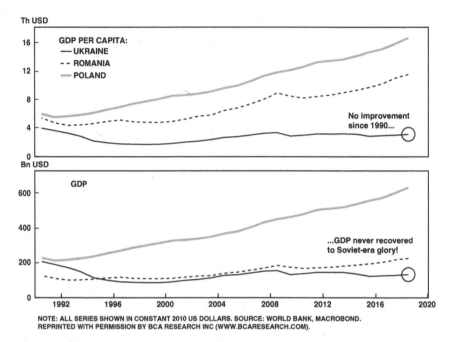

Figure 6.1   Ukraine: Europe's Argentina?

This "value-add" sphere imbalance – an immutable constraint for Russia – forced Moscow down the path of least resistance to its only remaining choice: military aggression. Compared to the EU's arsenal of benefits, it had few other options with which to appeal to the Ukrainians. These bargain-basement benefits weaken the Russian economy as well as the Russian value proposition to its client states. To co-opt a popular saying, Russia had no carrot, so it had to use the stick.

As Russian military involvement in Ukraine deepened, commentators wondered if Moscow would intervene directly to establish a land bridge to Crimea from the rebel-held areas of Donbas.[17] Such a bridge would have required another military intervention to seize the large city of Mariupol.

---

[17] Steven Pifer, "The Mariupol Line: Russia's Land Bridge to Crimea," *The Brookings Institution,* March 19, 2015, https://www.brookings.edu/blog/order-from-chaos/2015/03/19/the-mariupol-line-russias-land-bridge-to-crimea

Three main constraints prevented further Russian aggression:

Economic: Europe – Germany in particular – had the economic upper hand over Russia (Figure 6.2). Russia is more addicted to European demand for its natural gas than Europe is to Russian supply. Europe could theoretically go without Russian natural gas altogether, further diminishing the utility's essential quality. Germany and other core European states mostly use natural gas for heating – not electricity production or industry. And unfortunately for Russia, ample alternatives – from plug-in heaters to blankets – exist.

Political: Russian leadership could not assume that the median voter's preference for President Putin would last forever, particularly not in the face of the country's currency and economic weakness in 2015.

The idea that the Russian populace gives its leaders a blank check to pursue aggressive foreign policy is not rooted in historical evidence. In fact, Russia has a spotty history regarding public support for failed military campaigns: the Crimean War in the mid-nineteenth century, the 1904–1905 Russo-Japanese War, World

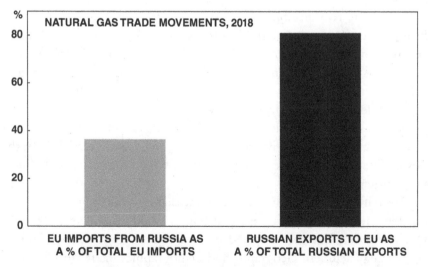

SOURCE: BP STATISTICAL REVIEW OF WORLD ENERGY 2019.
REPRINTED WITH PERMISSION BY BCA RESEARCH INC (WWW.BCARESEARCH.COM).

Figure 6.2   Germany has Russia by the pipelines.

War I, Afghanistan in the 1980s, and the First Chechen War in the early 1990s.

As the "time-in-power" constraint might have predicted, each of these military losses and dragged-out campaigns eventually led to popular backlash. They caused domestic political crises (if not outright revolutions), especially when accompanied by economic pain.

Geopolitics: A glance at a Ukraine map circa 2015 illustrates the pro-Russian rebels' paucity of success. The dividing line between the two groups ossified and remains the same in 2020. Even in Donetsk and Luhansk, the two *oblasts* where Russians and Russian speakers form an overwhelming majority, the actual rebel territorial gains amount to under 50% of the land area.

Russia's poor showing was a function of East Ukraine demographics and geography. Russians and Russian speakers combined may be the majority, but they are concentrated in high-density urban population centers. Ukrainian speakers dominate the rural areas, thus making military operations beyond the cities a challenge for the pro-Russian rebels. Overall, the people and land constrained pro-Russian rebels to less than 5% of the total Ukrainian territory.

There are two possible reasons why Russia stopped at 5% and why it did not employ more aggression to build the land bridge to Crimea and push beyond to the rest of Ukraine (as pundits predicted). Either Russia was an incompetent, third-world power incapable of fostering a successful insurgency – even on its very own borders – or Moscow made the only decision its constraints allowed.

President Putin and his team understood the costs if they committed to a serious military confrontation inside a vast hostile territory. Both hostile forces and a hostile local population would threaten supply lines via insurgency.

Even if I accept the conventional view that Russia's military is highly capable, the corollary assessment that Russia could easily defeat Ukraine in a war purely due to the spread in capabilities betrays a lack of military strategy acumen. Geography and demographics matter in Ukraine. Securing supply lines inside recently conquered territory over vast distances would be a challenge for any military – particularly Russia's, which has experienced no similar warfare for over 50 years.

I estimate that to establish a land bridge to Crimea, the military operation would have required 60,000–100,000 Russian soldiers for the initial invasion, securing supply lines, and pacifying the local population. Invading all of Ukraine would have required over 200,000 Russian soldiers. This show of strength would have overcommitted the Russian military and economy, playing right into the hands of its adversaries in the West.

Two constraints held Russia back from more military action: the geography of its sphere of influence and its own hard power capabilities, which fell well short of the glory days of the Soviet Union.

Given the stalemate in Ukraine and the paltry territorial gains in Donbas, President Putin pivoted to countering Islamic terrorism. On September 30, 2015, Russian military intervention in Syria began. Russian state-controlled TV also got to elegantly pivot its coverage away from a theater of war where Moscow was geopolitically constrained and where its military prowess fell short to one where it was not and did not.

Geopolitics: The Takeaway

While I worked at Stratfor, my favorite analysis that George Friedman ever produced was a piece on the Obama presidency. It was late 2008, and Barack Obama had won the election. It came to George to pen an analysis of what kind of a foreign policy Barack Obama would pursue during his next four years in power. The main variables were what Obama would do with the troops in Iraq, whether he would establish a *détente* with Russia, and whether he would close the Guantanamo Bay prison.

George's missive to clients had a disappointing thesis: Obama would largely follow George W. Bush's prerogatives. Troops would not be withdrawn from Iraq as quickly as people hoped, the *détente* with Russia would not work, and Guantanamo Bay would remain open.

Oh, to see the hate mail pouring in. The conservative clients were incensed. The hippie-liberal Obama couldn't hold a candle to the hawkish conservative! Of course he would make America tuck its tail between its legs and abandon Iraq! Of course he would make peace with Russia![18] And of course he would liberate the terrorists from Guantanamo Bay! Meanwhile, the liberal clients thought George was trolling them. How could Obama follow in the footsteps of a failed presidency?

Geopolitics constrained Obama from delivering on his campaign promises just as it had forced George W. Bush onto the path of least resistance, which at his inauguration became Obama's burden to bear. The impassioned hate mail indicated that our readers could not get past their political and ideological frameworks. Geopolitical constraints do not discriminate between party labels.

While geopolitics is a powerful constraint, I never grew comfortable using it in isolation. In my experience as an investment strategist, geopolitical *alpha* is rarely a product of only the geopolitical constraint. Nonetheless, it is powerful in certain contexts and should be kept in store for careful use.

---

[18] To recall for those with selective memories: back in 2008, it was Republican voters who held an extremely negative view of Russia, while Democrats were positive. By 2016, of course, the sentiment is diametrically opposite!

Chapter 7

Constitutional and Legal Constraints: The Constraint–Preference Hybrids

"Within our mandate, the ECB is ready to do whatever it takes to preserve the euro. And believe me, it will be enough."
— Mario Draghi, ECB president, July 26, 2012

I hesitate to write this chapter. This book is about material constraints and how they force policymakers down the path of least resistance, not the path that they have chosen themselves. And yet, this chapter is about a constraint that, more often than not, behaves like an optional preference.

Constitutional and legal constraints ought to be meaningful because in law-abiding societies, the law is a strong constraint to the individual citizen. No one wants a parking ticket, to end up in jail, or to be arrested for tax evasion. As a result, most individuals take the path of least resistance and operate within the constraints of the law.

But in policymakers' hands, these constraints are malleable. They get around laws more often than investors realize. When it comes to this particular subset of constraints, they are meant to be broken, especially in a crisis. In both Europe and the US, recessionary economic constraints forced policymakers to manipulate the legal constraints – and sometimes even the constitutional ones.

During the 2008–2009 Great Recession, the US banking system faced a liquidity Armageddon. Because their balance sheet collateral was worthless, banks abruptly stopped lending to each other and the real economy. Because the banks knew precisely what horse manure was on the books, they assumed that their counterparts were full of it as well. To suspend reality and allow banks to extend and pretend, the US Financial Accounting Standards Board (FASB) amended rule FAS 157, known as the "mark-to-market" regulation. This amendment allowed the banks to determine the value of their own assets on balance sheets.[1] Specifically, the ruling on April 2, 2009, allowed banks to assess the value of assets based on their own assumptions rather than on "observable inputs" (i.e., reality).[2]

Poof. In one fell swoop, the financial crisis was on its way to being mended!

Euro Area Crisis Averted

European policymakers not only amended the rules but ignored the EU constitution altogether. Article 125 of the Lisbon Treaty (and Article

---

[1] They arrived at a number using sophisticated quantitative approaches such as the cutting-edge SOOMA modeling, which stands for "Straight Out of My … Assets." This is a family show, folks!

[2] Kara Scannell, "FASB Eases Mark-to-market Rules," *The Wall Street Journal*, April 3, 2009, https://www.wsj.com/articles/SB123867739560682309.

104b of the Maastricht Treaty) expressly forbade bailouts of EU member states. As such, the first fiscal backstop involved interstate loans, rather than assuming full liabilities. On May 9, 2010, Euro Area members created the EU's first *de facto* bailout mechanism: the European Financial Stability Facility (EFSF). It was framed as an off-the-books special purpose vehicle (SPV). Eventually, the EU approved constitutional changes that allowed for the establishment of the more permanent European Stability Mechanism (ESM). But, at the height of the crisis, policymakers did more than rewrite and bend the law — they broke it.

Investors and corporate executives often get hung up on legal and constitutional technicalities. Don't! The constitution is not a suicide pact that dictates the operation of a country. Most of the time, other constraints come first. If the political capital exists, the economic and financial implications are meaningful. If the geopolitical imperatives are overwhelming, then policymakers will scrap or rewrite the rules. Quickly.

I discussed the Euro Area crisis in Chapter 4 through the lens of political constraints. It also exemplifies how political constraints are more restrictive than constitutional and legal constraints. The crisis only resolved once policymakers convinced the markets that they were, indeed, willing to do "whatever it takes." Setting up the EFSF was not enough. Only Mario Draghi was enough.

On July 26, 2012, Draghi uttered his famous line, "Whatever it takes." He did qualify the phrase with "within our mandate," giving a nod to the rules governing the ECB mandate. However, he also appended it with, "believe me, it will be enough."[3]

Draghi clarified that the ECB would bend its mandate to the preservation of the euro. Compared to the strength of all other constraints pushing against the euro's failure, a flimsy legal mandate was most easily broken. In 2011, Draghi used the Securities Markets Program (SMP) to intervene in the Italian and Spanish bond markets because their dysfunction was making appropriate monetary policy, and thus price stability, impossible. Eventually, the technocrats at the ECB defined Draghi's "whatever it takes" through a program called the Outright Monetary

---

[3] "Verbatim of the Remarks Made by Mario Draghi," *European Central Bank,* July 26, 2012, https://www.ecb.europa.eu/press/key/date/2012/html/sp120726.en.html.

Transactions (OMT). This was Draghi's "big bazooka" that the ECB never actually used.

When it comes to the ECB's economic Band-Aids, looking back at the Euro Area crisis from the thick of the COVID-19 pandemic is like looking back at medieval Europe from the twenty-first century. Draghi's successor, ECB President Christine Lagarde, is not just using a bazooka. She is throwing the kitchen sink, a clawfoot tub, and all sorts of other household appliances at the economy. Within days – not months or weeks – the ECB crossed any remaining lines that may have existed on use of unorthodox monetary policy. And with the Macron-Merkel consensus on a mutualized fiscal backdrop, the EU has crossed the ultimate red line.

Policymakers' ease in breaking legal constraints shows just how strong political, economic, and geopolitical constraints are. As long as there is geopolitical and political will along with logic for integration, European policymakers will do "whatever it takes" to preserve the Euro Area.

Trump and Trade

A constitutional lens of analysis does not always deal with laws to be ignored. Sometimes, extant laws push policymakers onto the path of least resistance. President Trump had an ambitious agenda in January 2017, from a comprehensive immigration overhaul to repealing Obamacare. However, with the Senate majority insufficient to break the legislative deadlock on most issues,[4] he was forced to focus instead on foreign policy and trade in his first term.

My teammate Matt Gertken and I huddled after the November 2016 election to produce a forecast of Trump's presidency. As we went over his priorities and campaign promises one by one, we realized many

---

[4] A Senate majority that the 2018 midterms eventually improved upon. But in losing the House of Representatives, Trump lost the ability to fully fund his most ambitious legislative policy: the "wall" on the southern border.

would die in Congress, even a Congress controlled by his own party. At the time, the consensus view was that Congress, chock-full of pro-trade Republicans and Democrats, would check Trump's most aggressive threats on trade.

This view did not sit well with our reading of history. President Nixon had imposed an import tariff on essentially all imports when he closed the gold window in 1971. And Obama had used tariffs, selectively, from the first month of his presidency.

Early in 2017, many investors were unfamiliar with the lack of constraints on the president's actions concerning trade policy. Article I, Section 8, and Article II, Section 2, of the US Constitution give Congress the power to govern trade. However, starting in the 1930s, Congress delegated its own authority to the executive branch via a number of legislative acts.[5]

This series of laws enacted over the past century gave Trump enough latitude to impose tariffs. The Trade Act of 1974 allows the US president to impose tariffs on countries as an effort to correct unjustified foreign trade practices. President Trump used Section 301 of the act against China. The Trade Expansion Act of 1962 allows the president to impose tariffs for the sake of national security, and the Trump administration used Section 232 to raise tariffs on a number of importers, including American allies like Canada.

President Trump also has the authority to declare an emergency and invoke the Trading with the Enemy Act of 1917, which allows the president to regulate all commerce and seize foreign assets. President Nixon used that act to justify a 10% surcharge tariff on all imports in 1971. He cited the Korean War – which had been over for *19 years* – as the emergency. Since the Korean state of emergency had never officially ended, Nixon used it as a reason to impose tariffs on all imports.

Because of Nixon's loose legal framework for the surcharge, Congress ended up passing the 1974 act. Much as the EU eventually

---

[5] President Roosevelt passed the first of these, the Trade Agreements Act of 1934, to help haul the US out of the Great Depression.

passed constitutional changes that allowed the EFSF to be replaced by the ESM, the US Congress retroactively normalized Nixon's policy.

Matt produced a table that listed all of the legislative acts that give the US president authority over trade. We threw it in our chart pack and pounded the proverbial pavement with the argument that Trump had no constraints to pursue a trade war with China. When the April 2017 Mar-a-Lago summit put the trade war on hold, the naysayers criticized our view. However, investors bullish on the US–China relationship misunderstood the point.

The *absence* of a legal and legislative constraint to trade war was the risk. At Mar-a-Lago, Trump's preference for deal-making prevailed. But if that preference changed, there would be no constitutional or legal constraint standing in his way. Betting on preferences, therefore, was folly.

On the hierarchy of constraints, constitutional and legal issues take the bottom rung. If these are the fulcrum constraints of your forecast, you are probably wrong.[6] A proper net assessment – a term I describe in Chapter 9 – never begins with a legal analysis. It begins with an understanding of the first-string constraints: political, economic, financial, and geopolitical. Only at the end do constitutional and legal matters come to the forefront. Like preferences, for policymakers they are subject to all other constraints.

In countries with loosely followed legal and constitutional norms, this constraint on policymakers is irrelevant, and I treat it as a pure preference in my constraint framework. Think of Russian presidential term limits, as an example.

I incorporate legal and constitutional constraints into my forecast only when all other constraints fail to elucidate the situation. In the case of US tax cuts, I had a high-conviction view that the political constraints to passing profligate tax cuts were virtually nonexistent.[7] Only when the political constraints did not help me eliminate any hypotheses did I turn to possible legal constraints: Republicans' ability to pass legislation that would blow out the budget deficit.

---

[6] You are likely going to be wrong, and you need to stop reading the aforementioned *Gyro Wedge*.

[7] See Chapter 3 for a reminder of this scenario.

Reconciliation and the Markets

Early on in President Trump's administration, he threatened to start a trade war with China, end the Iran nuclear deal, and repeal Obamacare. But the most market-relevant issue was whether he could follow through on passing the corporate tax cut. Many investors were unsure he could do this with the budget reconciliation process as his only tool. Most investors believed budget reconciliation only allowed legislators to pass revenue-neutral fiscal bills. Or did it?

Budget reconciliation – "reconciliation" for short – simplifies the process of passing a budget, and it was introduced by the Congressional Budget Act of 1974.[8] To illustrate why reconciliation mattered to Trump's budget cut aspirations, I first have to explain how the US Congress sets the budget.

If you think that this is a backward-looking analysis not worth your time, think again. A Biden presidency may hinge on the reconciliation process to fundamentally alter the way America's companies and investors do business. This is critical stuff (albeit still really boring).

The US Budget Process

The US budget process (Figure 7.1) begins when the US president submits a White House budget request to Congress. This step is ceremonial, as Congress has power over the appropriations process.

Congress considers the president's request – or doesn't – as it formulates a *budget resolution*, which both houses of Congress pass. But it is not submitted to the president and does not constitute law. The resolution sets out the guidelines for the budget process, which ideally produces an *appropriations bill*.

---

[8] I draw on several overviews of the budget reconciliation process in this chapter: David Reich and Richard Kogan, "Introduction To Budget 'Reconciliation,'" *Center on Budget and Policy Priorities,* November 9, 2016, https://www.cbpp.org/research/federal-budget/ introduction-to-budget-reconciliation; Megan S. Lynch, *The Budget Reconciliation Process: Timing Of Legislative Action* (Congressional Research Service, 2016); Lynch, *Budget Reconciliation Measures Enacted Into Law: 1980–2010* (Congressional Research Service, 2017).

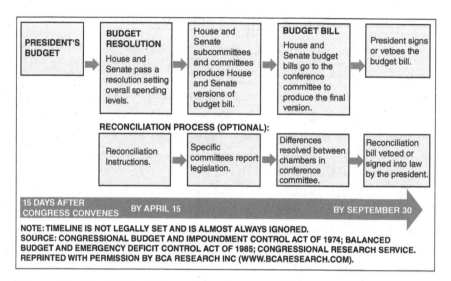

Figure 7.1   The US budget process: a fantasy time line.

The appropriations bill, also known as a "budget bill," cobbles together funding for the various federal government departments, agencies, and programs. Under a revised timetable in effect since 1987, both chambers of Congress are supposed to adopt the annual budget resolution by April 15. The date gives legislators sufficient time to then pass a budget bill by the start of the fiscal year on October 1. However, Congress has no obligation or punitive incentive to meet either of these deadlines.

In fact, Congress failed to pass a budget resolution for most of President Obama's two terms in office due to extreme polarization. As such, "continuing resolutions" funded the government. These resolutions extend pre-existing appropriations at the same levels as the previous fiscal year.

Under President Trump, the situation has not improved. The government shut down for three days in January 2018 and then again from late 2018 to early 2019. The latter was the longest shutdown in history – 35 days – due to the failure of President Trump and House Democrats to agree on an appropriations bill.

The Reconciliation Process

Within this legislative staring contest, the reconciliation process was originally introduced to simplify changing the law on the books, enabling Congress to bring revenue and spending levels into line with the budget resolution in a timely manner. It was so crucial to the prospects of the 2017 tax reform because it limits Senate debate to 20 hours. The limit prevents any senator from filibustering the final legislation that emerges from the reconciliation process.

Reconciliation enabled Republicans to prevent filibuster – without having the 60 votes to invoke cloture.[9] In the 2017 tax cut context, where the Republican Party controlled 52 seats, this feature of the reconciliation process allowed Republicans to pass legislation that would otherwise be filibustered in the Senate.

The reconciliation procedure is a powerful legislative tool that helps Congress pass controversial legislation, as long as such legislation affects government revenues or spending levels. Tax legislation falls under the first of these umbrellas.

George W. Bush used the reconciliation procedure to lower taxes in 2001 and 2003. His father, George H.W. Bush, used reconciliation to *raise* taxes in 1990 (to roll back some of Ronald Reagan's 1986 tax reform). The 1996 welfare reform – the Personal Responsibility and Work Opportunity Reconciliation Act – was also passed via the reconciliation process.

The one unifying feature of all reconciliation bills is that they must have an impact on the budget, by changing either the revenue or spending levels of the federal government. If the bill introduces extraneous provisions that deviate from the budgetary requirement, then these can be struck out by invoking the "Byrd rule." Waiving the Byrd rule requires an affirmative vote of three-fifths of the Senate, which is 60 votes. As such, it is equivalent to the 60-seat majority needed to invoke cloture, rendering the entire reconciliation process redundant.

---

[9] Cloture, an act that ends debate in the chamber, requires 60 Senate votes to invoke. Are you asleep yet? That's cool, this is a short chapter. Take a power nap and then crush it. The rest of the book really picks up from here.

While a detailed account of previously passed bills may read like dusty legal history, the closer the 2020 elections loom, it is only becoming more relevant.

Imagine the COVID-19 recession lowers the odds of a Trump second term. President Biden is inaugurated in January 2021, with a Democratic House *and* a slim majority in the Senate. (He picks that up thanks to the tailwinds of a recession and a median voter angry at the Trump administration for downplaying the virus threat.) The reconciliation procedure allows the newly elected President Biden to pass *all sorts* of legislation through the Senate chamber without a 60-seat majority. Just as Trump lowered corporate taxes with a bare minimum of a majority, Biden can increase them. Just as Obama passed Obamacare with a bare minimum of a majority, Biden can build on it. And, most relevant for investors, President Biden can use the reconciliation process – and a slim 50–50 tie in the Senate broken by his vice president – to raise capital gains taxes. And he most certainly will do that.

Reconciliation and the 2017 Tax Reform: So What?

The investment community struggled to map out how Republicans would pass tax cuts in 2017. When the Obamacare repeal failed midyear, investors balked. They could not understand how tax reform would succeed where the Obamacare repeal had failed. A constraint-focused comparison of the two events resolves the policy puzzle: strong political constraints prevented an Obamacare repeal. But laws designed to bypass those political constraints – reconciliation – enabled Republicans to cut corporate taxes. In this special case, legal constraints eliminated both interparty and partisan political constraints.[10]

Reconciliation was designed to fast-track the changing of America's complex tax laws. And it worked exactly as it should have for the 2017 tax cuts. But investors in 2017 still wondered about the forecasting bottom line: would tax cuts actually be stimulative?

---

[10] These events demonstrate the hybrid nature of legal and constitutional constraints. Like a non-Newtonian fluid (i.e., oobleck to those with kids), laws shift between two states – preference or constraint – depending on the environment.

Uncertainty over the act's effects abounded. Investors wondered whether the Tea Party would allow President Trump to douse what remained of America's fiscal prudence with gasoline and set it alight. They doubted whether the reconciliation process would actually allow lawmakers to pass a profligate bill. Wouldn't spending cuts, or revenue-raising "offsets," need to be included to justify the loss of revenue?

From 1980 to the 1990s, Congress used the reconciliation procedure for its intended purpose: *reducing* the deficit through reductions in mandatory spending, revenue increases, or both. Starting in the new millennium, Congress wielded the tool to expand deficits instead. The Bush-era reconciliation bills in 2001 and 2003 introduced large tax cuts.

Remember the Byrd rule from seven paragraphs ago?[11] In addition to ensuring the bill is budget-relevant, the Byrd rule also forces any provision to expire, or "sunset," if it increases the deficit beyond the years covered by the reconciliation bill.

In the case of the 2001 and 2003 bills, Bush-era tax cuts expired in 2011 (estate tax) and 2013 (which investors remember as the "fiscal cliff" of 2013). But the sunset period does not have to be 10 years. It could be a lot longer and make tax reform semipermanent. The 2017 tax cut established a sunset of 10 years, so most of its provisions will expire in the mid-2020s.

Following the Democratic Party sweep in the 2006 midterm elections, the Democrat-controlled Senate changed reconciliation rules to prohibit any deficit-increasing measures, regardless of the sunset clause loophole. However, the Republicans changed the rules back in 2015 after they retook the Senate in the 2014 midterm election.

The 2015 switch means that the procedural rules on the books allow deficits to be blown out via the reconciliation procedure. The limitless deficit possibilities enabled Republicans in Congress to be *fiscally profligate,* despite media punditry to the contrary. All this was happening at a time when, thanks to news reports and Republican rhetoric, most of my clients thought a budget-busting tax cut was impossible.

---

[11] No? Time for another nap.

How to Peddle a Budget-busting Tax Cut

One constraint remained that stopped the Obamacare repeal, and might still have halted the corporate tax cut: legislative math. While House Republicans seemed on board with a budget-busting tax cut, there was the off chance that some senators would dissent. Earlier in the year, three Republican senators refused to repeal Obamacare. A fiscal hawk could hold up the legislation; one opportunistic scavenger could rob the market of the succulent carcass of a fiscally stimulative tax cut.

In Chapter 3, I emphasized how the statements of Tea Party Representative Mark Meadows helped me predict a tax cut. But there was more to my forecast confidence than just statements from Tea Party Congress members.

As it happens, Republicans did have more tools in their bottomless policy toolbox to get the job done. In particular, they could rely on "dynamic scoring," the macroeconomic modeling tool based on the work of economist Arthur Laffer (of "Laffer curve" infamy).

Dynamic scoring estimates the outcome of tax cuts based on the theory that they pay for themselves. Headline government revenue lost through tax cuts is only half the story, as the cut's growth-generating consequences also contribute to the full economic picture. These consequences are known as the "macroeconomic feedback" of the cuts and include factors that actually add to revenues.

The Congressional Budget Office (CBO) would balk at dynamic scoring. But it was clear that "egghead, socialist economists" would not stand in the way of tax reforms. At worst, the CBO's score would force the Republicans to "sunset" tax reform legislation, but not scuttle it.

Pessimistic investors were not buying my constraint-based wares. In client meeting after client meeting, I was told that the Tea Party line of "revenue neutrality" would dismantle any stimulative impact of the tax cut. But investors were making a mistake by taking the rhetoric of revenue neutrality seriously.

The House Republicans did offer ways to offset tax cuts with revenue-raising measures: a border-adjustment tax, eliminating the deductibility of business interest payments and jettisoning the deduction for state and local income taxes for individuals. But such proposals were either draconian or insufficient to cover the cost of the tax cuts.

Policymakers' path of least resistance, therefore, was to bust the budget. That couldn't be helped. Then, force the measures to expire over the life of the budget-setting window, all the while using dynamic scoring to "prove" that the cuts would actually pay for themselves.

Constitutional and Legal Constraints: The Takeaway

Occasionally, then, knowledge of the legal and constitutional constraints are indispensable to accurate constraint analysis.[12]

The minutiae sometimes matter, especially in the forecasting field. Outside of *ad-hoc* constraint analysis, the forecaster's tendency is to simplify as much as possible so problems can be described in formulas and compared across time and events. Reconciliation does not fit such a convenient mold, and most clients I spoke with in 2017 did not understand its importance. Those that did claimed the Byrd rule prevented the use of reconciliation to pass budget-busting legislation. Or they remembered that the Democrats had changed the rules, ensuring that reconciliation bills could not widen the deficit – but did not recall that in 2015 the Tea Party Republicans – ironically! – had quietly tilted the rule back toward profligacy.

The reconciliation process is not the sole reason Congress could pass the 2017 tax cuts. President Trump exercised his median voter–fueled political capital on the austerity-obsessed Republicans. He had enough capital to bend them, particularly Tea Party members, to his will. The reconciliation process was only important because it allowed the investor to gauge the scenario's political constraints, i.e., whether they were strong enough to either prevent or enable the legislation to go through.

Be wary of any macro investment view that is overly technical, legal, or reliant on constitutionality. Remember the hierarchy of constraints. A good object lesson of such over-reliance is the impact of the 2016 UK referendum on EU membership. It was a nonbinding, consultative referendum and had dubious, if any, legal or constitutional power. However, it ultimately carried political weight, and so legal constraints bent to its much stronger political constraints.

---

[12] The knowledge acquisition will require boring research. Immensely boring.

Chapter 8

The Time Constraint: When Preferences Run Down the Clock

"Falsehood flies, but truth comes limping after."

Jonathan Swift

I wrote this book between January and April 2020, at the height of the COVID-19 pandemic. I am glad that I chose to write a framework book and not a forecast one.

My view of the upcoming decade is clear from the first chapter, and COVID-19 has not altered it: I expect the world to continue deglobalizing. I expect *laissez-faire* to give way to *dirigisme*. I expect Europe to remain integrated and in fact accelerate the process. And I expect the US and China to remain at each other's throats — albeit constrained from full economic bifurcation by multipolarity.

The COVID-19 pandemic will likely only reinforce and accelerate these themes – particularly the move away from the Washington Consensus and toward the Buenos Aires Consensus, especially in the US and UK. By the time this manuscript hits the shelves, I suspect the move will be obvious. The time to forecast the apex of globalization, the end of *laissez-faire*, the Buenos Aires Consensus, and the US–China conflict was back in the early 2010s, not 2020.

Yet the COVID-19 crisis teaches a methodological lesson, particularly when it comes to the limitations of the constraint framework. Like many other investors, I initially underestimated the global impact of the virus: I advised clients to hold cash but not to outright short the market in February.

The constraint framework has a blind spot: the power of market participants' collective psychology to run down the clock on constraint-based forecasts. This weakness is the only feature the constraint framework shares with traditional forecasting methods because they are all at the mercy of time – in any analysis, *alpha* generation depends on whether the forecast event happens too early, too late, or at just the right moment.

In the case of the constraint framework, the link most vulnerable to time is the *zeitgeist* of the median voter. Recall from Chapter 4 that political constraints – the most powerful and predictive – hinge on the median voter *preference*. Usually, this measure is large enough to be material: reliable; quantifiable; and – above all – a median, or *moderate*, representation of the collective. It is large enough that it discounts irrational or extreme views as outliers with little influence on policymaker action.

The predictability of the link weakens when the collective responds irrationally, *en masse*, to a single issue. Or when a few Twitterati dominate the discussion by "shouting" over the median voter. The outlier becomes the median in those moments of panic. The *zeitgeist* veers toward the extreme, and suddenly it's a median voter preference gone *wild*. Under these circumstances, the panic has the power to delay material, constraint-based outcomes. As a result, it can shift forecast time horizons. In this chapter, I examine this limitation of the constraint framework through the lens of the latest cases of mass irrationality: terrorism and the COVID-19 pandemic.

Material Constraints Versus Terrorism

In early 2014, President Barack Obama said the following about the Islamic State: "The analogy we use around here sometimes, and I think is accurate, is if a J.V. team puts on Lakers uniforms, that doesn't make them Kobe Bryant."[1]

That same month, the Islamic State seized Falluja, a major city in Iraq's majority-Sunni Anbar Province, and large portions of Ramadi, the capital of the province. By June 2014, the militant group conquered Mosul, Iraq's second-largest city. In mid-October, the Islamic State was fighting the Iraqi army and various Iran-allied Shia militias on the outskirts of Baghdad.

Obama's statement was eerily similar to President Trump's initial treatment of COVID-19. At a February 28 South Carolina rally, Trump referred to the virus as a "hoax" perpetrated by the media and the Democrats to scuttle the economy.[2]

My next view will probably get me hate mail from 90% of American readers: I kind of agree with Obama *and* Trump.[3] Yes, the Islamic State was capable spreading of terror, and no, the virus was not a hoax. Obviously, the statements were objectively wrong. However, both Obama and Trump were correct in their initial assessments that materially, the threats were overblown.

They were only wrong because in early 2014 and early 2020, the material reality did not matter. What mattered was the perception of that reality by the public, and thus the markets, for the foreseeable (forecastable) future. The public *lost its mind* when confronted by the rampaging, decapitating Islamic State and the rampaging, octogenarian-targeting COVID-19 pandemic.[4]

Obama's flippant comments on the Islamic State cost him, or at least his centrist peers, in the following two years. The Islamic State's rampage

---

[1] David Remnick, "Going the Distance: On and Off the Road with Barack Obama," *The New Yorker,* January 20, 2014, https://www.newyorker.com/magazine/2014/01/27/going-the-distance-david-remnick.

[2] Poppy Noor, "Trump Is Trying to Stop People from Seeing This Ad on His Response to Coronavirus," *The Guardian,* March 27, 2020, https://www.theguardian.com/world/2020/mar/27/donald-trump-coronavirus-response-us-advertisement.

[3] The remaining 10% are my fellow nihilists.

[4] The median age of death from COVID-19 is, almost universally, above 80.

across Syria and Iraq and the subsequent 2015 European migration crisis probably gave anti-establishment populists a major boost, contributing to the "Leave" outcome in the UK's 2016 EU membership referendum. It turned Geert Wilders and Marine Le Pen into contenders to lead the Netherlands and France, respectively. It allowed right-wing populist *Lega* to ascend to power in Italy. While it is difficult to ascertain how much the Islamic State's atrocities contributed to Trump's own electoral success, he certainly benefited from the terror attacks inspired by the group throughout his election campaign in late 2015 and 2016.

All that said, the Islamic State really *was* a low-quality terror group. While it managed to inspire – and occasionally directly conduct – terror attacks across a swath of the developed world, its methods were of a junior varsity skill level. Compared to Al-Qaeda, the Islamic State's low-quality, high-quantity attacks killed fewer people in the West, failed to target critical infrastructure, and eventually desensitized the Western public. As the public got used to the constant attacks, the "return on investment" of each subsequent attack fell.

On the conventional battlefield, the group proved to be a joke. Yes, the Islamic State had initial success against the demoralized Iraqi army. And it ran amok in the lawless deserts of Syria. But its threat was overstated. Its successes were only possible in the power vacuum of a civil war–ravaged Syria and Iraq. Still, at one point, "people in the know" were seriously contemplating the possibility that the Islamic State could invade Saudi Arabia.

Once the Islamic State was confronted by a loose coalition of the Popular Mobilization Forces (Iran-allied Shia militias in Iraq), Iran's elite Quds force, US special forces and air assets, and Russian air assets in Syria, the group crumbled within months. No nation-state had an interest in the Islamic State's success. Its threat as a terrorist organization was massively overstated because it lacked the kind of command and control that made Al-Qaeda a serious threat.

Writing at BCA Research at the time, I made these forecasts early on in the group's rampage. I bolstered these views with my high-conviction view that the 2015 Europe migration crisis would collapse in a year due to a number of material constraints. It didn't matter. The hate mail poured in. Some clients said I was "nuts" to my face.

Ultimately, the material, constraint-based analysis proved correct. The Islamic State was defeated with minimal effort from the world's powers and local regional players, terrorist attacks inspired by the group subsided (despite the return of many of its fighters home), and the migration crisis dissipated.

Still, I had underestimated the impact that social media would have on collective psychology. The videos of beheadings, migrants streaming across borders, and active shooters running amok across the world's major cities caused voters to believe that the threats of terrorism and mass migration were higher than their material reality.

The unforeseen length of time it took for my forecast to come true demonstrates the constraint framework's potential to be overly forward-looking for its own good. It allows a forecaster to see "around the curve," the curve being the prevailing narrative in the media. But the markets will respond to the narrative, not necessarily the constraint-based long-term forecast. So, beware of wielding the framework if you have a fiduciary duty to make money.

React as a tactical investor to the narrative and as a strategic investor to the constraints.

Material Constraints Versus COVID-19

This cautionary tale brings me to the COVID-19 pandemic that caused one of the largest bouts of volatility in the history of markets. As of March 2020, I assume it will produce a biblical, but astoundingly brief, recession.

My view of the COVID-19 market sell-off is not going to be popular. I think academics will study it, and the subsequent recession, for centuries as an example of "mass hysteria" on an order of magnitude similar to the one that culminated in the Salem witch trials.

But the investor's job is not to scoff at the irrationality of groupthink from an ivory tower, only to forecast the market. As such, my failure to turn massively bearish at the onset of the crisis in January stings. As my Islamic State forecast also demonstrates, focusing too much on the material reality, as opposed to the *zeitgeist* of market participants, is a failure of the framework to ascertain when, and for how long, its forecasts will be put on hold.

That said, constraints-based analysis can gauge whether the world will descend into a 1930s-style depression. This call is particularly important here in March 2020, as it is the difference between another 30–50% downside in equity markets – after they fell 36% already – and a bottoming in risk assets on March 23 (the latter being my view).

In the case of the COVID-19 pandemic, there are three broad constraints suggesting that the crisis is ultimately manageable, despite its severity:

- **COVID-19 targets the elderly:** There is a lot that we in March 2020 do not know about the virus. But what we *do* know is that the hospitalization and mortality rates are highly concentrated in the elderly portion of the population. The concentration of risk into a single category opens the door for less economically damaging management strategies. And if those strategies do not emerge, human behavior can adjust so that the most vulnerable know to self-isolate.
- **The cost of fear is not constant:** Fear is cheap, until it isn't. Over time, fear-led behavior will buckle under the rising socioeconomic costs of maintaining it. The "Unit Cost of Fear" will ultimately rise.
- **The median voter leans left:** The US median voter has abandoned *laissez-faire* policies and moved to the left on the ideological spectrum, as discussed in Chapters 1 and 4. As such, the policy response to the COVID-19 pandemic will be – and has been – much larger and faster than investors anticipate.

Writing in March 2020, this forecast is not obvious. The "flatten-the-curve" narrative has become a dominant approach to fighting the COVID-19 pandemic, which encourages a near-total shutdown of all economic activity. If pursued to its ultimate conclusion, it will cause a depression and thus prove me wrong.

Policymakers across the ideological and geographical spectrum cite the curve-flattening approach as their reason to impose broad lockdown measures. California's Governor Gavin Newsom specifically mentioned the need to "bend the curve" when issuing his mid-March statewide "stay-at-home" order. The view is so prevalent that I've heard it from friends, schoolteachers, and folks in checkout lines at pharmacies. My parents in Switzerland, sister in Milan, aunt in Vancouver … everyone is an amateur epidemiologist and supporter of flattening the curve.

While the World Health Organization (WHO) has most authoritatively pushed for flatten-the-curve policies, the most draconian measures draw inspiration from just two sources. One is an Imperial College London study using available COVID-19 data.[5] Another is a blog post.[6]

The data underlying the Imperial College London study is of poor quality. A study published in the peer-reviewed journal *Science* estimates that "86% of all infections were undocumented prior to January 23, 2020 travel restrictions" in China.[7] Given the paucity of testing in the US and other countries, the spread of COVID-19 is probably monstrously underestimated in America as well, which in turn suggests the US mortality and hospitalization rates are overstated. Another study, published in *Nature Medicine*, supports my view by suggesting that the mortality rate at the epicenter of the pandemic, Wuhan, was considerably lower than what is being reported by the WHO as of March 2020.[8] I suspect that additional studies over the next 12–18 months will confirm that these mortality rates are grossly overstated. My fearless forecast is that the ultimate mortality rate of COVID-19 will prove to be somewhere between 0.1% and 0.3%: higher than the flu, but lower than the widely quoted 2–3%.

The bottom line is that the world is crafting an indefinite public policy based on a linear extrapolation of extremely limited data.[9]

But not all data is limited. The world does know *something* about COVID-19. Data plentiful enough to be statistically significant shows

---

[5] Neil M. Ferguson et al., "Impact of Non-pharmaceutical Interventions (NPIs) to Reduce COVID-19 Mortality and Healthcare Demand," *Imperial College COVID-19 Response Team,* March 19, 2020, https://www.imperial.ac.uk/media/imperial-college/medicine/sph/ide/gida-fellowships/Imperial-College-COVID19-NPI-modelling-16-03-2020.pdf

[6] Tomas Pueyo, "Coronavirus: Why You Must Act Now," *Medium,* March 10, 2020, https://medium.com/@tomaspueyo/coronavirus-act-today-or-people-will-die-f4d3d9cd99ca.

[7] Ruiyun Li et al., "Substantial Undocumented Infection Facilitates the Rapid Dissemination of Novel Coronavirus (SARS-CoV2)," *Science,* March 16, 2020, https://science.sciencemag.org/content/early/2020/03/13/science.abb3221.

[8] Joseph T. Wu et al., "Estimating Clinical Severity of COVID-19 from the Transmission Dynamics in Wuhan, China," *Nature Medicine,* March 19, 2020, https://www.nature.com/articles/s41591-020-0822-7.

[9] John P.A. Ioannidis, "A Fiasco in the Making? As the Coronavirus Pandemic Takes Hold, We Are Making Decisions Without Reliable Data," *Stat News,* March 17, 2020, https://www.statnews.com/2020/03/17/a-fiasco-in-the-making-as-the-coronavirus-pandemic-takes-hold-we-are-making-decisions-without-reliable-data.

that it is *ageist*. It discriminates by age. The mortality rates across the world – which again, are likely overstated – vary by age cohort. While Figure 8.1 is data from May and June, we had plenty of data out of China and Italy in March to make this conclusion very early (Figure 8.1).

Hospitalization rates are largely in line with the mortality rates, according to the Imperial College London study itself – which again, probably overstates and skews all data to the bearish side (Figure 8.2).

If those above the age of 60 make up 68.2% of symptomatic cases requiring hospitalization, it is prudent to ask why age-specific policies are not part of the arsenal in fighting COVID-19.

Before I pick up on this thread again, let me emphasize my actual area of expertise. I analyze geopolitics and politics from a market and economic perspective. My job is to produce research that projects the macroeconomic implications of political policies and geopolitical events.

So, let me do my job and forecast the implications of a draconian curve-flattening policy.

If G20 economies embrace indiscriminate flatten-the-curve policies, particularly if they do so *indefinitely*, they will cause a depression. Not a 2008-style Great Recession, but a 1930s-style Great *Depression*.

Unlike the "Chinese approach," which was an absolutist model of quarantine and containment, a flatten-the-curve policy accepts that COVID-19 infections will not be brought to a sudden halt. It suggests that countries drag out the pandemic – and presumably social distancing policies – long enough to keep the hospitalizations and tests below the healthcare system's capacity. "Long enough" probably translates to the entirety of the 18 months that it would take to produce a vaccine.

This approach will drag out the economic uncertainty over the course of the summer, perhaps longer. Such uncertainty will end all business investment, which, thanks to the 2019 US–China trade war, was weak to begin with. It will lead to the firing of large numbers of workers in anticipation of lower revenues. No amount of stimulus will deter companies, particularly the small- and medium-sized enterprises that employ the vast majority of American workers, from firing their workforces.

COVID-19: DEATH RATE BY COUNTRY

	SPAIN		ITALY		SWEDEN		SWITZERLAND		KOREA		JAPAN		CHINA	
	AGE	DEATH RATE (%)	AGE	DEATH RATE (%)	AGE	DEATH RATE (%)	AGE	DEATH RATE (%)	AGE	DEATH RATE (%)	AGE	DEATH RATE (%)	AGE	DEATH RATE (%)
	0–9	0.2	0–9	0.2	0–9	0.3	0–9	0.5	0–9	0.0	0–9	0.0	0–9	0.0
	10–19	0.3	10–19	0.0	10–19	0.0	10–19	0.0	10–19	0.0	10–19	0.0	10–19	0.2
	20–29	0.2	20–29	0.1	20–29	0.1	20–29	0.0	20–29	0.0	20–29	0.0	20–29	0.2
	30–39	0.3	30–39	0.3	30–39	0.2	30–39	0.1	30–39	0.1	30–39	0.2	30–39	0.2
	40–49	0.6	40–49	0.9	40–49	0.4	40–49	0.1	40–49	0.2	40–49	0.3	40–49	0.4
	50–59	1.5	50–59	2.7	50–59	1.3	50–59	0.6	50–59	0.7	50–59	0.7	50–59	1.3
	60–69	5.1	60–69	10.6	60–69	5.4	60–69	3.4	60–69	2.5	60–69	3.5	60–69	3.6
	70–79	14.5	70–79	26.0	70–79	22.1	70–79	11.6	70–79	9.8	70–79	9.8	70–79	8.0
	80–89	21.2	80–89	32.9	80–89	35.3	>80	28.4	>80	25.4	>80	18.9	>80	14.8
	>90	22.2	>90	31.0	>90	40.0								
	AS OF MAY 22. SOURCE: SPANISH MINISTRY OF HEALTH.		AS OF JUNE 15. SOURCE: ISTITUTO SUPERIORE DI SANITÀ.		AS OF JUNE 22. SOURCE: PUBLIC HEALTH AGENCY OF SWEDEN.		AS OF JUNE 22. SOURCE: FEDERAL OFFICE OF PUBLIC HEALTH OF THE SWISS CONFEDERATION.		AS OF JUNE 22. SOURCE: KCDC.		AS OF MAY 27. SOURCE: TOKYO KEIZAI.		AS OF FEBRUARY 11. SOURCE: CHINESE CDC.	

REPRINTED WITH PERMISSION OF CLOCKTOWER GROUP, L.P.

Figure 8.1 COVID-19 is ageist.

AGE	% SYMPTOMATIC CASES REQUIRING HOSPITALIZATION	% HOSPITALIZED CASES REQUIRING CRITICAL CARE	INFECTION MORTALITY RATE
0 to 9	0.1%	5.0%	0.00%
10 to 19	0.3%	5.0%	0.01%
20 to 29	1.2%	5.0%	0.03%
30 to 39	3.2%	5.0%	0.08%
40 to 49	4.9%	6.3%	0.15%
50 to 59	10.2%	12.2%	0.60%
60 to 69	16.6%	27.4%	2.20%
70 to 79	24.3%	43.2%	5.10%
80+	27.3%	70.9%	9.30%
SOURCE: IMPERIAL COLLEGE STUDY. REPRINTED WITH PERMISSION OF CLOCKTOWER GROUP, L.P.			

Figure 8.2   Hospitalization and fatality rates.

The uncertainty will also lead to drastically lower revenues. If I project the current situation in the restaurant sector, revenues for large parts of the economy will go to zero (Figure 8.3). Such a catastrophe will in turn infect hospitality, airlines, fitness, healthcare (non-COVID-19 related, of course), etc. And as workers in these sectors lose their jobs, they will need fewer goods and services from other sectors. The chain reaction will be of nuclear proportions.

This outlook is a level of economic retrenchment unseen in any recession, not even during the Great Depression. Analysts are dealing with an economic calamity that cannot be reasonably forecast. If data from China is replicated in the rest of the world – and then prolonged due to the open-ended social distancing encouraged by *Flattenistas* – a depression is almost guaranteed.

A dislocation of this magnitude beyond *one or two months* would cause a permanent loss of consumer demand. The US consumer – comprising about 15% of global GDP – is particularly at risk. A prolonged recession that mutates into a depression could lead to a "demand hysteresis" (as opposed to merely a labor hysteresis), where consumers permanently retrench due to the combination of the COVID-19 exogenous shock and permanent impairment of their balance sheets. Given that a large swath of America has a negative savings rate, those balance sheets will be impaired within weeks. Days now.

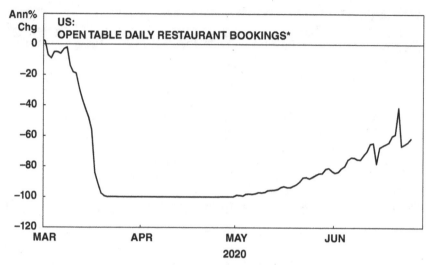

***INCLUDES PHONE, ONLINE, AND WALK-IN DINERS. SOURCE: OPEN TABLE.
REPRINTED WITH PERMISSION OF CLOCKTOWER GROUP, L.P.**

Figure 8.3   Revenue is going to zero.

But wait, human lives are in the balance. Wasn't a recession due anyway? So what if stocks fall another 30% and we have to tighten our belts for a ~~decade~~ year or two? It will be worth it if we prevent even one COVID-19 death.

But a deep recession will potentially kill *more* people than COVID-19, and not just from the well-known recessionary effect of rising suicides. A 2016 *Lancet* study posited that an excess of 260,000 cancer-related deaths occurred in OECD economies due to the 2008 Great Recession.[10] That mortality surplus is just from cancer, and just from the 2008 Great Recession. What would a *depression* do?

For that, I turn to Greece. A 2018 *Lancet* study concluded that the Greek mortality rate increased between 2010 and 2016 by 17.8%

---

[10] Mahiben Maruthappu et al., "Economic Downturns, Universal Health Coverage, and Cancer Mortality in High-income and Middle-income Countries, 1990–2010: A Longitudinal Analysis," *The Lancet* 10045, no. 388 (May 2016), https://doi.org/10.1016/S0140-6736(16)00577-8.

(Figure 8.4). This was three times higher than that of Western Europe, at a time when worldwide mortality rates were declining.[11]

A 20% jump in the mortality rate in the US would mean, on average, about 2.5 to 3 million extra deaths *annually*. And unlike COVID-19, those deaths would not be concentrated among the elderly cohort, as the Greek experience under depression showed.[12]

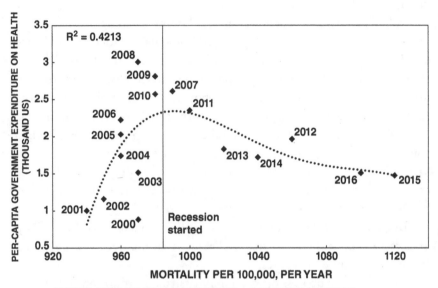

SOURCE: WORLD BANK, MACROTRENDS, LANCET PUBLIC HEALTH.
REPRINTED WITH PERMISSION OF CLOCKTOWER GROUP, L.P.

Figure 8.4 Mortality rate increase in Greece.

---

[11] Stefanos Tyrovolas et al., "The Burden of Disease in Greece, Health Loss, Risk Factors, and Health Financing, 2000–16: An Analysis of the Global Burden of Disease Study 2016," *The Lancet Public Health* no. 8, 3 (August 2018), https://doi.org/10.1016/S2468-2667(18)30130-0.

[12] I am also being highly optimistic by suggesting that the US mortality rate would rise by the same equivalent as that of Greece. In my humble view, the quality of life of the median Greek – pre-2010 – was much higher than the quality of life of the median American today. I would therefore expect the US mortality rate to jump 30%–40% thanks to a Greek-level depression. Two reasons for this bold claim: a significant lack of reality-defying beachfront property (per capita) in the US and a significant supply (per capita) of guns.

And that fatal disaster is only the *second*-order effect of a depression. For third- and fourth-order effects of a depression, I defer to the politics and geopolitics of the 1930s. As in that decade, in 2020 there is a multipolar distribution of power, an isolationist US, and multiple challenger powers looking to carve out a sphere of influence. With such a similar historical model to go by, it does not take much imagination to extrapolate a 2020s depression to its conclusion: deglobalization, populism, jingoism, and finally a world war.[13]

Policymakers may therefore pause before handing over the keys of public policy to epidemiologists (and bloggers). Doctors and nurses deserve our support, especially at a time when a pandemic is going to stretch the healthcare system and require healthcare professionals to make Herculean sacrifices. Yet their priorities do not include preventing an economic depression. More importantly, they are not constrained by the possibility of one. They have taken the Hippocratic Oath, which constrains them to focus instead on first-order effects of a medical crisis. Save lives now, let someone else deal with the consequences. They are not trained to worry about – nor do we want them to be distracted by – second-, third-, and fourth-order effects.

But doctors don't make public policy. Policymakers do. And policymakers are constrained by a material reality that includes a depression in its various possible outcomes.

An economic depression is such a massive constraint on policymakers that the trajectory of flatten-the-curve policy will ultimately have to change.

Non-linearity and COVID-19

How can policy possibly change when a virus does not? To answer this question, we need to descend into the world of data, which by the summer had given us a fuller picture of the COVID-19 outbreak. As I mentioned above, my March forecast of the eventual mortality rate was somewhere around 0.1% to 0.3%. How could I have confidently made

---

[13] Jingoism is nationalism taken to its belligerent extreme.

this forecast at the beginning of the outbreak, especially when the World Health Organization (WHO) settled at a much higher number, 3.4%?

My initial forecast was guided by the simple fact that, early on in any outbreak, the number of cases will be massively understated, whereas the deaths will generally not be. In advanced economies, people do not die in the streets. They die in hospitals where their deaths are recorded, and autopsies performed. As such, the numerator of the mortality rate – deaths – was going to be close to reality, whereas the denominator – the total number of infected – would be woefully underreported early on in the crisis.

We also had pretty good data out of China and a trickle of studies that ultimately became a cacophony of research suggesting a much lower mortality rate. As with previous outbreaks – the H1N1 influenza in 2009 and Ebola in 2014 – the initial reporting of the mortality rate was overstated.[14]

Not only did I fully expect the mortality rate to be massively overstated, my experience tracking the 2014 Ebola outbreak reminded me early in the COVID-19 outbreak to be wary of epidemiological modeling. The Centers for Disease Control and Prevention (CDC) forecast in 2014 concluded that 1.4 million people would get infected with Ebola and that 100,000 would be dead *within months*.[15] Instead, ultimately only 28,646 were infected, with 11,323 deaths. Why the discrepancy?

Obviously, modeling is difficult, particularly in nonlinear environments like a viral outbreak. But what was particularly difficult for the CDC to get right was a change in human behavior. Through excellent public health reaction and individual behavior change, the Ebola outbreak was mitigated. I expected the same would be the case with COVID-19.

But there is another reason why early modeling was so egregiously alarming. I suspect that there was an element of public service in the

---

[14] I was also fortunate to have paid very close attention to both outbreaks. In 2009, I was in charge of Stratfor's research on the H1N1 outbreak and in 2014, I took a deep interest in the Ebola outbreak at BCA Research.

[15] *Washington Post*, "Ebola cases could skyrocket by 2015, says CDC," http://apps .washingtonpost.com/g/page/national/ebola-cases-could-skyrocket-by-2015-says-cdc/ 1337/

modeling. They were supposed to be scary so that people would, in the end, change their behavior.

Take the valiant effort by the CDC to convince young people that they are not invulnerable to COVID-19. Just as I was explaining to clients and investors that the median age of death was essentially the same as *life expectancy* in most countries, the CDC came out with a breathless analysis that the youth was in danger as well. In mid–March, new data from the CDC suggested "young adults" are being hospitalized in the US at higher rates than internationally? As a result, several media outlets – leading with the *New York Times* – reported that "young adults" are being hospitalized in the US at an elevated rate.[16] Figure 8.5 was published accompanying the report.

I could write an entire *chapter* about this chart! Having excelled during my long career in the "sell side" of the financial industry, I know a manipulated chart when I ~~make~~ see one. The CDC report was either written by a high school student with a poor grasp of mathematics or is an outright piece of ~~propaganda~~ PR.

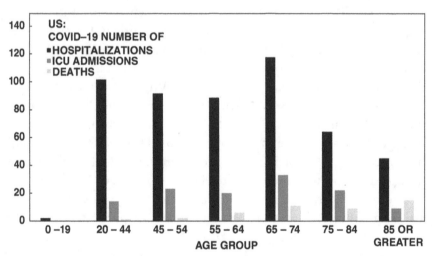

NOTE: BASED ON DATA FROM FEBRUARY 12 TO MARCH 16, 2020.
SOURCE: US CDC.
REPRINTED WITH PERMISSION OF CLOCKTOWER GROUP, L.P.

Figure 8.5   Is the CDC manipulating data?

---

[16] Pam Belluck, "Younger Adults Make Up Big Portion of Coronavirus Hospitalizations in U.S.," *New York Times,* March 18, 2020, https://www.nytimes.com/2020/03/18/health/coronavirus-young-people.html.

The data in Figure 8.1 of this chapter, sourced from individual countries' health agencies, segregates hospitalization and mortality rate by age cohorts of 10 years. But the CDC study invents a new category: the "young adult" category of 20–44 years.[17] This lopsided category indicates that, according to the CDC, it is empirically acceptable to have one age cohort encompass 25 years where the rest include merely 10.

The 20–44 cohort could have a higher rate of hospitalization for those in the 40–44 age range. It also happens to be the largest demographic cohort, so it would make sense for rates of hospitalizations to be high. But hold on … the chart doesn't even report a "rate." It reports hospitalizations in *absolute numbers*. The sheer number of methodological errors in one chart reveal the preference of its creators: manipulation.

There is no other way to explain the CDC reporting than as an effort to get Millennials and Gen Z-ers to take social distancing policies seriously. In this case, the CDC's ends do not justify their means – and the means are not even effective. Publishing manipulated data will not help fight COVID-19, nor will it endear the public to the federal agency that has already bungled America's rollout of testing capacity.

By the summer, another data discrepancy began to appear: a divergence between new cases and deaths. I first noted the divergence in Swedish data, but it appeared to have gone global by June (Figure 8.6).

Now, there may be a lag in deaths, but I doubt that the number would ultimately peak at the same level as early in the crisis. In Sweden, the petri dish that gave us a mirror into the world post-opening, the lag appeared to be almost *two months* long (Figure 8.7)! Either lingonberries cure COVID-19, the untrustworthy Swedes are manipulating the data, or there is something more structural going on.

If I had to guess, I would suggest that three things are going on:

- **More testing**: Yes, more tests *do* produce more cases. Unfortunately, this thesis has become the rallying cry for the Trump administration, which now confirms to many readers that I sit at home with a MAGA hat perched on my head while slowly caressing the last batch

---

[17] In other news, I'm a Young Adult!!! Woohooo!

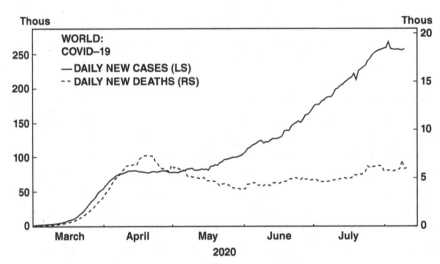

NOTE: BOTH SERIES SHOWN AS A 1–WEEK MOVING AVERAGE.
SOURCE: WHO, EUROPEAN CDC, MACROBOND.
REPRINTED WITH PERMISSION OF CLOCKTOWER GROUP, L.P.

Figure 8.6   Disconnect between deaths and cases goes global

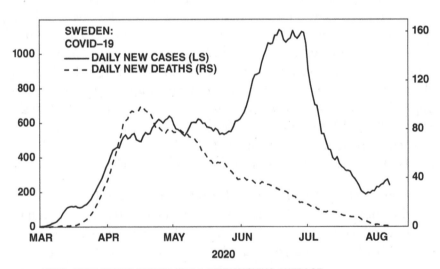

NOTE: BOTH SERIES SHOWN AS A 1–WEEK MOVING AVERAGE.
SOURCE: PUBLIC HEALTH AGENCY OF SWEDEN.
REPRINTED WITH PERMISSION OF CLOCKTOWER GROUP, L.P.

Figure 8.7   Sweden: the petri dish for COVID-19

of hydroxychloroquine.[18] While many of US states have not experienced a tick up in cases as percent of tests, the "Party States" – the US states where you would enjoy a cold brew poolside during the Memorial Day weekend – did.

- **Viral load**: Scientific research suggests a link between the severity of COVID-19, the disease, and the initial viral load of the SARS-CoV-2 virus.[19] In lay terms, this means that getting sick from a milk carton while grocery shopping is different from having someone sneeze in your face in the office. Given that social distancing policies have reduced the number of indoor super spreader events – like sporting events – while human behavior has adjusted to the risks of the virus, odds are that high viral load infections have been mitigated. In late May, the head of the San Raffaele Hospital in Milan, Alberto Zangrillo, said that *"the swabs that were performed over the last 10 days showed a viral load in quantitative terms that was absolutely infinitesimal compared to the ones carried out a month or two months ago."*[20] The *Reuters* article carrying his comments bore a misleading headline: "New Coronavirus Losing Potency, Says Top Italian Doctor." Unsurprisingly, media in the US trotted a series of epidemiologists to discredit the silly Italian.[21] The virus causing COVID-19 has not changed, they quickly retorted! It is still as potent as ever! That's true, but the doctor in charge of one of Italy's best hospitals – and thus presumably *an expert on COVID-19* – did not claim that the virus actually "lost potency." He simply said that the viral load of infections was "infinitesimal" compared to what he observed on a daily basis in February and March. If true, it would go a long way to explaining

---

[18] I don't. I bathe in nihilist indifference instead.

[19] Carl Heneghan et al., "SARS-CoV-2 Viral Load and the Severity of COVID-19," March 26, 2020, https://www.cebm.net/covid-19/sars-cov-2-viral-load-and-the-severity-of-covid-19

[20] *Reuters*, "New coronavirus losing potency, top Italian doctor says," https://www.reuters.com/article/us-health-coronavirus-italy-virus/new-coronavirus-losing-potency-top-italian-doctor-says-idUSKBN2370OQ

[21] *Reuters*, "WHO and other experts say no evidence of coronavirus losing potency," dated June 1, 2020 https://www.reuters.com/article/us-health-coronavirus-who-transmission/who-and-other-experts-say-no-evidence-of-covid-19-losing-potency-idUSKBN23832J

the ongoing divergence between severity of the increase in cases and increase in deaths in the US and Sweden.

- **Human behavior**: I initially thought that policymakers would ultimately legislate a vertical distancing strategy, one that isolated the elderly from the rest of the population. That forecast was apparently too draconian for politicians to contemplate, but not for the actual elderly to implement. Data out of Florida suggested by the summer that the elderly have shifted their behavior (Figure 8.8). A vertical strategy of containment may *de facto* be happening thanks to human behavior changes.

Ultimately, this discussion is not merely theoretical. As the US opens, the R0 – the rate of infectiousness – is going to rise. Figure 8.9 shows that there is a correlation between the Dallas Fed Mobility and Engagement Index and COVID-19 R0. If hospitalization and mortality rates begin to approximate the elevated levels from April, an R0 meaningfully above 1 will again induce a panic. But if the impact of COVID-19 has been blunted, then the population can slowly desensitize to the risks

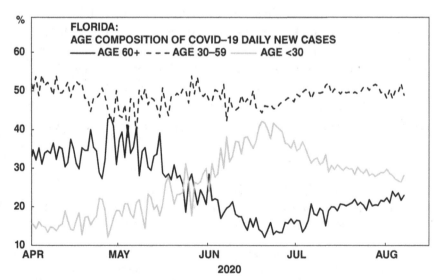

SOURCE: FLORIDA DEPARTMENT OF HEALTH.
REPRINTED WITH PERMISSION OF CLOCKTOWER GROUP, L.P.

Figure 8.8   Elderly: not stupid

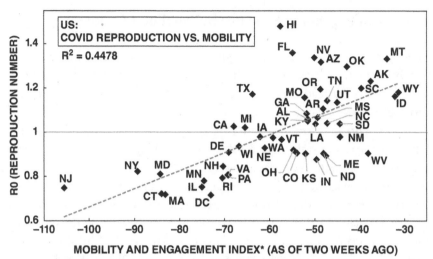

Figure 8.9 Opening the economy is leading to new infections

of a rising R0. In effect, daily new cases become irrelevant from the market's perspective.

As a geopolitical forecaster, I have to bathe myself in nihilist indifference. The novel coronavirus clearly produced a public health crisis that was much worse than the common influenza. However, it was a level of risk, concentrated in a particular age cohort, that the population would eventually become desensitized too. Many investors that I spoke with over the course of 2020 were aghast at this forecast. They themselves did not want to see their elderly parents suffer and die. I didn't either! I love my parents! But that is irrelevant to my job of forecasting the markets.

Not only did data throughout 2020 suggest that the initial forecasts and models of COVID-19 were wrong, many investors also kept focusing on the virus, instead of the policy response initiated to respond to it. This was a major mistake.

Gargantuan Stimulus: Nuthin' But a *G* Thang

Had flatten-the-curve policies from March and April continued indefinitely, as many *Flattenistas* had hoped, the economy would have been in dire straits. Instead, the outbreak lost potency as hospitalizations and mortality rates apparently began to lag the severity of new infections. Investors who kept trading based on daily new cases missed the point. The gargantuan stimulus raised to respond to the crisis became the most important piece of investment news.

Not only was the economy on pace to recovery, the pace was extraordinary. A V-neck forecast was too cautious. We were experiencing an I-neck recovery. While most investors focused in the early stages of the crisis on the sub-sectors that were "going to zero" – airlines, restaurants, cruise lines, rent-a-car agencies, etc. – the reality is that the combined weight of these sectors in the economy is merely 5.4% of GDP. And even then, they remained at "zero" for only a brief moment, with a recovery of even the most beleaguered sub-sectors underway by May.

Far more relevant than these ancillary parts of the economy where the carnage is indeed vast are durable goods, housing and car sales, which experienced a brisk recovery. Particularly impressive had been the surge in personal consumption on recreational goods & vehicles. It suggested that expenditure not spent on one part of the economy – travel, restaurants, leisure – had been redirected towards another (Figure 8.10).

The recovery in durable goods consumption has been nothing short of extraordinary. While it took durable goods consumption *six years* to recover to the 2007 highs after the GFC, it took merely two months this time around. Anyone who still thinks that the post-COVID-19 rally had been "retail led" or based on "non-fundamentals" should carefully study Figure 8.11.

What most bears missed is that the main story of 2020 is not COVID-19, but the gargantuan stimulus that has followed it. In particular, that stimulus did not merely rely on the Fed. Monetary stimulus has been subservient to the fiscal, which is real and fundamental. This isn't a "money printing" rally. It is a rally based on fundamentals. The

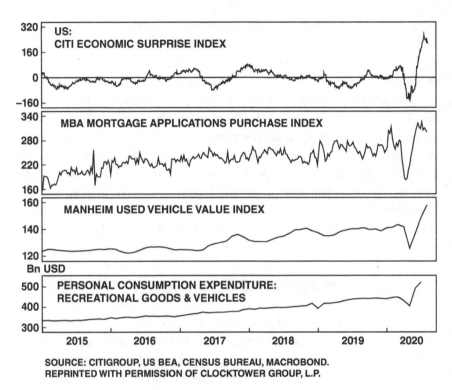

SOURCE: CITIGROUP, US BEA, CENSUS BUREAU, MACROBOND.
REPRINTED WITH PERMISSION OF CLOCKTOWER GROUP, L.P.

Figure 8.10   A Robust Recovery Is Afoot

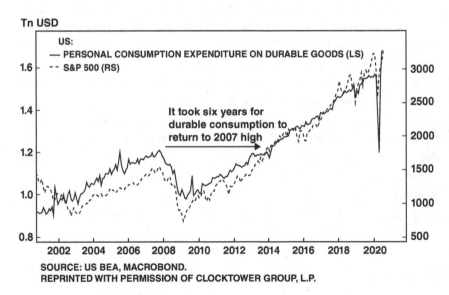

SOURCE: US BEA, MACROBOND.
REPRINTED WITH PERMISSION OF CLOCKTOWER GROUP, L.P.

Figure 8.11   An *I*-Neck Recovery

fiscal side of the economy is the definition of economic fundamentals. It is the **G** in the GDP equation, which states that GDP = C + **G** + I + NX. There is nothing manufactured, or "printed" about this recovery.

Despite the recovery, I expect \$1.5-\$3.5 trillion worth of additional fiscal stimulus by the end of the year and likely more stimulus in 2021 to avoid a fiscal cliff. That is how powerful the Buenos Aires Consensus paradigm is in this cycle. Investors should therefore expect new highs in early 2021. Selloffs are opportunities to put money to work and take advantage of the profligate paradigm. This is a fiscal-led market. It is not about the Fed, or COVID-19, valuations, technicals, or anything else. As Snoop Dogg and Dr. Dre would say, *it ain't nuthin' but a G thang*.

Time is the Achilles' Heel of the Constraint Method

Over the past decade, my clients' number-one criticism of the constraint framework has been that policymakers are not rational. This point is not a major flaw of the framework. Even an irrational policymaker cannot run through a wall. The framework focuses on material constraints, and no amount of irrationality can alter reality.

Had clients instead pointed out that the collective *population* can be irrational, I would have had a harder time justifying that flaw. As the examples of terrorism and COVID-19 illustrate, fear creates its own reality. There is a *reflexive* relationship between the median voter – the public at large – and reality. If every voter suddenly demanded a teal Hyundai Sonata, I am pretty sure that they would get one.

A deranged, confused, or simply mistaken policymaker is quickly brought back to reality by constraints – one of which is the median voter. But a hysterical society becomes a material constraint in itself; the median voter reins in policymakers, but society – the median voter – has no such immediate force constraining its actions. As a result, the time it takes for an entire society to return to sanity is unknowable, and impossible to forecast.

If median voters believe that COVID-19 will kill them and their children, that belief *is* a material constraint. Policymakers have to respond to such a fear with measures that may cause an economic depression. The mass hysteria of voters is an imminent constraint, but an economic depression is further afield, further down the risk curve. As such, even a rational policymaker, grounded in material reality, can use the shorter-term constraint as a reason – and in fact could be forced – to pursue policies that may have disastrous long-term implications.

This chapter tests whether I can successfully use the constraint framework to forecast the behavior of a society. I can.[22] In 2014–2015, I held a controversial view that Western populations – particularly Europeans – would become desensitized to terrorism. I believe that a similar desensitization is now occurring with the coronavirus. While COVID-19 is a dangerous business, the mortality rates are almost certainly overstated, and they are highly differentiated by the age cohort. By the end of the summer, I suspect that parents who were worried about their kids' health will be screaming at the district superintendents that children are practically immune.

The real constraint that will break the public's enthusiasm for flatten-the-curve policies is of course not the frustration of home-schooling. The real constraint is money and, in particular, the lack of it. The vast majority of Americans are not savers, despite the aggregate saving rate being elevated. At some point (I suspect with the first round of layoffs), that constraint will kick in and change the *zeitgeist* of the nation.

In addition to the constraints of childcare and money, the particulars of COVID-19 also represent an important material constraint to prolonged public fear. If this virus were an airborne, Ebola-like virus, my view would not be the same. It is tough to see how the population would become desensitized to a 30% mortality rate. But one that is likely to settle somewhere around 0.3% – three times more potent than the flu – is unlikely to end Western civilization as we know it.

---

[22] Just not the behavior's end date.

The age of social media has created a high-volatility context for narratives. It is a narrative accelerant, an amplifier of the most extreme ones. In the cases of both the Islamic State and COVID-19, it allowed the alarmists to come to the forefront at the expense of more measured voices. It has also created a viral panic equal to – possibly greater than – the pandemic. But social media narratives die as quickly as they flare up. Their half-life is shorter than media-driven narratives of the past. As such, markets may react with great sensitivity, but they can also recover just as quickly.

In February, as I was writing this manuscript, I felt pretty down on myself. I missed the opportunity to turn mega bearish.

In late March, however, I turned maniacally bullish. Using the framework of material constraints, I posited that data would turn on the virus, given social distancing and non-linearity of human behavior. Meanwhile, my view that the US was transitioning from the Washington to the Buenos Aires Consensus gave me a high conviction view that policymakers would stimulate in a much more meaningful way than in 2009.

When all is said and done, decades from now, investors will look back at 2020 and realize that it was the beginning of a new paradigm. The most important macro chart of 2020 will not be the epi curve of COVID-19, but rather Figure 8.12, a chart that visualizes the transition from the Washington Consensus to the Buenos Aires Consensus. It depicts how, in the months following the 2008-2009 Global Financial Crisis, monetary policy stimulus was quickly followed by the guardrails of austerity. Then, when President Trump stimulated fiscally from 2017 onwards, the extra government spending was immediately followed by the guardrails of a hawkish monetary policy.

In 2020, monetary policy is a slave to the master of fiscal policy. The two lines are moving in lockstep on Figure 8.12. In my view, this will not ease up in 2021, as the incoming Biden administration would not want to usher in its government with a massive fiscal cliff. And if President Trump wins, it is almost guaranteed – given his first term – that he will not turn towards austerity. As we discussed in previous chapters, this has nothing

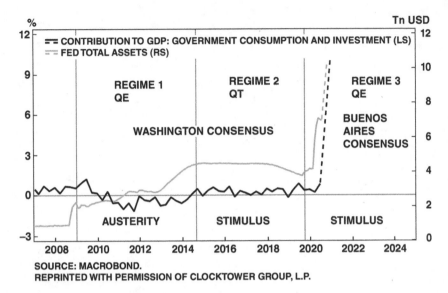

Figure 8.12   The Buenos Aires Consensus

to do with policymaker preferences, but rather the sentiment among median voters that the tenets of the Washington Consensus – namely fiscal prudence – are no longer relevant.

The Buenos Aires Consensus paradigm will lead to a year or two of orgies in asset markets, with new highs likely to follow in early 2021. However, it can't all just be milk and honey from here on out. I would expect inflation to start rising faster than investors expect. While not negative for equities in its early stages, the 2020s will eventually become stagflationary.

Part Three

OPERATIONALIZATION

Chapter 9

The Art of the Net Assessment

I n the first section of this book, I presented the theory behind the constraint framework and why geopolitics matters for investors. Chapters 4–8 introduced the constraints that really matter, those that sometimes matter, and the weakness of the framework. In the next three chapters, I *operationalize* the framework. How do investors put it to work and generate *alpha*?

The first step is to learn the art of the net assessment. The term comes from the US Defense Department's work on long-term strategic analysis, produced by the Office of Net Assessment (ONA).

A net assessment *nets* out the conclusions of competing analytical approaches. Normally, it is US military forecasters who apply net assessments to adversaries or critical risks over a long-term period. For example, the ONA may produce a net assessment of risks posed by North Korea or climate change.

I left the operationalization of the constraint framework for Chapters 9–11 because investors cannot produce net assessments without understanding what *assessments* are being *netted*. Chapters 4–8 focus on the material constraints that influence policymaker behavior – the very factors that an investor or C-suite executive needs to *net* out in analysis.

The different time horizons, or lenses, for geopolitical forecasting each require a different kind of net assessment. So before diving into examples, I will define the purview of each lens.

Three Lenses of Geopolitical Forecasting

"Geopolitical forecasting" is a catchall term that many investors use to describe a factor not *sui generis* to the market or macroeconomics. This broad label obfuscates what is and is not in the wheelhouse of geopolitical analysis.

The constraint framework can be used to analyze any number of challenges across different time horizons. The US's targeted killing of Major General Qasem Soleimani? Yes, there is a market-relevant, constraint-based net assessment for that. Prospects of a leftward turn in the US elections? There is a market-relevant, constraint-based net assessment for that too. Climate change as an investment thesis? Yes, there is even a market-relevant, constraint-based net assessment for that.

There are three lenses of forecasting that investors have to become comfortable with:

- **Discrete Event:** The targeted killing of Major General Qasem Soleimani is a great example of a nonmarket, non–macroeconomic event that an investor has to deal with at a moment's notice – in a reactive and tactical manner. Hopefully you, a newly indoctrinated constraint framework analyst, are "ready" for it by already having an off-the-shelf net assessment. In this chapter, I illustrate the constraints keeping the US and Iran at arm's length. If you are caught with your geopolitical pants down on a particular issue, you can enlist consultants to cover you. Frame your questions so that the answers they provide inform your constraint framework: "Yes, we all know that the Quds force are ideologues who hate America, but what can they *do* about it, given X, Y, and Z (the constraints)?"
- **Cyclical:** The second type of net assessment is focused on the cyclical time horizon. To produce this analysis, know the geopolitical

calendar over the course of the next 12–18 months. Assign someone on your team to produce a calendar of all political and geopolitical events that may be market-relevant: elections, summits, referenda, budget deadlines, fiscal cliffs, notable military exercises, etc.[1] If you see an important election ahead, produce a net assessment of that country in advance of the event. Monitor the mutability of constraints on policymaker preferences as they enact policy decisions that could move markets, either positively or negatively.

- **Around the Curve:** For long-term forecasts, I like to focus on themes, not country- or region-specific economies. In my past life as a sell-side strategist, I produced forecasts on several long-term themes:

Will the Euro Area survive and European integration continue? My forecast was a 2011 analysis titled "Europe's Geopolitical Gambit: Relevance Through Integration." Will US–China tensions escalate into a market-relevant conflict? I responded in 2013 with "Sino-American Conflict: More Likely Than You Think." Is globalization sustainable? I analyzed the question in 2014, penning "The Apex of Globalization – All Downhill from Here." Will *laissez-faire* economics survive? I tried to answer in a 2015 net assessment titled "The End of the Anglo-Saxon Economy."[2]

These forecasts were products of theme-based net assessments well outside the view of investors. Few investors in 2013 cared about US–China tensions, not when Europe was falling apart. In 2015, nobody wanted to talk about political risks in the US when Hillary Clinton was presumed to succeed President Obama and Greece was playing a high-stakes game of chicken with Germany. But it is useful to purposefully focus on the themes that are out of sight, especially if they have lain dormant for a while. Their expiration date may be closer than the consensus thinks.

---

[1] Or, you can rely on the geopolitical calendar by my former teammates at BCA Research, the best in the business.

[2] All of these analyses are available on request, courtesy of the fine folks at BCA Research.

To prepare for each of these geopolitical lenses, investors looking to be proactive should follow these three steps:

1. **Discrete Event:** Focus on several topical risks that could upend markets where a reactive analysis may be required. Every January, while the world is still recovering from New Year's Eve, I like to sit down and write the five risks likely to require a reactive net assessment.

2. **Cyclical:** Develop a constraint-based net assessment of major economies that you are invested in or would like to invest in. Starting with the G20 is a good idea. In this chapter, I illustrate what such a net assessment may look like with a close examination of India.

3. **Around the Curve:** Write down five assumptions about today's investment environment taken as gospel by most of your peers. One in 2020 is the idea that the world is weathering secular stagnation, a deflationary environment characterized by low interest rates. How confident are you in this forecast? Does it make sense to produce a net assessment? In the fallout of the COVID-19 recession, will secular stagnation be confirmed, or will governments' overwhelming economic stimulus signal the end of the stagnation thesis?[3]

Net Assessment: The Bayesian Prior

A solid net assessment sets "priors" ahead of any forecasting exercise. It creates the initial probabilities of an event occurring or of a relevant economy outperforming some benchmark (either arbitrary or set by its peers). In early 2016, I penned an analysis on the coming Brexit referendum that correctly ascertained that the odds of a Brexit event were higher than the market assumed.

The fancy term for the method I used is finding the Bayesian prior, or Bayesian probability. A net assessment sets the "prior probability": the

---

[3] My high-conviction view is that it will lead to an inflationary environment over the next decade. Secular stagnation will be vanquished, but at a cost.

subjective process through which the analyst assigns the probability of an event occurring based not on the historical record but a thorough net assessment.[4]

Take the 2016 Brexit analysis example. To assign a probability to the "Leave" campaign winning, I did not look at previous independence referenda or the frequency with which they produced a secessionist outcome because my sample size would be too small to be statistically significant. There is no natural law of secession, and similar events are not similar enough upon closer examination. The 1995 Quebec independence referendum is far from a referendum on EU membership. The 1975 UK referendum on European Community membership was a different time, different context. Neither the quantity nor the quality of available historical data was enough to be statistically significant. Had I applied this frequentist inference approach, I would have assigned 10% to Brexit occurring, as only 1 in 10 noniterative referenda go against the established, consensus view.

A net assessment approach allows the analyst to net out all of the constraints identified in Chapters 4–8. The result produces a subjective prior probability of an event occurring. But, even more crucially, the net assessment produces a fulcrum constraint on which to focus. It can suggest the critical pieces of data to monitor that would indicate a change in the net assessment, requiring the analyst to adjust probabilities. These "data streams" give investors a sense of what they need to monitor to keep their probabilities up-to-date and accurate. To keep track of those "data streams," I suggest keeping a checklist.

In the case of the Brexit analysis, polling is an obvious data stream to monitor. In the case of 2017 tax cuts passing, it might be statements of fiscal conservatives in the House and the Senate. In the case of the 2020 COVID-19 crisis, where median voter opinion is the fulcrum constraint, a critical data stream might be the number of op-eds lamenting the economic costs of curve-flattening policies, coupled with Google Trends mentions of "depression," "back to work," or "why is my internet slow."

---

[4] There are many books to read on Bayesian probability. But if you want one that will not drown you in math, I recommend *The Signal and the Noise* by Nate Silver.

Or, as discussed in Chapter 8, it may be the growing gap between new cases rising in a slew of second waves and a flatlining number of deaths, a gap that ultimately leads to the daily new cases no longer leading the market.

It is useful to call this part of my framework Bayesian, as that is precisely what the net assessment is designed to do.[5] The net assessment is not where constraint-based analysis ends, but where it begins. Yes, the assessment provides some prior probability to help gauge whether there is any geopolitical *alpha* to harvest. But the real key is that it identifies the data streams that will impact the fulcrum constraint of any given geopolitical activity. If the data flowing through those streams change, probability should change with it, as illustrated in Figure 9.1.

Now that you have a more complete knowledge of how to integrate the net assessment into a constraint-based analysis, here are some examples.

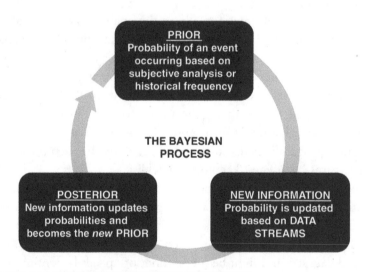

Figure 9.1   The Bayesian process.

---

[5] Still, I hesitate to call it so because it describes only the beginning of constraint-based analysis.

India Net Assessment: An Investment Thesis Built on Mean Reversion

The defining feature of India is that it is difficult to define. Its history, diversity, geography, and size make generalizations – and thus pithy net assessments – unsatisfying.

As of 2020, many investors embrace India as the "next big thing." The sweeping 2019 general election has produced even more political capital for Prime Minister Narendra Modi's reformist administration. And yet, the past five years of structural reforms – which would otherwise produce optimism – had a mixed impact on macroeconomic data.

My net assessment of India focuses on investment opportunities over the medium and long term. It concludes that there is strong support for the thesis that Indian consumers should continue to lead the way for the economy, but there is mixed support for the thesis that the country is on the cusp of a breakout *à la* the East Asian "Tigers."

What Is Keeping India from Mean Reverting?

India's typical geopolitical narrative is that its ethnic diversity and geography make it a difficult country to control, no matter who is in charge. As such, India's nation-building has been massively delayed by its heterogeneity and added complexity of its democracy, leading to the fractured and regionalized polity of 2020.

But India is not the only heterogeneous country in the world, a fact that the typical narrative does not account for. There is a simpler explanation for India's relative modern poverty: imperialism.[6] India and China were the two largest economies for much of the past two millennia. This position changed with the Age of Discovery, which kicked off European military, economic, and technological domination.[7]

---

[6] Shashi Tharoor, *Inglorious Empire* (London: C. Hurst & Company, 2017).
[7] David Abernathy, *The Dynamics of Global Dominance* (New Haven, CT: Yale University Press, 2000).

For India, that domination began about a century earlier than it did for China.[8]

In the wake of imperialism, centralized and socialist government played a role in delaying India's catchup. Whereas China shifted its focus to free-market reforms in 1978, India did not let go of the command economy until the early 1990s.

The promise of India, therefore, is in *mean reversion* (Figure 9.2). With the command economy of the twentieth century and the extractive rule of European empires in the rearview mirror, both India and China have had much of the past 75 years to re-establish their previous trajectories. China is well on its way to accomplishing mean reversion.

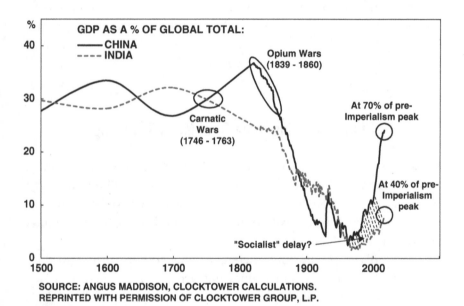

SOURCE: ANGUS MADDISON, CLOCKTOWER CALCULATIONS.
REPRINTED WITH PERMISSION OF CLOCKTOWER GROUP, L.P.

Figure 9.2   India's investment thesis is built on mean reversion.

---

[8] The British East India Company established a trade monopoly over India at the conclusion of the Carnatic Wars (1746–1763) against the French East India Company and various independent rulers. The British Crown did not formally take over the East India Company until 1858. In contrast, British domination of China began with the First Opium War (1839–1842) and only became entrenched with the 1858 Treaty of Tientsin, which concluded the Second Opium War.

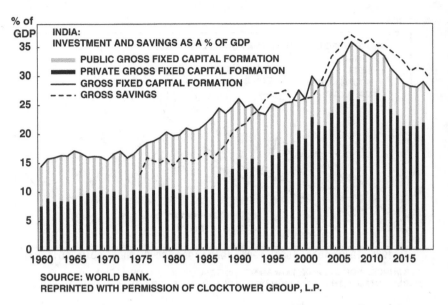

SOURCE: WORLD BANK.
REPRINTED WITH PERMISSION OF CLOCKTOWER GROUP, L.P.

Figure 9.3   Why the dropoff in investment amid a reformist government?

India, however, only arrested its decline in the share of global output in
1985, and it remains well below China in terms of global GDP share.

Underinvestment is the fulcrum constraint that has held India back
thus far. Prior to the election of Narendra Modi's reformist government
in 2014, gross fixed capital formation – investment in fixed assets by the
business sector, government, and households – reached a peak in 2007,
as did the gross national savings rate (Figure 9.3). The lack of growth
is doubly problematic for a country that has historically underinvested,
with gross fixed capital formation lagging behind its Asian peers for half
a century (Figure 9.4).

Underinvested: India's Fulcrum Constraint

There are three ways to spur investment in the economy. The government can raise taxes – or capture the profits generated by state-owned
enterprises – and spend the revenue on investment. The domestic corporate sector can be incentivized to invest. Or foreigners can invest on
their own. All three options face challenges.

% of GDP

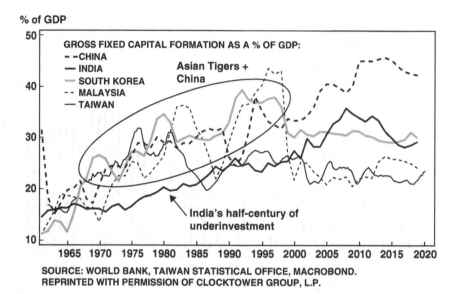

Figure 9.4   India has a lot of catching up to do.

1. **Individuals are undertaxed:** India scores poorly in international comparisons of government tax revenue (Figure 9.5). While the introduction of the goods and services tax (GST) in 2017 was a major reform, India still needs a comprehensive reform of property, personal income, and corporate taxes. Only 53 million individuals, just 5.6% of the population, pay personal income tax. For many wealthy families in India, this narrow tax base constitutes "tax terrorism" – as recounted to me by the scion of a particularly wealthy Indian family – that justifies keeping assets abroad. Families keep as much as 70% of their assets outside the country.[9] While capital flight has always been the case in India, the unsettling part is that nothing has changed under Modi, despite his pro-market rhetoric. The data does not justify Indian elites' angst. Various tax deductions help the wealthy avoid taxes, as does the lack of a robust real estate tax and the astonishingly low marginal income tax rate relative to EM peers

---

[9] Families avoid capital controls by designating one family member as a nonresident Indian, enabling them to take more wealth out of the country.

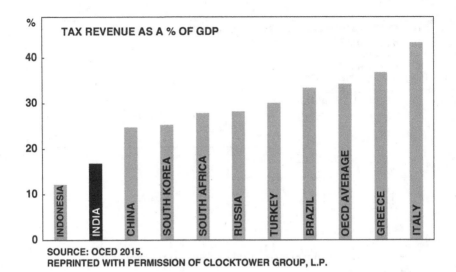

SOURCE: OCED 2015.
REPRINTED WITH PERMISSION OF CLOCKTOWER GROUP, L.P.

Figure 9.5 India needs to raise more taxes.

(Figure 9.6). So why the lack of confidence? I suspect that the lack of a redistributive mechanism deepens already-high income inequality and fuels incentive for capital flight, as elites may fear that the gravy train will end due to populist backlash (Figure 9.7).

2. **Corporates are overtaxed:** Given the paltry household tax base, the corporate tax rate in India has traditionally been very high, even by developed-world standards. However, the Modi government managed to reduce corporate taxes for small and medium enterprises to 25% in 2016 and to 22% for all remaining firms in 2019. India's effective corporate tax rate is now around 25%, in line with the rest of the world. However, only about 100 firms, totaling 0.012% of India's 800,000 companies, comprise more than 40% of corporate tax collection.

3. **Foreign domestic investment (FDI) is muted:** While the stock of inward FDI has risen nearly four times over the past decade, the pace of inward FDI has slowed since 2008. According to the OECD FDI regulatory restrictiveness index, India remains one of the most restrictive countries for FDI, although it has seen considerable improvement under the Modi administration.

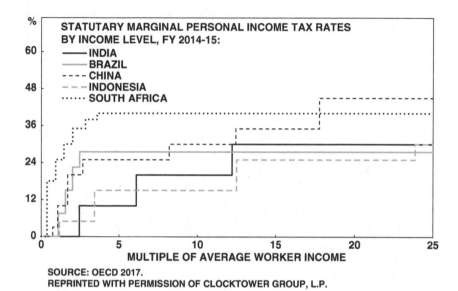

Figure 9.6 India: a sneaky-great place to be rich?

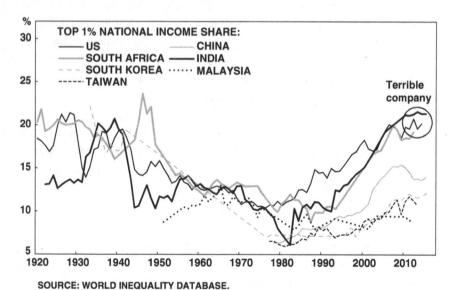

Figure 9.7 India – a very poor country – is more unequal than America.

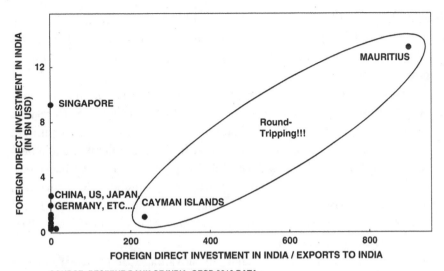

SOURCE: RESERVE BANK OF INDIA, OECD 2018 DATA.
REPRINTED WITH PERMISSION OF CLOCKTOWER GROUP, L.P.

Figure 9.8   One of these things is not like the others.

Nothing brings all of the above factors together quite like the role of Mauritius in India's FDI "round-tripping."[10] Figure 9.8 shows that Mauritius is India's largest source of FDI … by far! This is astounding given that the tiny island nation is the world's 123rd largest economy, and India is the sixth.

There are several problems with Mauritius being India's largest investor, aside from optics. First, it suggests that some unknown portion of inbound FDI in India is simply a derivative of tax evasion and thus not greenfield investment.[11] Second, it means that Mauritius' share

---

[10] Adrienne Klasa, "Round-tripping: How Tiny Mauritius Became India's Main Investor," *Financial Times*, October 30, 2018, https://www.ft.com/content/b2a35d1e-c597-11e8-86b4-bfd556565bb2.

[11] An Indian corporation looking to avoid prohibitive domestic corporate taxes will invoice its exports to Mauritius, where it does not have to pay any taxes. Some, but not necessarily all, of the proceeds are then imported back to India, recorded as FDI.

of India's 2020 FDI – 30% – had nothing to do with actual foreign investors reflecting an optimistic vision of India's future. Third, this tip-of-the-iceberg figure begs the question of what share of such profits remains *outside*.

What cements my negative prior bias toward India is that the stagnation of investment – along with a reduced pace of FDI growth relative to GDP – has occurred despite Narendra Modi's reformist government. Since Modi's revolutionary 2014 victory, India's manufacturing as a percentage of GDP and its share of global exports (Figure 9.9) have both either stagnated or fallen. Even more troubling, these trends occurred in the context of rising labor costs in China, a potential tailwind for India. The 2019 US–China trade war was another tailwind, yet it is not clear that India capitalized on it.

Why has India failed to take full advantage of Modi's reformist government and a favorable geopolitical context? Cosmetically, the improvements in the investment environment are substantial. The

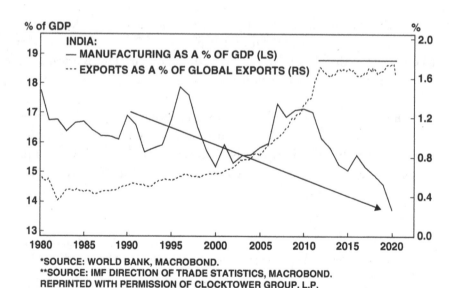

SOURCE: WORLD BANK, MACROBOND.
SOURCE: IMF DIRECTION OF TRADE STATISTICS, MACROBOND.
REPRINTED WITH PERMISSION OF CLOCKTOWER GROUP, L.P.

Figure 9.9   Exports have stagnated while manufacturing is collapsing.

government often cites that India has moved up 30 spots in the World Bank's Doing Business report, the largest single move in the ranking ever.

The answer comes down to labor and real estate regulation. As for the optimism of the World Bank survey results, they can be gamed by the government. The Modi government focused on the easiest reforms that it could accomplish specifically to move up in the rankings, not to actually fix the underlying problems in the economy. In doing so, Modi transformed India into a good test-taker, but not a learned student of structural reform.

Labor laws are complex and strict, especially for manufacturing businesses. India scores high on the OECD employment protection legislation index, even compared to some developed market (DM) economies (Figure 9.10).[12] Firms with more than 100 employees have to obtain government approval to dismiss just one of them. On the real estate front, laws are difficult to amend. They fall under the purview of states and complex communities, not the federal government.

As the 2020 COVID-19 pandemic is hitting India when its GDP growth was already slowing, Modi is unlikely to focus on reforms. Economic performance will become a prohibitive constraint to painful tax and labor reforms. Modi planned but failed to pass such reforms in his first term, as the GST required all of his political capital. To pass, labor and land reforms will need to be watered down by a messy legislative process. Prospects of land reform are even grimmer. It is a prerogative of the states, and the ruling Bharatiya Janata Party (BJP) has controlled 21 out of 29 state legislatures (17 since December 2019) – more than enough votes to enact reforms. If it planned to do so, the BJP would have moved on to land reforms over the past few years. Their absence is a cautionary flag indicating no reforms are forthcoming.

---

[12] The OECD index of employment protection is a synthetic indicator of the strictness of regulation on dismissals and the use of temporary contracts. Data range from 0 to 6, with higher scores representing stricter regulation.

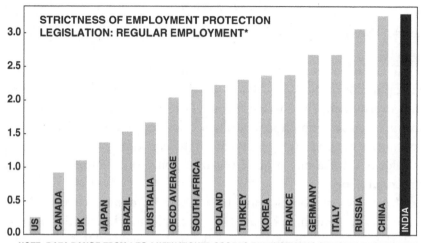

Figure 9.10   India needs new labor laws.

Why Is Investment the Fulcrum Constraint?

The most optimistic narrative for India is that it could replicate the East Asian miracle. It could "mean revert" to its past glory as a leading global economy.

Three factors underpinned the rapid rise of the East Asian economies in the 1970s and Southeast Asia in the 1990s: high domestic savings levels that translated into high rates of gross capital formation, high productivity growth rates (which followed such investment), and a geopolitical environment conducive to export-oriented industrialization.

On the savings front, India remains behind its Asian peers. Its gross national savings rate is below that of the oft-cited Asian miracles at just 28.5%, compared to China's 45.8%. India's financial system remains underdeveloped, making it difficult for banks to intermediate private savings and investment. Banking assets as a percentage of GDP are half that of other Asian economies. While productivity did break out in the

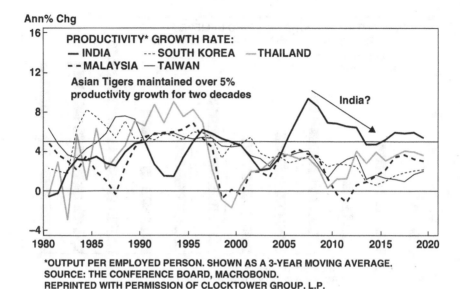

Figure 9.11   Strong productivity performance has stalled.

mid-2000s, it has again stagnated despite the reformist government in charge (Figure 9.11).

In addition to less savings, India may have a smaller global customer base than its twentieth-century predecessors. The country is unlikely to enjoy the type of geopolitical tailwinds that helped East and Southeast Asian economies export their way to prosperity. Voters in developed nations are beginning to sour on trade (Figure 9.12). As I discussed in Chapter 1, middle classes in the developed world saw limited gains in real wage growth during the most intense phase of globalization. Given the resultant reduced global demand, India is unlikely to receive the type of welcome China's opening elicited, especially in the 1990s.

India's macro and geopolitical context raises the odds that Dani Rodrik's 2015 thesis of *premature deindustrialization* may come true before investors' eyes.[13] Rodrik – a Harvard economist and notable critic

---

[13] Dani Rodrik, "Premature Deindustrialization," *National Bureau of Economic Research* Working Paper No. 20935, February 2015, https://www.nber.org/papers/w20935.

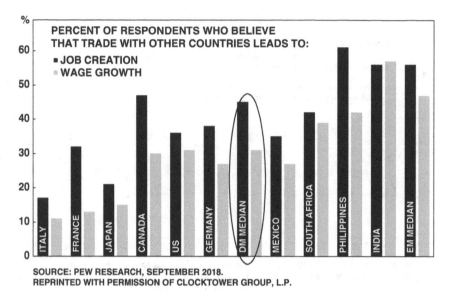

Figure 9.12   The West is souring on trade.

of globalization – argues that due to the combination of automation and East Asia's competitiveness in low-cost manufacturing, developing economies were reaching a peak in manufacturing at a much lower level of wealth.

For countries like India, premature deindustrialization "blocks off the main avenue of rapid economic convergence in low-income settings, the shift of workers from the countryside to urban factories where their productivity tends to be much higher."[14]

Rodrik argues that services-led growth – particularly IT and finance – could replace manufacturing for India. But such industries "do not have the capacity to absorb – as manufacturing did – the type of labor that low- and middle-income economies have in abundance."[15] Services are difficult to export in large volumes due to their local nature as well as nontariff barriers to trade, which means that their growth is capped at the domestic rate of income growth. As a result, the service industry's real cap is at the rate of India's *productivity* growth. A high

---

[14] Rodrik, "Premature Deindustrialization," 23.

[15] Ibid., 24.

level of productivity growth is a must in such a services–led scenario. Another constraint to service-led growth of exports is that artificial intelligence (AI) and big data may soon replace the global demand for India's back office and call center services.

India is already facing some of the challenges that Rodrik identified in 2015. There is not enough demand for labor in its service sector: out of a population of 1.34 billion, only 500 million people are employed in India, with another 300 million of working age and yet unemployed. Around a third of the labor force is employed in the services sector, where the *per-capita* income in 2018 was about US$7,900, comparable to countries like Thailand and South Africa. However, the other 70% of India's population is employed in the agricultural and industrial sectors, where *per-capita* income was much lower and where real rural wages "grew" at −0.3% between FY2015 and FY2018 (Figure 9.13).[16]

Every month, close to a million youths reach working age in India. It is difficult to see how the services sector will be able to absorb all of them over the next decade. Anecdotal evidence, shared with me by

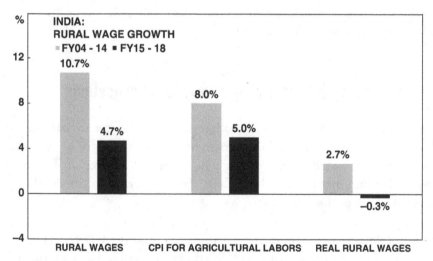

Figure 9.13   Shocking performance of rural wages.

---

[16] A *big* thank you to Ritika Mankar for her help with this analysis.

India-based investors, cited numerous examples where the government would post a call for jobs only to be overwhelmed by the demand.[17]

Foreign investors constantly hope that reformist Modi will live up to his credentials. Despite two surprising electoral victories, he continues to fall short. From my constraint-based perspective, the investment community is putting too much faith in the man and his preferences, and not enough in the power of the median voter. No matter Modi's preferences, he is constrained by the Indian median voter. And she would not support painful reforms amid a global recession, given rampant income inequality and poor employment prospects.

Without investment and productivity growth, India could still grow based on robust consumption, which is set to increase as the population continues to grow. However, such growth will not be high-quality growth that sees the country move up the manufacturing and export value chain. An economy addicted to consumption would also ensure that India's current account deficit remains a persistent constraint to high-quality growth. A rise in consumption without an accompanying increase in productive capacity would therefore either widen the country's current account deficit or increase domestic inflation as domestic demand overwhelms domestic supply.

India Net Assessment: Investment Implications

A global macro manager I spoke with regarding India argued that Indian equities are, from a long-term perspective, a "screaming buy ... it is just not clear whether the scream will be due to elation or despair." Several bullish managers outlined their optimistic thesis in late 2019 as a combination of the following:

- **Trade war insurance:** India is insulated from the US–China trade war and from a global trade slowdown in general, as exports are merely 11% of its GDP.

---

[17] The most jarring of the anecdotal examples was a posting for 63,000 jobs in the national railway service that saw *19 million applicants*. Apparently getting a job with India's national railway is less likely than getting into an Ivy League university.

- **Chinese reform insurance:** China's move away from fixed asset investment is positive for India because it is a low-income economy that imports almost all of its commodities. As China's demand for commodity slows, India's costs should ease as a consequence.

These fail-safes are no longer factors in 2020. There are long-term constraints to the US–China trade war, as I pointed out in Chapter 5. Meanwhile, the COVID-19-induced recession has reduced prices of commodities for India, but it is not clear that this event is good for the country. A global recession is unlikely to see Indian assets outperform, and the COVID-19 recession has elicited so much epic fiscal and monetary stimulus out of the West and China that commodity prices will probably rise before long, especially food. On the contrary, India may struggle if the long-term consequence of the COVID-19 stimulus is inflation, as I think it will be.

A global recession is bad news for the country's assets. But the fulcrum constraint to a positive performance of the country's markets and economy is its lack of domestic investment. If India struggled to attract foreign investment in 2019, when the twin tailwinds of the US–China trade war and Modi's electoral victory filled its sails, investment stimulus will likely not improve going forward.

Absent these bolstering tailwinds, domestic political risks may actually rise over the rest of Modi's term. Instead of focusing on painful structural reforms, Modi has turned to nationalism and populism. His change in focus is consistent with my suspicion that median voters are not looking for "short-term pain, long-term gain" policies. Although labor and land reforms are languishing, Modi has pivoted to reform the country's citizenship laws – reforms opponents say disenfranchise Muslims. They elicited protests starting in late 2019 that continued into 2020. Ethnic and religious tensions, a structurally impaired investment environment, and an imminent global recession create a toxic brew for India's mean reversion prospects.

Could the sell-off be a buying opportunity? India has a lot of positives going for it. Unfortunately, its policymakers have limited capacity to execute painful reforms. At some point, investors have to stop and ask themselves what those delays suggest. Modi's hesitation to pursue painful reforms may reveal the constraint of the Indian median voter preference.

This net assessment gives investors a road map for investing in India. The first fork in the road is that its fulcrum constraint to high-quality growth, and thus profitable investment, is ... the lack of investment. To resolve this constraint, policymakers need to fix land and labor factors. Instead of expending his 2019 political recapitalization on that goal, Modi focused on social policies that elicited unrest that could grow throughout 2020. The global recession in 2020 will probably only cause Modi to double down on populism at the expense of market-friendly policies.

The verdict? As of early 2020, investors should not invest in India yet. *Regardless of valuations.*

The point of an investment-relevant net assessment is to boil everything known about an economy down to the fulcrum constraint. From there, it is simple to monitor the data streams of that one constraint and use them to gauge when conditions may shift. In the case of India, the net assessment reveals that the country is woefully underinvested. Without investment, India will probably not experience high-quality growth.

On top of that, I identify the key issues to follow the data streams of labor and land reforms. If they occurred, it would indicate a shift in India's fulcrum constraint of underinvestment, prompting me to change my mind about the country's prospects. But, given the government's focus on populist social reforms at a peak of its political capital, I doubt that India is about to embark on market-friendly policies.

I spent little time on India's geopolitical constraints because I am optimistic on this front. America's rivalry with China has made India a valuable US ally, as President Trump's high-profile India tour in 2020 demonstrates. Meanwhile, its traditional rival Pakistan is no longer a match for India's hard power. Future tiffs with China could even prompt Modi to "sell" painful structural reforms as necessary from a national security perspective. As such, the rivalry with China is not necessarily a negative.

Nonetheless, geopolitical risks abound in the long term for India. Climate change represents a global threat, but it is particularly problematic for India. The costs of climate change are not equally distributed.

From the evidence gathered by the scientific community thus far, developing economies have born and will continue to bear the brunt of the burden.

Without a meaningful change in carbon emissions over the next decade, which I do not expect will happen, India is likely to see further economic drag from climate change.

War in the Middle East: Net Assessment

Iran's attack on Saudi Arabia's Aramco energy facilities in September 2019 and the American targeted killing of Major General Qasem Soleimani in January 2020 raised the prospects of a US–Iran war. Oil prices spiked both times, 15% following the first incident and 4.6% following the second. Both spikes proved transient due to geopolitical constraints and because global demand was impaired.

The US – the only actor in the region with enough firepower to counter Iran – has geopolitical constraints preventing it from fighting a major war against Iran in 2020. Without troops on the ground in Iraq, there is no sustainable way to counter Iran's growing regional hegemony. These geopolitical constraints not only mean that a prolonged kinetic action between the two countries is unlikely but also that the US will eventually (again) accept Iran's regional hegemony.

The historical context demonstrates why such a forecast is likely.

The Obama administration agreed to the Joint Comprehensive Plan of Action (JCPOA) with Iran in 2015 because the US sought to extricate itself from the Middle East. The US chose retreat to reduce resources committed to the Middle East – where America's national interests were in decline – and to pivot to East Asia, where national interests were increasingly challenged by China (Figure 9.14). While the Obama administration managed to free up resources, it did little with the available maneuvering room as the "pivot to Asia" fell flat.

US national interests were declining in the Middle East for more reasons than just energy independence. True, increasing domestic oil

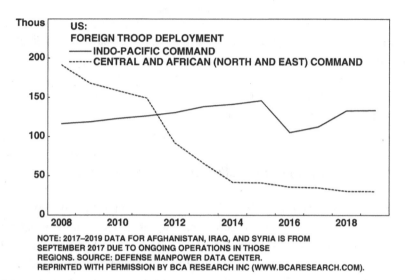

NOTE: 2017–2019 DATA FOR AFGHANISTAN, IRAQ, AND SYRIA IS FROM
SEPTEMBER 2017 DUE TO ONGOING OPERATIONS IN THOSE
REGIONS. SOURCE: DEFENSE MANPOWER DATA CENTER.
REPRINTED WITH PERMISSION BY BCA RESEARCH INC (WWW.BCARESEARCH.COM).

Figure 9.14   The JCPOA allowed the US to deleverage.

production has a lot to do with it, as does declining reliance on direct
energy imports from the Organization of the Petroleum Exporting
Countries (OPEC). But in 2015, the US also no longer faced any direct
national security threats from rivals in the Middle East, whereas China
(and to a certain extent Russia) represented significant regional and
global hegemonic challenges.

Iran threatened American allies in the region, but that is much different from a threat to the US homeland itself. Obama's decision to pivot
away from the Middle East created the constraint of limited troops in
the area.

The other constraints to a US-initiated war with Iran are the domestic and geopolitical contexts:

- **Politics:** On the domestic front, the median voter's exhaustion with
  wars in the Middle East constrains policymakers from engaging a
  sophisticated military rival like Iran. As of mid-2019, while 82%
  of Americans have an unfavorable view of Iran, only 18% support
  military action against it, and 65% are concerned that the US would

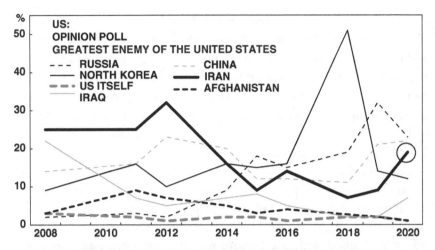

NOTE: THE SURVEY ASKS THE FOLLOWING QUESTION, "WHAT ONE COUNTRY
ANYWHERE IN THE WORLD DO YOU CONSIDER TO BE THE
UNITED STATES' GREATEST ENEMY TODAY? [OPEN-ENDED]"
SOURCE: GALLUP. REPRINTED WITH PERMISSION OF CLOCKTOWER GROUP, L.P.

Figure 9.15   Americans do not want a war with Iran.

be "too quick to use military force." Most importantly, Americans
now consider Iran as merely "one of many" enemies, and it is no
longer clearly the greatest enemy, as was the case 2008-2013. It is
third on the list of enemies behind Russia and China. In 2012, it
was literally Public Enemy Number One at 32% (Figure 9.15).[18]

- **Geopolitics:** Since the 2015 JCPOA, the geopolitical context of the
  Middle East remains unconducive to an American military response.
  Thanks to the US's own intervention in Iraq – and the subsequent
  regional imbroglio that followed – Iran has been the largest benefi-
  ciary of America's blood, sweat, and treasure.

The collapse of the Saddam Hussein regime – which was dominated
by Iraqi Sunnis, a minority in the country – created a power vacuum in
the country that Shias filled, some of whom are allied with Iran.

---

[18] "Iran," *Gallup*, July 15–31, 2019, https://news.gallup.com/poll/116236/iran.aspx.

As of 2020, the Iraqi government is made up by a coalition of the Fatah Alliance and Sairoon. Both strengthen Iran's relationship with Iraq and provide political and military deterrents for any kind of US presence in the area.[19] While the Sairoon leader Muqtada al-Sadr is mostly moving away from Iran and adopting an Iraqi nationalist position, al-Sadr was hosted in Iran days before the Aramco attack, which the US traced back to Iran's Grand Ayatollah Ali Khamenei and the Islamic Revolutionary Guard Commander Qasem Soleimani.

Iran is cultivating a comprehensive Middle East sphere of influence. In addition to Iraq slipping into Tehran's orbit, Iran also strengthened its influence in Syria and Lebanon thanks to Sunni militancy (i.e., the Islamic State), targeting Shias. Iranian sympathy is present in Yemen, where it is allied with the Houthi militants who claimed responsibility for the Aramco attack and are at war with Saudi Arabia. Iran also gained influence in Qatar, which suffered for its close ties to Tehran in 2017. It was embargoed by its fellow members of the Gulf Cooperation Council.

These are the political and geopolitical constraints that bind the US in 2020, and they put the country in a weak position in the Middle East. President Trump pulled out of the JCPOA so he could leverage sanctions to force Tehran to negotiate a new deal. But geopolitical constraints make an alternative, more advantageous deal for the US impossible. The JCPOA was a "bad deal" because the US was never negotiating from a position of power. Its multiple wars in the Middle East have exhausted Washington's political and geopolitical capital. It can no longer maintain enough troops in the region to deter Iranian influence in Iraq, which is the *geopolitical epicenter of the region.*

Without the option of re-engaging Iran for influence in Iraq, the US is constrained into reducing its physical presence and settling for a *détente* with the Islamic Republic. The signing of the JCPOA was not just the Obama administration's dovish politics. It was the optimal path of least resistance, given growing constraints on US maneuvering room

---

[19] The Fatah Alliance is the political arm of the Iranian-backed Popular Mobilization Forces (PMF). Sairoon, or the Alliance Toward Reforms, is a political alliance led by the Shia cleric Muqtada al-Sadr, whose militias fought a bitter insurgency against the US.

in the region. There are simply bigger fish to fry for the US, specifically its budding tensions with China in the South China Sea.

The US faces considerable constraints to an armed conflict with Iran. An attack against Iran would likely invite a Tehran retaliation against Saudi production facilities, which Iran already demonstrated are vulnerable (2019 Aramco drone strike). Iran could also directly target US troops in Iraq and Syria, where the two adversaries have been tacitly allied since 2014 in the war against the Islamic State militants. In January 2020, Iran already demonstrated its willingness to retaliate on US troops in the immediate aftermath of Soleimani's death.

American allies in the region may take the retaliatory heat off of a shrinking US military presence. But Saudi Arabia and Israel do not have the capacity to mount a successful attack on Iran and take matters into their own hands.

Israel has no strategic bomber force that would make an air war against Iran feasible. It would have to use fighter jets (F–15E Strike Eagles, F–16 Fighting Falcons, and 18 F–35 Lightning IIs) to reach Iranian targets, and they require complicated refueling operations.[20] The Israeli air force is capable of conducting such an attack but would likely require around 50–70 fighter jets to both conduct suppression of enemy air defense (SEAD) operations *and* hit enough Iranian military and industrial targets to make the attack worthwhile.

While the Saudis have enough jets to conduct a similar attack and are geographically closer to Iran, they have never conducted anything so sophisticated. The only experience that the Saudi air force has had in striking ground targets is against the hapless Houthi rebels.

Iran is not hapless. It possesses the Russian S–300 air-defense system, operational since 2017. While the S–300 is less sophisticated than the S–400 – which Russia refuses to sell to Iran – it is sophisticated enough to handle most of the fighter jets that Saudi Arabia or Israel would be able to throw at Iran. Iran also possesses a competent air force, including

---

[20] Refueling operations would not just be complicated logistically, but also diplomatically as the refueling would likely take place in Saudi airspace. The idea that Israeli jets would refuel in the skies over Mecca on their way to strike targets in a Muslim country is an interesting thought exercise.

20 MiG-29s. It is not good enough to deter an attack, but it guarantees casualties in any non-US-conducted raid.

The US is therefore constrained from taking the conflict to the kinetic level due to domestic politics and geopolitical logistics. Because of its reduced ground troops, the US is unwilling to support air strikes with a commensurable military ground force in Iraq. Such ground troops would be necessary to prevent a potential Iranian counterattack against Saudi territory. Meanwhile, American allies in the region do not have the military force to attack Iran without US aid. If they had, Israel and Saudi Arabia would have already collaborated on a joint attack in 2011, when Israel came very close to doing so on its own (but backed off, likely due to an analysis similar to this one).

Despite the rhetoric and the passive-aggressive back-and-forth between the US and Iran throughout 2019 and 2020, my forecast is that thanks to geopolitical constraints, in the long term, the US has to come back to a *détente* with Iran. As long as the US keeps the focus on China and Russia – two global powers – it has to make peace with Iran. That peace will necessarily include giving Iran some influence in the Middle East. What of America's allies in the region, Saudi Arabia and Israel? They will simply have to learn to live with a suboptimal outcome. However, thanks to their sophisticated military forces and an overall security guarantee from the US, they will be fine. Angry. But fine.

However, a risk to this forecast does exist. There is some non-negligible probability that the US and Iran engage in tit-for-tat retaliation that gets out of hand, crosses some undefined red line, and produces a prolonged kinetic action. As the example of the Islamic State in Chapter 8 demonstrates, the threat of terrorism is a powerful mover of the median voter and, as a result, could also spur on policymaker action.

When producing a net assessment of a discrete event – in this case a US–Iran conflict – it is useful to organize the various possible scenarios into a decision tree. The diagram gives investors a visual representation of the constraint-defined path of least resistance to policymaker actions. It formalizes choices available to policymakers and offers the investor a chance to apply conditional probabilities to a succession of policy options.[21]

---

[21] Conditional probability is dependent on other events happening first, while subjective probability is derived from the forecaster's personal judgment.

I show a simple decision tree in Figure 9.16. I produced it in early 2018 to illustrate the limited – but still meaningful – odds of a US–Iran war due to the reimposed oil embargo. The first step of the forecast was the physical loss of Iranian oil exports. There was some possibility that Europeans would not comply with the embargo or that Iran would open back-channel negotiations with the US to avoid the sanctions. To these two outcomes, I assigned only 5% and 15% probability. The greatest probability went to the scenario where the rest of the world complied with US sanctions, severely reducing Iranian oil exports (80% subjective probability).

That 80% probability, the main scenario, then split into three possible paths: Iranian retaliation via rhetoric, concrete kinetic action somewhere in the Middle East, or both kinetic retaliation and a full restart of its nuclear program.

Step I: The US reimposes sanctions against Iran.

Step II: Iran retaliates against US sanctions.

Step III: The US retaliates against the Iranian retaliation.[22]

Scenario 1 (36% conditional probability): An uneasy status quo emerges, where Iran benefits from a geopolitical risk premium on oil prices but suffers the loss of exports.

Scenario 2 (24% conditional probability): The US ratchets up military and economic pressure on Iran.

Scenario 3 (20% conditional probability): Scenario 2 fails to move Iran, and it continues to use kinetic actions to retaliate against sanctions, drawing the US (or Israel) into an attack against its nuclear facilities.

Scenario 4 (5% probability): There is a trade war between the US and the EU because Europeans failed to implement the US oil embargo.

Scenario 5 (15% probability): The US and Iran negotiate a *détente*.

Given this analysis was produced in May 2018, the time line at the bottom of the diagram and the ultimate probabilities were not far off

---

[22] Yes, this decision tree is starting to sound an awful lot like the plot to *Romeo and Juliet*. But all's fair in love and (trade) war.

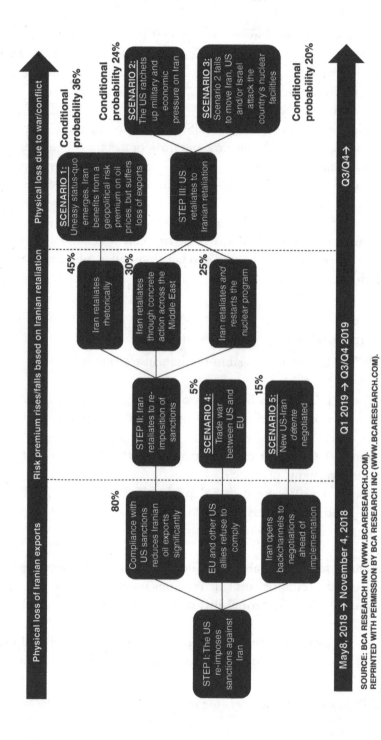

Physical loss of Iranian exports · Risk premium rises/falls based on Iranian retaliation · Physical loss due to war/conflict

Conditional probability 36%

SCENARIO 1: Uneasy status-quo emerges. Iran benefits from a geopolitical risk premium on oil prices, but suffers loss of exports

Conditional probability 24%

SCENARIO 2: The US ratchets up military and economic pressure on Iran

SCENARIO 3: Scenario 2 fails to move Iran, US and/or Israel attack the country's nuclear facilities

Conditional probability 20%

STEP III: US retaliates to Iranian retaliation

45% — Iran retaliates rhetorically

30% — Iran retaliates through concrete action across the Middle East

25% — Iran retaliates and restarts the nuclear program

STEP II: Iran retaliates to re-imposition of sanctions

5% — **SCENARIO 4:** Trade war between US and EU

15% — **SCENARIO 5:** New US-Iran *detente* negotiated

80% — Compliance with US sanctions reduces Iranian oil exports significantly

EU and other US allies refuse to comply

Iran opens backchannels to negotiations ahead of implementation

STEP I: The US re-imposes sanctions against Iran

May8, 2018 → November 4, 2018 · Q1 2019 → Q3/Q4 2019 · Q3/Q4 →

SOURCE: BCA RESEARCH INC (WWW.BCARESEARCH.COM).
REPRINTED WITH PERMISSION BY BCA RESEARCH INC (WWW.BCARESEARCH.COM).

Figure 9.16 Iran–US conflict decision tree (May 2018).

from what actually took place. An all-out US–Iran war was correctly assigned a non-negligible, but not the highest, probability. The actual outcome – put in motion by Iran's attack on Aramco facilities and US targeted killing of Soleimani – was somewhere between the first two scenarios. An "uneasy status quo" emerged, but the US did also "ratchet up military and economic pressure on Iran."

This net assessment would have correctly given investors a conservative bias following both the Aramco facility attack and the targeted killing of Iranian general. Both times, the correct call was to short the spike in oil prices. The global macro context of the subdued demand for oil also helped.

Net Assessment: The Takeaway

The purpose of a net assessment is to identify one or several fulcrum constraints that define one's forecast. In the case of India's cyclical net assessment, assigning probabilities would not have produced a helpful frame of analysis. Rather than setting a probabilistic prior, the assessment sets my prior bias: to remain bearish India until its policymakers resolve underinvestment via land and labor reforms.

In case of discrete events, such as a possible US–Iran war, investors should try to produce a net assessment that concludes in a set of scenarios that analysts can apply probabilities to. A decision tree becomes a highly useful tool, as I have found visualizing scenarios and their probabilities is the best way to operationalize the constraint framework. It illustrates the concept that constraints lead policymakers down a "path of least resistance."

In *Expert Political Judgment*, Tetlock posits that forcing forecasters to think in probabilities improves forecast performance. Investors should assign subjective probabilities to their forecasts because the more specific the subjective probability, the better the forecast is likely to be.

In my experience, Tetlock's directive and theory prove true, especially when combined with the decision-tree tool.

The combination of conditional probability and decision trees can sometimes have interesting and unintended outcomes – which skew toward a more accurate assessment. Following a net assessment analysis in late 2019 of a no-deal Brexit outcome, I thought that my subjective probability of Brexit was 15%. But when I visualized the scenarios through a decision tree and applied conditionality to several decision paths, I came to a probability of just 4%. The process of visualizing the various paths increased my confidence that a no-deal Brexit would not happen.

Net assessments are meant to be changed. The point of a net assessment is to produce the Bayesian prior – a probability or a bias – that is the starting point of the forecast. However, as information changes, that probability or bias changes with it. As such, the net assessment is the *netting* of all the constraints at hand. It does not conclude the hard work. In fact, the hard work has only begun.

Chapter 10

Game Theory – It's Not a Game!

I t is relatively easy to produce a cyclical, constraint-based net assessment. Sure, it takes a lot of research, but the subject is simple and discrete. The real challenge is to operationalize competing sets of constraints, such as when two countries or multiple sets of policymakers face off against one another.

The multiplayer and competitive factors in these circumstances make game theory a useful tool of analysis. Game theory allows the forecaster to formalize choices and the conditional probability of events. However, a formalized model where each choice is assigned a precise mathematical value does not guarantee a correct – accurate – forecast. Precision is not the same as accuracy, and the presence of one (mathematical precision) does not guarantee the presence of the other.[1] Game theory–based

---

[1] Matt Parker, *Humble Pi: A Comedy of Maths Errors* (New York: Penguin, 2019).

predictions are only as good as their empirical and contextual knowledge foundations. Without a solid base, they can be detrimental, even downright stupid.

In graduate school, I read some *really* stupid game theory papers. Political scientists – some of whom are essentially failed economists or mathematicians – would pick a topic, seemingly at random, to "formalize." The outcome was often mathematically elegant, but empirically … well, inaccurate, and therefore useless in application.

From their mistakes, I learned how important it is to *know something* about the topic at hand – something concrete and empirical – before attempting to formalize it. As such, I hesitate to discuss game theory in this book. I don't actually use it that often. But because I see investors use it all the time when navigating geopolitics, I decided to include this chapter as a guide for the dos and don'ts of game theory. At the very least, it provides the observer with some ways to recognize a well-researched game theory analysis.

Before You Play the Game, Set the Gameboard

The key to game theory is in assessing which actor holds the greater capability to change its rival's expected utility function. To calculate expected utility, take the weighted average of all possible outcomes under certain circumstances.[2]

Investors often overstate the role of material power in forcing capitulation and changing the rival's expected utility. In the contest between the US and China, investors throughout 2018 and 2019 argued that the US had enough material leverage to force China to accept onerous terms in the trade war. This did not happen. The Phase One deal, concluded in late 2019, was not much different from the May 2018 agreement that Beijing offered Washington. In other words, the extra 18 months did not really budge Beijing from its original position. Why? Because material power was not the only factor on the gameboard.

---

[2] $U(w) = ln(w)$, assuming that the utility is logarithmic, which is most often the case where material outcomes are concerned.

When assessing relative power, investors should consider three factors that measure an actor's relative capability:

- **Material balance of power:** In the case of the US–China trade war, the material balance of power favors the economy that is less leveraged to trade – clearly the US (Figure 10.1) – and the country that is the "customer" in the relationship – again, the US (Figure 10.2).
- **Risk tolerance:** The actor willing to risk more is the one with *greater interests* at stake. For this factor, the balance of power is more equally distributed. China had reason to stress stability in 2019 given its 70-year anniversary celebration as the People's Republic of China. But the US was heading toward a general election, meaning it had the greater interests at stake should US–China relations go south. It is not clear what the transmission mechanism between a US recession and a trade war would be, but the economy was clearly nearing the end of the cycle even before the COVID-19 outbreak. The yield curve inverted in 2019, signaling approaching recession, and animal spirits were already weak.
- **Credibility:** The reputations of the players matter. Do the actors involved have follow-through? President Trump gained global street cred early on in his term by being especially tough on North Korea. However, the renegotiated US–Korea Free Trade Agreement only marginally benefited the US while the United States–Mexico–Canada Agreement (USMCA; "NAFTA 2.0") fell far short of the White House's initial "ask." Therefore, President Trump's bark appeared stronger than his bite from Beijing's vantage point. For China, establishing credibility and signaling a high risk tolerance were critical to national security. As a result, it maintained its credibility throughout negotiations. Any sign that it had reached its pain threshold on trade could prove fodder for US decision-makers eager to force a Beijing behavioral change in future conflicts, whether on trade or geopolitics.

With the addition of two factors, China wins the capability game two to one. But balance of capabilities alone does not help resolve the trade war puzzle. China and the US are not only confronting each other, but

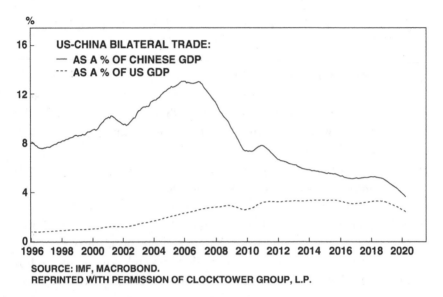

Figure 10.1   The US is less leveraged to trade …

also the competing interests in geopolitical and domestic arenas. They are playing a "two-level game."[3] Two-level game theory posits that domestic politics creates acceptable "win-sets," which are then transported to the geopolitical theatre. These win-sets, if lost, become constraints to policymaker action. As Figure 10.3 illustrates, politicians cannot conclude foreign agreements that are outside of those domestic win-sets. For a win-win outcome, all four arenas must align.

All of these points combined result in Figure 10.4, which illustrates the competing "tolerance curves" of China and the US. The figure suggests that the Chinese economy – saddled with the constraints of export dependence and an addiction to the American consumer – has a lower pain threshold than the US economy. The difference between the pain thresholds is determined purely by material power.

Although China's pain threshold may be lower, its internal politics, focus on the real economy (as opposed to the equity market), and lack of an election calendar mean it has fewer domestic political constraints

---

[3] Robert Putnam, "Diplomacy," 427.

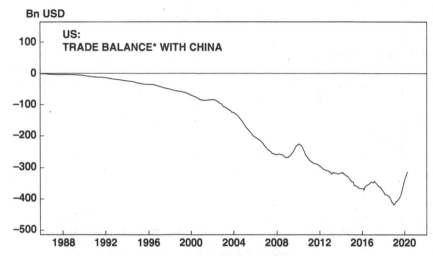

Figure 10.2   ... and clearly the customer.

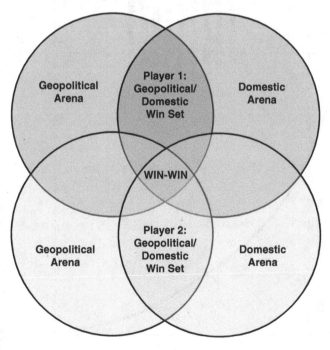

Figure 10.3   Two-level game.

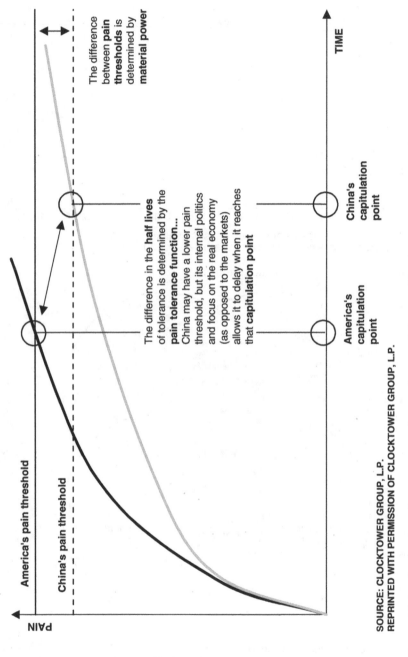

Figure 10.4 Competing tolerance curves show only part of the gameboard.

than the US.[4] As a result, it has sufficient political capital to delay when it reaches the capitulation point.

Game theory is a powerful tool, but investors have to be careful in wielding it. Setting the gameboard is as important as playing on it, as it reveals material factors are not the only constraints in play. Often, analysts have to play three-dimensional chess when determining which side is more constrained on the domestic front, especially when considering domestic politics and interest groups.

Beware Simplistic Games

In early 2015, Greek voters gave SYRIZA and its leader, Alexis Tsipras, the mandate to govern Greece and negotiate with Europe. Tsipras appointed Yanis Varoufakis, an economist and game theory expert, to be his finance minister. At the height of their battle with Brussels, many market commentators flagged their "game of chicken" as likely to produce a negative outcome.

For those who are not fans of James Dean movies, a "game of chicken" refers to a scenario where two young men, each behind the wheel of a hot rod, drive straight at one another to prove their bravery and win the heart of a young woman. The one that swerves – the "chicken" – proves unworthy of wooing the lady thanks to his high levels of risk aversion and self-preservation (a signal to the potential mate that he will fail later in life, obviously). The one that keeps driving straight wins.

The game of chicken is indeed the most dangerous form of game theory. In a world where both actors assume rationality in their opponent, each has an incentive to drive straight and not swerve. This brand of reckless obstinacy means that the bottom-right outcome in Figure 10.5 – the costliest and least optimal for *both* actors – has a high probability of occurring.

In the case of Greece in 2015, however, Athens was massively constrained by its material reality: a subpar mode of transport. Using

---

[4] In Chapter 4, I noted that the strongest constraints to policymaker action are political, and the two-level game theory supports this view. They play a key role in determining an actor's capability on the global stage.

		PLAYER A: SWERVE	PLAYER A: STRAIGHT
PLAYER B	SWERVE	(X,X) (TIE,TIE)	(X–1,X+1) (LOSE,WIN)
PLAYER B	STRAIGHT	(X+1,X–1) (WIN,LOSE)	(X–10,X–10) (CRASH,CRASH)

SOURCE: BCA RESEARCH INC (WWW.BCARESEARCH.COM). REPRINTED WITH PERMISSION BY BCA RESEARCH INC (WWW.BCARESEARCH.COM).

Figure 10.5 Regular game of chicken.

constraint-based analysis, Figure 10.6 illustrates the game much more accurately. The adjusted outcomes show that game theory is useless without first correctly assessing each actor's *relative power,* which includes material balance of power, risk tolerance, and credibility.

In the case of Greece, Tsipras was facing considerable political, economic, and geopolitical constraints to leaving the EU. These constraints lowered his vehicle's horsepower relative to Angela Merkel's.

On the political front, polls throughout 2015 showed that over 60% of the Greek public supported Euro Area membership. On the economic front, an exit from the Euro Area would have produced a massive depreciation of the drachma, accompanied by a massive rise in prices because the Greek economy imported its energy needs, as we discussed in Chapter 5. Yes, there was the off chance that a depreciation would lead to foreign investment and an export boom, but not before the angry median voter forced Tsipras out of power. On the geopolitical front, Greece had no alternative to Europe, no other ally to fall back on. When Tsipras signaled that Greece would consider Russian financial support in exchange for a geopolitical alliance, President Vladimir Putin rebuffed him.

MERKEL, DRIVING A G-CLASS MERCEDES-BENZ

TSIPRAS, RIDING A TRICYCLE	SWERVE	STRAIGHT
SWERVE	(X,X) (TIE,TIE)	(X–1,X+1) (LOSE,WIN)
STRAIGHT	(X+1,X–1) (WIN,LOSE)	(X–∞,X–5) (DEATH,BODY PAINT DAMAGE)

SOURCE: BCA RESEARCH INC (WWW.BCARESEARCH.COM). REPRINTED WITH PERMISSION BY BCA RESEARCH INC (WWW.BCARESEARCH.COM).

Figure 10.6 2015 Greek crisis game of chicken.

The logic behind my view that Greece was bluffing in 2015 is strong, and steadfast empirical evidence supports it. German Chancellor Angela Merkel and Tsipras may have been heading straight for each other, but they were doing so in different vehicles. While Merkel was driving a G-Class Mercedes-Benz SUV, Tsipras and Varoufakis were pedaling a tricycle.

Game Theory: The Takeaway

Game theory is often mentioned but rarely applied correctly in the investment community. There is too much *prima facie* theorizing going on. I have read too many game theory–reliant reports on investment that go little beyond material power.

To properly set up a game, investors first have to produce a comprehensive net assessment of the actors whose interaction is being formalized. Accurate information about the actors is key. The game of chicken between Greece and Germany relies on the net assessments in Chapter 5, where I explained the constraints faced by policymakers in both Berlin and Athens.

In Chapter 5, I showed that during the sovereign debt crisis, a Euro Area exit for Greece would have been folly. At the same time, I illustrated that Berlin did not want the Euro Area to collapse. By 2015, the odds that a Greek exit would produce such an outcome were much lower. Thanks to the ECB's actions to ring-fence Mediterranean economies against bond vigilantes, combined with the fact that Greek sovereign debt had been cleansed from Europe's banking sector, Berlin felt it could play hardball with Athens and not risk a dissolution of the entire Euro Area. A constraint-based analysis bolstered by deep contextual knowledge of each actor's relative capabilities proved the game of chicken was not quite so high-stakes as it seemed in 2015. Those who invested based on this dire Euro Area prediction lost the game.

A way to update this game for 2020–2021 conditions would be to consider a similar confrontation between Italy and the EU. Italian policymakers are certainly not riding a tricycle. They are behind the wheel of a finely crafted Italian supercar. Much safer than a tricycle, for sure, but still no match for the G-Class Benz.

While Italy has a much larger economy than Greece, the reality of material constraints is still cogent. As such, investors should expect to see Italian populists consistently bend their Euroscepticism once they come to power, as the *Lega* party did during its brief time in power between June 2018 and September 2019. The main difference between Greece and Italy is that Germany will have to accommodate Italy more than it did Greece. As such, the COVID-19 recession is likely to see Germany cross a number of red lines that it never did with Greece, including the adoption of some form of debt mutualization.

Without a thorough net assessment and in-depth knowledge of the matter at hand, game theory is dangerous. The mathematics can produce a false sense of confidence in the forecast. An accurate assessment of the players and gameboard is key. Investors should therefore only engage in game theory once they have produced painstaking research to underpin their net assessment.

Chapter 11

Geopolitical Alpha

F or much of the past decade, I've worked in finance as a strategist, which requires me to think in narratives and themes but not actually pull the trigger on trades. A navigator plots the course for the airplane, but a passenger wouldn't want him behind the controls actually flying the thing. The execution of investment themes is left for the pilots, the investment professionals who know how to structure a trade to take advantage of a well-articulated strategy. Those are the true "ballers and shot callers" of the financial profession who always humble me, particularly when it comes to implementing my forecasts in the actual marketplace.

I make this distinction lest readers confuse my framework for a trading rule.[1]

---

[1] I also stress it so my friends can stop asking me what stocks to buy. I have no idea!

But what I *do* know how to do is beat the market on geopolitics. The market is not very good at pricing geopolitical risks and opportunities because its behavior is dictated by investment professionals (and retail investors), who all have different time horizons. While they may have good reason to both sell and buy Apple stock at the same time – likely due to their differing time horizons – volatile market reactions indicate they don't know how to price geopolitics. I see a fundamental skills mismatch that creates an opportunity for those investors willing to broaden their skill set.

In Chapter 1, I asserted that the global community of investors has become over-professionalized and overquantified. The CFA curriculum has no section dedicated to simple concepts in political science. It has no case studies to test investors' reactions to the ups and downs of legislative negotiations on fiscal spending. As such, the market consistently over-reacts to geopolitical events as investors try to feel their way through a framework they lack the skills to navigate.[2]

Educated industry colleagues, clients, and friends have asked me the most bizarrely basic questions. What does a Senate do? What is a nation-state? Who elects the EU president? Does the resignation of the German president matter? Not to mention questions that reveal a shocking level of ignorance concerning foreign political systems. Their blind spot is not because they are stupid or poorly read. It simply takes a *lot* of hard work to become an investment professional, and for many of them, spending time on politics and history is a luxury they cannot afford.[3]

---

[2] Ongoing COVID-19-related volatility is similar. Although the initial event – the pandemic itself – is not precisely geopolitical, it does fall under the rubric of noneconomic/finance risks. The pandemic has now evolved into a geopolitical issue, however, as investors have to both assess the spread of the disease and the policy response to the economic calamity.

[3] There are many finance professionals who do know how to conduct a quality, informed geopolitical analysis. Global macro hedge funds have been incorporating geopolitical and political analysis into their discretionary idea generation for half a century. However, they are a tiny sliver of the broader community. For most investors, geopolitics is new and exotic.

This skills mismatch and knowledge gap mean that geopolitical analysis may be the final frontier for the typical investor, and that there is *alpha* to be harvested in betting against the market. In this book, I introduced a framework for analysis that is particularly good at ignoring the noise generated by social media and news. While the media and policymaker preferences distract each other (as well as ill-equipped investors), a disciplined analyst can focus on material constraints to action.

But this new perspective does not mean that investors should plow headlong into forecasting political events. The key to harvesting geopolitical *alpha* is betting against the spread, not trying to predict who wins the game.

In sports betting, the astute gambler does not try to predict the outcome of a game. He is indifferent toward the winner of the match because he cannot simultaneously be a gambler and a fan. Success instead lies in "beating the spread" or choosing an "over/under" on the "line" set by the casino.

Some of my worst calls as an investment strategist have been when I forgot this point and tried to bet on who wins the election. And some of my best calls have been when I bet against the bookie: the market.

Take the 2016 UK referendum on EU membership. In March 2016, I argued that the probability of Brexit was closer to 50% than the 30% that the currency and political betting markets had priced in. I did not actually forecast that Brexit would occur. I wrote an analysis in early 2016 asserting that the risk of Brexit was massively understated, but that the Bremain side would win in a tight referendum.

Swing and a miss, right? Wrong! I don't get paid to make forecasts for the sake of politics. I get paid to make forecasts for the sake of the market. Because I thought the market was overly complacent, I recommended a strategy in UK currency, gilts, and equity markets that made money when Brexit did happen.

My approach to politics and geopolitics makes me a terrible dinner guest with "normal people." For noninvestors – and many investors who can only think ideologically[4] – politics is about winning and losing,

---

[4] And are therefore terrible investors.

about politicians doing the wrong or the right thing. They assume there *is* a right and a wrong – one clear side in which to invest not just money but their hearts and moral standards. But I will bear the dirty looks across the dinner table because my approach allows me to confidently check my work in a field where most are flying blind.

Few political analysts know how to ascertain whether their forecast is correct. One of the most frustrating things about working in the political risk industry was the revisionist performance reviews. A forecast that "the Bashar al-Assad regime would be destabilized by the Arab Spring" can be both right and woefully inadequate at the same time. Sure, Assad has faced a civil war, but he still runs Syria and has beaten back most challengers!

In contrast to politics, markets provide brutal, immediate feedback. Right away, they tell forecasters if they're right because the results of their views are either in *green* or in *red*. As such, converting my geopolitical forecasts into trade recommendations has been liberating.

Tensions between Iran and the US are overstated and materially constrained?[5] *Short oil after it rallies 15% following the attack on Aramco facilities.*

If I'm in *green,* my forecast was sound.

Marine Le Pen's odds of winning are massively overstated in the 2017 French presidential election? *Go long EURUSD in Q4 2016.*

Then I watch how the market checks my work.

In this chapter, I demonstrate how I use the constraint framework to generate geopolitical *alpha*. I first review my 2016 analysis on the odds of Le Pen winning the French election. I then go over the process itself, combining the constraint framework with the net assessment process.

Chocolate Labrador Brian Versus Marine Le Pen

As I wrote this book, my 13-year-old chocolate lab was dying. He had a great life.[6] Born on a small farm outside of Austin, Texas, he spent

---

[5] As discussed in Chapter 9.

[6] At least, *I* think he did. He may disagree …

most of his life in Quebec frolicking in snow. He passed away the same day that I took him to see the Pacific Ocean for the first time in his life. Brian helped me raise my three kids. He has been a nanny, a maid, and a couch. And for that, I thank him.

What Brian didn't realize was that he had also been my analytical crutch whenever I grew frustrated with clients and colleagues. I have no idea how many elections Brian could have won, but it is a *lot*. Whenever I reached the end of my patience, my go-to retort to some doubting Thomas was, "My chocolate Labrador, Brian, can beat Candidate X in Election Y."

In late 2016, investors were nervous. Victories for both the Leave side in the UK's EU referendum and Donald Trump had upended their entire framework for thinking about politics. As I talked to clients around the world – both sophisticated and not – I had a shocking revelation: investors were assigning a higher probability to the election of Marine Le Pen *because* of the anti-establishment victories in the UK and the US.

This logic was wrong on several levels. Investors had failed to account for just how different France was in terms of its political and geopolitical constraints. Sure, the English-speaking median voter was headed in a populist direction, but I have never known the French to follow trends established in the Anglo-Saxon world! I had a clear framework to explain what happened with both the UK and US Anti-establishment votes. The median voter in the Anglo-Saxon world was moving away from the *laissez-faire* establishment, as discussed in Chapter 1. Populist outcomes were therefore likely in those countries–but not necessarily in France.

In fact, the French median voter was moving away from Euroscepticism – a shift that was the fulcrum constraint to Marine Le Pen's victory. Popular opinion changed because, by late 2016, the migration crisis in Europe was over. Yet almost every investor I talked to was unaware of the clear data on this point (Figure 11.1). The media could not pivot away from the narrative that got them so many clicks, so they kept hammering home the "Europe will be over-run" narrative. But outside the newsrooms, both the median voters and politicians in Europe knew that the migration crisis had ended.

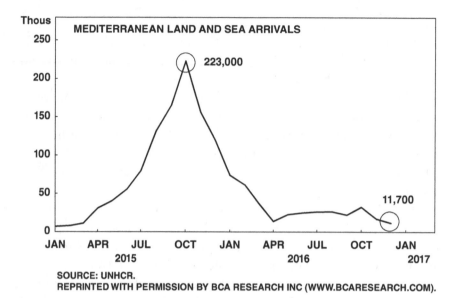

Figure 11.1   Ready my chart: the migration crisis is over.

The French public in particular was eager for reform. I had the toughest time convincing investors of this view, as most were both Anglo-Saxon and rather anti-French! Instead of investing with their heads, many were investing with stereotypes. But after conducting a net assessment of France – just as in-depth as the net assessment of India in Chapter 9 – I concluded that the median voter in France was looking for change. Polls showed that a "silent majority" wanted reforms. Even Marine Le Pen, a populist, tried to capitalize on the shift of the median voter by promising to cut the size of the state and reduce the retirement age. Not very populist of her! Investors ignored this shift, too busy obsessing over her EU and euro policies.

But her view toward European integration is precisely why Le Pen was unelectable. Despite moving toward the median voter on supply-side reforms, Le Pen made a critical blunder. She remained intellectually wedded to her long-held Eurosceptic preference, campaigning on a promise to exit the Euro Area. Her ideological loyalty to

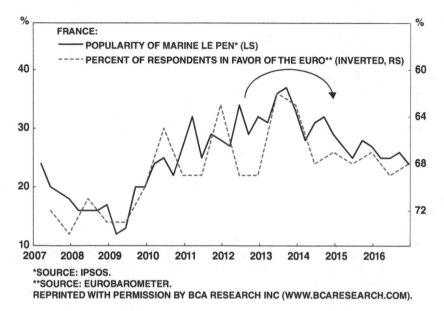

Figure 11.2 The euro was Le Pen's foil.

this position was a mistake, given France's median voter constraint. Le Pen's long-term support levels were almost the perfect inverse of the country's support level for the common currency (Figure 11.2).

From the results of my constraint-based net assessment, I concluded Marine Le Pen was not a viable candidate. She would get crushed in the second round of the vote by literally anyone – yes, even Brian the Lab. The subsequent government would enact a slew of reforms to close the unit labor cost gap between France and Germany (Figure 11.3).

More broadly, investors were catastrophizing Le Pen's candidacy. With two months to the French election, investors were assigning Le Pen a higher probability of winning than they had assigned at the corresponding time to Brexit or Trump's victory (Figure 11.4). This forecasting error was astounding, especially given that Emmanuel Macron's lead over Le Pen at that point was *30%!* Compare this gap to the one between Clinton and Trump (Figure 11.5).

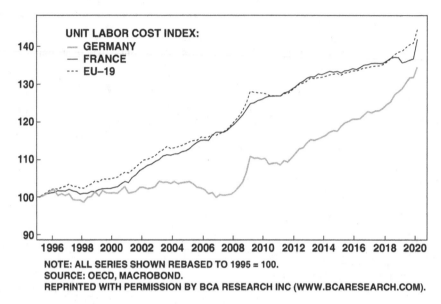

NOTE: ALL SERIES SHOWN REBASED TO 1995 = 100.
SOURCE: OECD, MACROBOND.
REPRINTED WITH PERMISSION BY BCA RESEARCH INC (WWW.BCARESEARCH.COM).

Figure 11.3   Structural reforms are coming to France.

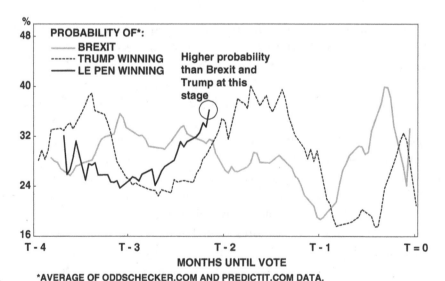

*AVERAGE OF ODDSCHECKER.COM AND PREDICTIT.COM DATA.
REPRINTED WITH PERMISSION BY BCA RESEARCH INC (WWW.BCARESEARCH.COM).

Figure 11.4   This chart is insane …

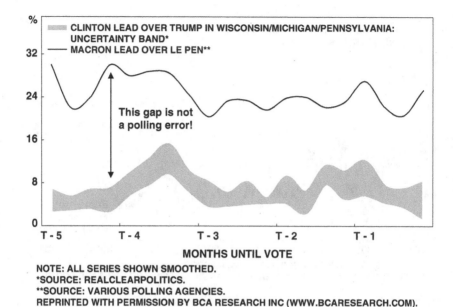

Figure 11.5   … given this chart!!

The market had lost its mind, and I was reaping all the benefits. Despite clear problems with electability and strategy, investors were distracted by poor-quality analysis reliant on historic stereotypes. They bet a 20%–30% electoral lead in the French election would evaporate in three months. I couldn't believe my luck. The bookies, overreacting to a Patriots loss the week before, were expecting the Miami Dolphins to beat Tom Brady … in New England … *in December.* Mortgage your house, pawn off your own mother, and put money on that line!

I sat down with my BCA colleague Mathieu Savary – a much better investment tactician than me – and we came up with two trades with which to take advantage of my strategy and maximize geopolitical *alpha.* The first trade, long EURUSD call, was easy enough for anyone to figure out. The euro bottomed on December 20, 2016, and rallied 21% to a peak of 1.250 on January 25, 2018. But the real gem, which required Mathieu's subtle touch, was to go long French industrials/short German industrials (Figure 11.6). The chart speaks for itself.

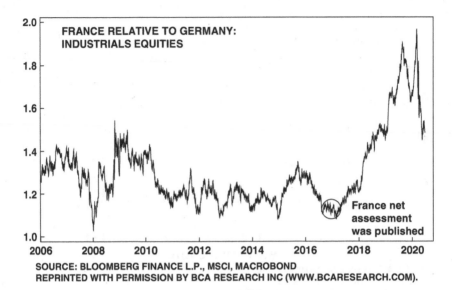

SOURCE: BLOOMBERG FINANCE L.P., MSCI, MACROBOND
REPRINTED WITH PERMISSION BY BCA RESEARCH INC (WWW.BCARESEARCH.COM).

Figure 11.6   Industrials: buy France/short Germany.

"So, You Want to Go Long Socialism and Short Capitalism"

The market's reaction to Marine Le Pen's candidacy, and my subsequent forecast, show that geopolitical *alpha* is easiest to harvest when investors confuse stereotyping for analysis. Emotions, anti-French bias, headlines, and a focus on the broad set of the possible – rather than the constrained set of the probable – caused investors to massively overstate the odds of a Le Pen electoral victory.

I *love* these opportunities. Give me your tired, your poor, your preference-led investors yearning to breathe ideologies! They are easy to bet against when geopolitics are in question.

At the end of my sell-side career in late 2018, I did one final round of my clients in New York and Connecticut. The salesperson ushered me into the office of a legendary hedge fund manager who had made his name in emerging markets (EM). I was particularly bearish on EM in 2019, but I thought there was some *alpha* to be generated in Mexico and Brazil.

As in France, investors' loss (of median voter perspective) was my gain. I thought investors were overly bullish on Brazil and overly bearish on Mexico. In both countries, the 2018 elections had seen voters turn to anti-establishment candidates due to concerns over violence and corruption. In the wake of these elections, I was skeptical that the Brazilian median voter had suddenly become an acolyte of Reagan and Thatcher or that the Mexican median voter had become a Trotskyite.

Investors expected Brazilian President-elect Jair Bolsonaro to prevail and pass market-friendly reforms, but he had a high hurdle to clear in the constraint of Brazilian legislative math. He had to convince a traditionally fractured Congress to pass a complex and painful pension reform. In other words, Bolsonaro had to show that he could *do something* in order to justify a rally that had *already happened* in Brazilian assets.

In Mexico, President Andrés Manuel López Obrador (AMLO) remained constrained by the constitution, the National Supreme Court of Justice, and political convention that Mexico is right of center on economic policy (an outwardly left-wing president had not won an election since 1924). Like Bolsonaro, AMLO had to prove that he could overcome his constraints in order to justify a sell-off that had *already happened*.

My point is not that AMLO was a positive, in the absolute, for Mexico. His decisions to scrap the Mexico City airport plans, sideline the finance ministry from key economic decisions, and threaten a return to an old-school PRI-era statism was indeed deeply concerning from a market perspective.[7] Similarly, I was not of the view that Bolsonaro was, in the absolute, a negative for Brazil.

But the *relative* investor sentiment was overly bullish Bolsonaro versus AMLO, especially given both presidents' strong political constraints. Ever faithful to my constraint framework, I weighted those

---

[7] PRI is the *Partido Revolucionario Institucional,* or Institutional Revolutionary Party, which governed Mexico from 1929 to 2000.

constraints more heavily than the leaders' stated economic preferences. I also observed that they faced respective median voters who were diametrically opposed to their economic agendas – Bolsonaro was facing a left-leaning median voter, whereas the Mexican median voter was center-right (at least according to polling).

The macroeconomic context supported my relative view. I thought China would fail to stimulate as much as investors hoped and that the US–China trade war would become a serious risk to investors. If this scenario played out, high-beta countries like Brazil would suffer, while an economy that is joined at the hip to the US, like Mexico, ought to outperform EM peers. My view on USMCA negotiations also happened to be bullish Mexico.

With everything aligning, I recommended a long MXNBRL trade to capture this sentiment gap between the two EM markets. Not only did it make sense given geopolitical constraints, but the market was also screaming for a long MXN trade. For the first time since I had been of legal drinking age, investors would be receiving positive carry on Mexico relative to Brazil (Figure 11.7).

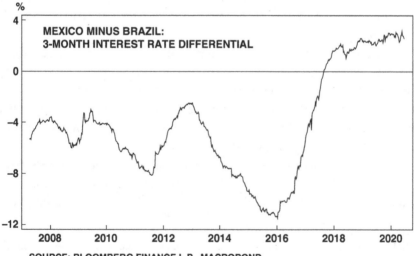

SOURCE: BLOOMBERG FINANCE L.P., MACROBOND.
REPRINTED WITH PERMISSION BY BCA RESEARCH INC (WWW.BCARESEARCH.COM).

Figure 11.7 Mexico has positive carry vs. Brazil.

I was super stoked that I had at least *one* positive story to tell on EM.

At the end of AMLO's term, Mexico would not be better off – economically – than Brazil at the end of Bolsonaro's. I wasn't making an absolute call. Imagine that AMLO and Bolsonaro are two NFL teams facing off against one another. The casinos set the line at Bolsonaro crushing AMLO by two touchdowns. I wasn't betting that AMLO would win the game, just that he would narrow the spread. Maybe he would lose by one touchdown, more likely by a field goal.

* * * * *

So, here I am … at the end of my sell-side career, facing the EM legend with a clear, well-thought-out view of how to make money over the next 12 months. I enter his spacious boardroom, shaking hands with him and his second-in-command. We exchange pleasantries and, as we sit down, he says, "So, you're going to tell me how that communist is going to ruin Mexico, right?"

I chuckle earnestly and say, "No, I actually think you should go long the Mexican peso! Let me show you something … "

As I open my chart pack to deliver my *strategery*, I see Legend's second-in-command lean back, out of his boss's peripheral vision, and slowly shake his head. Maybe. I'm not sure. The movement was almost imperceptible. *Ah hell, who cares … it's my last meeting on the sell side, let me crush it.*

Forty seconds into my pitch, I notice that Legend's knuckles are white. He stops me.

"Hold on, kid. You're telling me you want to go long communism and short capitalism?"

Uh-oh.

I look at the two gentlemen in front of me, confused. The second-in-command is telepathically telling me to zip it. He is literally sweating.[8]

---

[8] Apparently, I was in the office of Bolsonaro's main fan on Wall Street. I had no idea. The man was an old-school, *Journal*-reading, *laissez-faire*-worshipping Ayn Rand capitalist. And the thought that I should waltz into his boardroom and suggest he put his hard-earned dollars behind a "communist" over a "capitalist" brought him close to a brain aneurysm.

Legend says, "I mean ... this is just the dumbest f-ing thing I've heard year-to-date."

It's December.

Normally, such a client judgment would really hurt my feelings.[9] But I am checking out of sell side and heading to the beaches of California and don't give a damn. I say, "Well, given that I am the only one here who actually lived under communism, I think that, yeah ... I probably know what I'm talking about."

* * * * *

He didn't buy what I was selling.

Now let me assure you, this man *is* a Legend. He has made more amazing calls in his career than you, me, and a hundred other investors combined will ever make. But his bias and ideology were his kryptonite on this trade.

This is what is amazing about geopolitical *alpha*. When I invest based on geopolitical analysis, I am not just investing against peers. Even some of the greatest minds in finance are shooting from the hip, relying on stereotypes and meetings in smoke-filled rooms with deputy finance ministers who tell them what they want to hear. In the constraint framework, *all* preferences are subject to constraints − not just those of the actors, but those of the analyst as well. Everyone has preferences, but users of the constraint framework have the tools to question the pragmatism in others' as well as their own.

I am no legend, but I bested one that day. Long MXNBRL returned 11.2% from December 14, 2018, when I made the recommendation, until the end of 2019.

Geopolitical *Alpha*: The Takeaway

The constraint framework gives investors a way to think about geopolitics that is data-driven, focused on the observable, and rooted in the material world. While the media and the pundits focus on policymaker

---

[9] I may be a nihilist, but I'm not made of stone!

preferences or the dominant narratives, investors can focus on what is actionable: constraints.

Preferences are optional and subject to constraints, whereas constraints are neither optional nor subject to preferences.

The net assessment is the starting point to operationalize this framework. In Chapter 9, I presented examples of two net assessments: a cyclical one and a reactive one. In Chapter 4, I also made a net assessment of where the US median voter is going, arguing that *laissez-faire* was done. Start getting ready for *dirigisme* (at best), and outright socialism at the extreme. The explosion of fiscal stimulus is only the beginning.

A net assessment rooted in constraints provides investors with several points of reference. The fulcrum constraint(s) and associated data streams provide the investor with the right metrics to watch. If they change, the view needs to change. Most importantly, a net assessment provides the solid foundation for further analysis: a prior probability for an event or its multiple scenarios. The odds of a US–Iran kinetic conflict are 20% – non-negligible, but less likely than an uneasy truce.

A net assessment can also give investors enough information to choose a bias. My net assessment of Brazil in 2018 gave me a negative bias for the coming year, whereas my net assessment of Mexico gave me a bullish bias. The net assessment of India gives me a bearish bias. This is not an implicit bias rooted in stereotypes or out-of-date tropes, but rather one I chose deliberately that is grounded in research.

Armed with a net assessment and a *prior* view, investors can make the final gamble and compare it to market pricing and action. What do the valuations say about assets that would be impacted by the geopolitical event under examination?

In this chapter, I illustrated the process of harvesting geopolitical *alpha*. In the case of Brexit, there was much *alpha* to harvest as the market was ignoring risks of a Leave victory. In the case of Brazil and Mexico, investors were leaving positive carry on the table purely because of ideological preference. And in the case of the euro, investors were overstating odds of a Marine Le Pen victory.

Geopolitical analysis is rarely effective in a vacuum. In each case of a successful investment call, I've also relied on valuations and market sentiment. As such, just producing a net assessment is not enough. Your assessment has to be out of consensus, or the market may have already priced it in. The constraint framework gives you an edge because it allows you to think outside of the preference-led box.

Chapter 12

Conclusion

In March 2020, popular opinion – spearheaded by the media – might deem it beside the point to write a book about geopolitics and investing. A book on epidemiology and investing may be more appropriate.

But geopolitics is central to the COVID-19 pandemic and its ultimate effect on the economy and markets. In Chapter 8, I argued the curve-flattening narrative will ultimately succumb to economic constraints: the pressure to restart the economy. Figure 12.1 summarizes that chapter's conclusions, and only half-jokingly.

As a reminder of my main thesis in Chapter 8, most voters are *not* savers. Or, if they are, their savings is not enough to nurse them through a depression-level economic dislocation. Therefore, investors should expect a revolt against the indefinite curve-flattening narrative to occur sooner rather than later – at the "desensitization point for debtors" in Figure 12.1. While your sample may be skewed if your friends, family, and colleagues are "savers" – certainly if you are an investor they are – most people are "debtors" on the diagram. Twitter and Instagram are not representative of the median voter in this respect.

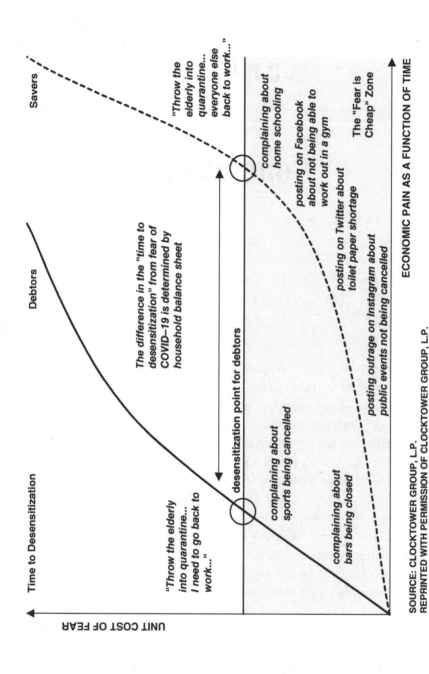

The figure contains the following labels:

UNIT COST OF FEAR

Time to Desensitization

Debtors

Savers

"Throw the elderly into quarantine... I need to go back to work..."

"Throw the elderly into quarantine... everyone else back to work..."

The difference in the "time to desensitization" from fear of COVID–19 is determined by household balance sheet

desensitization point for debtors

complaining about bars being closed

complaining about sports being cancelled

posting outrage on Instagram about public events not being cancelled

posting on Twitter about toilet paper shortage

posting on Facebook about not being able to work out in a gym

complaining about home schooling

The "Fear is Cheap" Zone

ECONOMIC PAIN AS A FUNCTION OF TIME

Figure 12.1 Constraints to flatten-the-curve narrative will grow.

This book has little to teach about pandemics, but it does provide a framework to forecast policy reactions to anything. A recession, terrorism, trade war, pandemic, alien invasion. It does not matter. A correct read of constraints will always beat a forecast based on preferences or one that extrapolates the current narrative and dominant sentiment linearly into the future. Such reductionist linearity might be common in abstract models, but it is harder to find in material reality.

Though COVID-19 is on everyone's minds at the time of writing, I want to end with a broader conclusion and highlight what this book has to teach investors and non-investors alike: leave ideology and unfounded bias out of policy discussions. Even if you run a think tank or a political advocacy interest group, you can find something useful in the constraint framework. Its unique perspective enables you to perceive reality – without the rose-colored glasses of personal preference. If you know where things stand materially and where they are going, your efforts to change them for the better will be more successful.

Take climate change. If you think it is a dire scenario, then you need to understand the constraints on reducing carbon emissions.[1] Once you develop a clear, nonideological, constraint-based forecast of policy, you will discover the fulcrum constraint that must change to generate the outcomes you want.

Personally, I will not be the agent of any change, only its observer. I posited in Chapter 3 that a special circle of forecasting hell is reserved for the self-important, op-ed-writing forecaster. I spend a lot of time meditating on my biases and bathing myself in nihilism. I would probably make a terrible motivational speaker. And I try, really hard, not to become outraged by stupid policymaking.

I wrote this book because my framework has allowed me to make sense of the world and occasionally generate *alpha*. I hope others who use it will find similar success, but it won't work for everyone, and it is definitely not a foolproof method. As I illustrated with COVID-19 – only the most important investment matter of 2020– a too-rigid focus on material constraints does have its pitfalls. Sometimes collective psychology can create a material reality of its own.

---

[1] You may be wondering what these constraints are. Too bad. It's Chapter 12, folks, and I will not expand on climate change here.

But in the long-term, like old age, material constraints are unde-feated. The problem for investors is that, before the long-term arrives, you can lose all your money. As Keynes remarked in the 1930s, "markets can stay irrational longer than you can remain solvent." Betting against time is the Achilles' heel of any investment framework and why invest-ing is an art, not a science. As is the case for the practitioner of any art form, I may strive for perfection, but I can only hope to approach it asymptotically.

From one artist to another, I hope this book helps you add the hue of geopolitical analysis to your palette.

Acknowledgements

I f I narrow the acknowledgements down to just those who helped me write this book, I should start with the trio of nationalists that destroyed my country: Slobodan Milošević, Franjo Tuđman, and Alija Izetbegović.[1] Thanks to their brand of ethno-populism, my homeland no longer exists, 150,000 people are dead, Yugoslavia is not dominating international hoops, and I am not a gynecologist like pretty much every other male in my family (shout out to my cousin Ljuba, carrying on the tradition!). Their warmongering made a lasting impression on a young kid who should have been playing with LEGOs and watching cartoons. Instead, I developed an analytical mind to make sense of the harrowing world around me.

So hey, thanks, guys!

I wrote this book in part because, to be honest, I want my grandkids to be able to pick up a book their grandpa wrote, rather than go through thousands of PDFs I generated while working in investment research.

---

[1] Special mention goes to Saddam Hussein and Ruhollah Khomeini! My first introduction to geopolitics was as a three-year-old in Baghdad, where my family lived briefly. The very first conversation I remember having as a sentient being was with my mom, who was trying to explain why Iranian Scuds were flying over our heads.

I also miss academia. By introducing investors to my framework over the past decade, I've fulfilled my passion for generating those "aha" moments in clients, colleagues, and friends in the industry. These moments bring me as close to teaching as I will ever get. Nothing makes me happier than when a client or colleague turns the tables and uses the constraint framework to prove me wrong.

There are many people who have helped me live my life and build my career. An immense thank-you goes to my partner and boss, Steve Drobny, who willed this book into existence. I have never met anyone with as much unconditional confidence in my abilities as Steve (other than my mom). He pushed me to put my thoughts on paper and has given me invaluable feedback throughout the process. He is a patient mentor and friend, and his only failure is at teaching me to surf, but that may be due to the fact that I have the balance of a beached whale.

The greatest thank you goes to my wife, Crystal. My finance career was constrained before it started. I mean, I can't do math! I took three economics classes in college. I still pantomime with my hands to figure out whether the curve steepening or flattening is bullish or bearish. To overcome my weaknesses, I've played catchup learning an industry that I parachuted into late in life. Over the past decade, my wife has helped me overcome this constraint by taking up the slack in every other responsibility that I have as a parent, husband, and human being. Crystal is the inspiration behind everything I do.

Thank you to my parents, Predrag and Gordana Papic. My dad was my first teacher in geopolitical analysis, and he would conclude every forecast with, "It's all Hollywood anyway." (True!) My parents sacrificed a lot for me to be where I am. If I do half as good a job at parenting as they did, I will have succeeded. The jury is out thus far. My mom, my sister, Maja, and my aunt, Vesna, deserve a special place in the Marko Papic Hall of Fame. They have all listened to my BS for longer than anyone else. And somehow, they survived it! Big thank you to my uncle Zoran, who embraced me like a son when I left Europe for the beautiful British Columbia, as well as my entire family in Belgrade (uncle Pavle and aunt Nataša).

I wrote this book from the ocean-view offices of the firm that Steve invited me to join: Clocktower Group. Thank you to all of my teammates at the firm. The other partners – Tyler Hathaway, Wei Liu, Benjamin Savage – gave their approval for Steve to let me crash the party.

Ashton Rosin helped me learn what it is that I am supposed to do in this job. While writing, I relied on my teammates Kaiwen Wang, Ekaterina Shtrevensky, and Ben Novak. I owe a debt to Kaiwen, who helped hold down the fort on my day job while I wrote. Let's keep *crushing* it.

The intellectual muses I have relied on throughout my career contributed to this book.

My BCA Research and Stratfor teammate, Matt Gertken, reviewed the text and scrubbed out the hyperbole. Without Matt, I would have become *persona non grata* in several countries and made far too many inappropriate jokes. Matt and I started working on the same day and have been intellectual brothers ever since.

My friends Dan Green, Jay Reinfrank, Noel Muller, Bayless Parsley, and Charlie Tafoya are the other muses. Dan helped with the math section and has, throughout my life, inspired me to reach my full potential. Jay Reinfrank is the reason I have a career in finance. The Jerry Maguire memo from the Introduction and Chapter 1 was a blend of our ideas, and he was there at the inception of the framework. Noel Muller has been an intellectual sounding board longer than anyone. He has also ensured that I did not drown, self-immolate, or get eaten by bears while meditating in the BC wilderness we both call home. Charlie Tafoya showed me everything there is to know about private markets and technology. And of course, there is Bayless, who gets a special mention in Chapter 3.

A large part of this book consists of research I wrote for BCA Research in Montreal. I owe a debt of gratitude to all of my colleagues at the firm, but especially: Anastasios Avgeriou, Emin Baghramyan, David Boucher, Santiago E. Gomez, Melanie Kermadjian, Jesse Anak Kuri, Jim Mylonas, Chester Ntonifor, and Mathieu Savary. They are my friends and teammates who, over a decade, grew up with me into the baller strategists we are.

My BCA mentors, David Abramson, Peter Berezin, Arthur Budaghyan, Dhaval Joshi, Ian MacFarlane, Mark McClellan, Doug Peta, Francis Scotland, and Chen Zhao also deserve many thanks. I still look back on our daily meetings in my early years at the firm, when as a starstruck young strategist I watched these macro mavens discuss the markets. And without Bashar Al-Rehany, Martin Barnes, and Nicky Manoleas, I would still be "blogging" somewhere in Texas.

My clients, colleagues, and friends in the global macro club that is the financial community have pushed me to refine my framework and humbled me with their intellect and creativity. This book is written for them (though many do not need its insights), especially Kenneth Andersen, Raphael Arndt, Louis Bacon, Whitney Baker, Achin Batra, Scott Bessent, Tony Boeckh, Antonia Bothner, Ziad Boustany, John Burbank, Ahmad Butt, Drew Casino, Christopher Chan, Jim Chanos, John Coates, Paul Danis, Charles Davidson, Mehul Daya, José Luis Daza, Pete Dilworth, Frédéric Dion, Barry Eichengreen, Volker Engelbert, Tit Andrej Erker, Gary Evans, Marc Faber, Hans Fahlin, Jonathan Fayman, Peter Fletcher, Dave Foraie, Christopher Forbes, Stephan Gabillard, Jonathan Gashalter, Stephen Gilmore, Anna Golubovic, Ian Gordon, Nicola Grass, Mike Green, Paul Greenham, Karl-Theodor zu Guttenberg, Elias Haddad, Cyrus Hadidi, Aljoscha Bjorn Grischa Haesen, Daniel Hepler, Alex Hess, Neels Heyneke, Ziad Hindo, Lisa Hintz, John Ho, Mike Hurley, Stephen Jen, David Kalk, Jitania Kandhari, Marc Keller, Mark Koenig, Kosta Kotsaboikidis, Zach Kurz, Franck Lacour, Andrew Lyon, Costas Lyras, Sebastian Mallaby, Michael and Yvonne Marsh, Mike Mayo, Dan McCollum, Nuno Amado Mendes, Jawad Mian, Brian Milner, Rafer Mitri, Oleg Mogilny, Andrew Moll, Shea Morenz, Jay Namyet, Russell Napier, Paul O'Brien, Ali Ojjeh, Juan Correa Ossa, Angkit Panda, Omar Paz, Andrew Pearse, Neil Phillips, Jean-François Pepin, Magesh Pillay, Rajeeb Pramanik, Benjamin Preisler, Marlene Puffer, Alex Purewal, David Ross, Henri-Paul Rousseau, Steve Saldanha, Ben Samild, Walter Schadenfroh, Zach Schreiber, Aaron Schuler, Murray Scott, Tatiana Semenova, Danilo Simonelli, Ilan Solot, Marc-André Soublière, Jeremy Stein, Barry Sternlicht, Jayne Styles, Maxime Tessier, Mario Therrien, Parvinder Thiara, Cullen Thompson, Barbara Tong, François Trahan, Mark Trevena, Ronny Turiaf, Ion Valaskakis, John Valentino, Zoltán Varga, Alice Wang, Yan Wang, Marco Willner, Mike Wissell, Ed Wolfe, David Zervos, Felix Zulauf, and many more. Any omissions are an innocent oversight on my part.

In the geopolitical analysis community, the main thanks goes to R.P. Eddy, the CEO and founder of Ergo, who, from our first meeting years ago, has mentored me more than he knows. Eddy runs the best geopolitical consultancy in the world, and his curated community of clients is a club that every investor must join. I am also a big fan of Mark Rosenberg, the CEO and founder of GeoQuant, which sits on the other side of the methodological spectrum from Ergo. Mark taught me alternate paths to systematic geopolitical analysis. He has created a quant-driven geopolitical consultancy that may revolutionize how we look at political risk (and put qualitative dinosaurs like me out of business!). George Friedman, my first-ever boss in the private sector, was the original wielder of the constraints framework, and I learned a lot from him about geopolitical analysis. Ian Bremmer, Charlie Cook, Alastair Newton, Nate Silver, Philip Tetlock, and Peter Zeihan have all been inspirations to my career. As Grand Puba said, "I wouldn't be here today if the old school didn't pave the way."

Melissa Lesh, the editor of this book, took up residence in my brain for three months. We became a hive mind without having ever met in person. She did more than just edit; she helped significantly reframe several chapters. If you need an editor, please reach out to her. She is a pro. Thanks also to the wider Team Papic that gave me the time to focus on my work, namely Rajeev Anand, Eva Stefanova, and Kristyna Sykorova.

I also want to thank my teachers. Above all, Grant Perry was an inspiration and mentor to me while at Stratfor. I will miss Grant immensely. Ivanka Anastasijević helped me as a young child to navigate the insanity of a country in its death throes. Larry Roetzel and Heather Gatley gave me confidence in my writing abilities, even though I learned English from movies, the Simpsons, and computer games. Yves Tiberghien was the first teacher to push me to strive for the best version of me. Robert Johnson, who opened my eyes to political theory, would be proud of Chapter 2 (I think … I *hope*). Barbara Arneil taught my first political science course, and Michael Byers showed me what self-initiated research looks like. At the University of Texas, I thank the Department of Government for all their time and resources, particularly Zoltan Barany, Wendy Hunter, Robert Moser, Peter Trubowitz, and Kurt Weyland. And though I only met Professor John Mearsheimer later in life, he has forever changed how I perceive the tragedy of Great Power politics.

I dedicate this book to my lost homeland, a country that no longer exists. There is an emptiness in my source code that, I think, makes me a strong geopolitical analyst. My bug – lack of a place to call home – has become a feature of my framework. Without a home, there can be no home bias. As a result, I remain objective when forecasting the future, and I can teach others how to do the same. You don't really need to have your homeland descend into an orgy of suicidal violence to forecast geopolitics. But it helps.

There is nothing to thank my children for, not yet. Instead, an apology is in order. I am sorry, Eva, Pascal, and Isabella, for often putting my career before your needs. You are lucky to have the mother that you have. Life is full of sacrifices, a product of constraints. I have worked very hard so that one day, you can look back at what Dad has done as inspiration for your own effort.

Remember: *do or do not, there is no try.*

Finally, thank you to Brian the Chocolate Lab, a foil to populists the world over.

This book has been written to the soundtrack of DJ Skee, Bijelo Dugme, old-school hip-hop, and a massive dose of brain-melting EDM.

Bibliography

Abernethy, David B. *The Dynamics of Global Dominance*. New Haven: Yale University Press, 2000. https://www.jstor.org/stable/j.ctt32bqtv.

Allison, Graham. *Destined for War: Can America and China Escape Thucydides's Trap?* Boston: Houghton Mifflin Harcourt, 2017.

Anton, Michael. "The Trump Doctrine." Accessed February 23, 2020. https://foreignpolicy.com/2019/04/20/the-trump-doctrine-big-think-america-first-nationalism/.

Bell, Eric Temple. *An Arithmetical Theory of Certain Numerical Functions*. Seattle: University of Washington, 1915. https://hdl.handle.net/2027/coo1.ark:/13960/t0cv52v93.

Belluck, Pam. "Younger Adults Make Up Big Portion of Coronavirus Hospitalizations in U.S." *New York Times,* Mar 18, 2020. https://www.nytimes.com/2020/03/18/health/coronavirus-young-people.html.

Bennister, Mark, Paul 't Hart, and Ben Worthy. "Leadership Capital: Measuring the Dynamics of Leadership." *SSRN,* December 15, 2013. https://papers.ssrn.com/sol3/papers.cfm?abstract_id=2510241.

"Bernhard Von Bülow on Germany's 'Place in the Sun.'" *German Historical Institute* 3 (1897): 1074–1083, http://germanhistorydocs.ghi-dc.org/pdf/eng/607_Buelow_Place%20in%20the%20Sun_111.pdf.

Bialek, Stephanie, et al. "Severe Outcomes among Patients with Coronavirus Disease 2019 (COVID-19) – United States, February 12–March 16, 2020."

Morbidity and Mortality Weekly Report 69, no. 12 (March 18, 2020). https://www.cdc.gov/mmwr/volumes/69/wr/mm6912e2.htm?s.

Black, Duncan. "On the Rationale of Group Decision-making." *Journal of Political Economy* 56, no. 1 (February 1948): 23–34.

"Boris Johnson: 'I'd Rather Be Dead in a Ditch' Than Ask for a Brexit Delay," *BBC News video*, 0:33, September 5, 2019. https://www.bbc.com/news/av/uk-politics-49601128/boris-johnson-i-d-rather-be-dead-in-a-ditch-than-ask-for-brexit-delay.

Buhi, Jason. "Foreign Policy and the Chinese Constitutions during the Hu Jintao Administration." *Boston College International and Comparative Law Review* 37, no. 2 (Spring 2014): 241–279. https://search.proquest.com/docview/1663666068.

Burgess, Robert. "The Daily Prophet: Carville was Right about the Bond Market." *Bloomberg*, January 29, 2018. https://www.bloomberg.com/news/articles/2018-01-29/the-daily-prophet-carville-was-right-about-the-bond-market-jd0q9r1w.

Carpenter, Ted Galen. "Are the Baltic States Next?" *The National Interest*, March 24, 2014. https://nationalinterest.org/commentary/are-the-baltic-states-next-10103.

Ciminelli, Gabriele. *The Political Costs of Reforms*. IMF Staff Discussion Note. Vol. 19. Washington, DC: International Monetary Fund, 2019.

Cohen, Eliot A. "America's Long Goodbye: The Real Crisis of the Trump Era." *Foreign Affairs* 98, no. 1 (January 1, 2019): 138.

Constanze Stelzenmüller. "At Last: The Trump Doctrine, Revealed." *The Brookings Institution*, June 5, 2017. https://www.brookings.edu/blog/order-from-chaos/2017/06/05/at-last-the-trump-doctrine-revealed/.

Darley, J.M. and C.D. Batson. "From Jerusalem to Jericho: A Study of Situational and Dispositional Variables in Helping Behavior." *Journal of Personality and Social Psychology* 27, no. 1 (1973): 100–108.

Department of Thought and Theory. "China's Realistic Response and Strategic Choices After the Great Changes of the Soviet Union." *China Youth Daily*, July 31, 2006. http://m.wyzxwk.com/content.php?classid=13&id=7392.

Development Research Center of the State Council, People's Republic of China. *China 2030: Building a Modern, Harmonious, and Creative Society Washington*, DC: World Bank, 2013.

Downs, Anthony. *An Economic Theory of Democracy*. 1st ed. New York: Harper & Row, 1957.

Dunsmuir, Lindsay and Doina Chiacu. "Republican Meadows: Tax Plan Does Not Have to Be Revenue Neutral." Edited by Jeffrey Benkoe. *Reuters*, March 26, 2017. https://www.reuters.com/article/us-usa-obamacare-meadows/republican-meadows-tax-plan-does-not-have-to-be-revenue-neutral-idUSKBN16X0L9.

Elagina, Diana. "Distribution of Russia's Natural Gas Exports by Destination Country 2016." *Statista,* November 5, 2019. https://www.statista.com/statistics/305394/russian-natural-gas-exports-by-destination/.

Farivar, Masood. "Armageddon and the Mahdi." *Wall Street Journal,* March 16, 2007. https://www.wsj.com/articles/SB117401728182739204.

Ferguson, Neil M., et al. *Report 9: Impact of Non-pharmaceutical Interventions (NPIs) to Reduce COVID-19 Mortality and Healthcare Demand.* London: Imperial College London, 2020. http://hdl.handle.net/10044/1/77482.

Ferguson, Niall. *The House of Rothschild.* New York: Penguin, 1998.

Flake, Jeff. *Conscience of a Conservative: A Rejection of Destructive Politics and a Return to Principle.* New York: Random House, 2017.

Friedman, Thomas L. "A Plan to Get America Back to Work." *New York Times,* March 22, 2020. https://www.nytimes.com/2020/03/22/opinion/coronavirus-economy.html.

Friedman, Uri. "The Libyan Stalemate Suggested by Google Earth." *Yahoo News,* July 15, 2011. https://news.yahoo.com/amphtml/libyan-stalemate-suggested-google-earth-215655107.html.

Gillespie, Patrick. "Argentina Election More Uncertain as Pollsters Go Dark." *Bloomberg,* June 26, 2019. https://www.bloomberg.com/news/articles/2019-06-26/argentina-s-election-faces-more-uncertainty-as-pollsters-go-dark.

Gilpin, Robert. *War and Change in World Politics.* Reprint. Cambridge: Cambridge University Press, 1995.

Goldberg, Jeffrey. "A Senior White House Official Defines the Trump Doctrine: We're America, Bitch." *The Atlantic,* June 11, 2018. https://www.theatlantic.com/politics/archive/2018/06/a-senior-white-house-official-defines-the-trump-doctrine-were-america-bitch/562511/.

Gollom, Mark. "Analysis: Post-Gadhafi Libya Faces Enormous Challenges." *CBC News,* August 23, 2011. https://www.cbc.ca/amp/1.1022710.

Gowa, Joanne and Edward D. Mansfield. "Power Politics and International Trade." *The American Political Science Review* 87, no. 2 (June 1, 1993): 408–420.

Hanke, Steve H. "The World's Greatest Unreported Hyperinflation." *Cato Institute,* May 7, 2007. https://www.cato.org/publications/commentary/worlds-greatest-unreported-hyperinflation.

"Hard Power." *Oxford English Dictionary,* 2011.

Heuer, Richards J. *Psychology of Intelligence Analysis.* Washington: The Central Intelligence Agency, 2015. https://www.cia.gov/library/center-for-the-study-of-intelligence/csi-publications/books-and-monographs/psychology-of-intelligence-analysis/PsychofIntelNew.pdf.

Hobsbawm, Eric J. *Nations and Nationalism since 1780.* 2nd ed. Cambridge, MA: Cambridge University Press, 1997.

Hotelling, Harold. "Stability in Competition." *The Economic Journal* 39 (1929): 41–57.

Huntington, Samuel P. *The Third Wave: Democratization in the Late Twentieth Century.* Norman: University of Oklahoma Press, 1991.

Huntington, Samuel P. *Political Order in Changing Societies.* New Haven: Yale University Press, 1968.

Ioannidis, John P.A. "A Fiasco in the Making? As the Coronavirus Pandemic Takes Hold, We Are Making Decisions without Reliable Data." *Stat News,* March 17, 2020. https://www.statnews.com/2020/03/17/a-fiasco-in-the-making-as-the-coronavirus-pandemic-takes-hold-we-are-making-decisions-without-reliable-data/.

"Iran." *Gallup,* accessed March 28, 2020. https://news.gallup.com/poll/116236/iran.aspx.

Joint Economic Committee. *A Symposium on the 40th Anniversary of the Joint Economic Committee, Hearings before the Joint Economic Committee: Congress of the United States: Ninety-Ninth Congress: First Session.* Washington, DC: US Government Printing Office, 1986.

Keynes, John Maynard. *The Economic Consequences of the Peace.* New York: Harcourt, Brace and Company, 1922.

Kindleberger, Charles. *The World in Depression, 1929–1939.* History of the World Economy in the Twentieth Century. Vol. 4. Berkeley: University of California Press, 1975.

Klasa, Adrienne. "Round-tripping: How Tiny Mauritius Became India's Main Investor." *Financial Times,* October 30, 2018. https://www.ft.com/content/b2a35d1e-c597-11e8-86b4-bfd556565bb2.

Krugman, Paul. "Ending Greece's Bleeding." *New York Times,* July 5, 2015. https://www.nytimes.com/2015/07/06/opinion/paul-krugman-ending-greeces-bleeding.html.

Lakner, Christopher, et al. "Global Income Distribution: From the Fall of the Berlin Wall to the Great Recession." *World Bank Working Paper No. 6719,* December 2013, http://documents.worldbank.org/curated/en/914431468162277879/pdf/WPS6719.pdf.

Levine, Adam Seth, Robert Frank, and Oege Dijk. "Expenditure Cascades." *SSRN,* September 13, 2010. https://papers.ssrn.com/sol3/papers.cfm?abstract_id=1690612.

Levy, Jack S. and Katherine Barbieri. "Trading with the Enemy during Wartime." *Security Studies* 13, no. 3 (December 2004): 1–47. doi:10.1080/096364 10490914059. http://www.tandfonline.com/doi/abs/10.1080/09636410490 914059.

Li, Ruiyun, et al. "Substantial Undocumented Facilitates the Rapid Dissemination of Novel Coronavirus (SARS-CoV2)." *Science* (March 16, 2020).

Liberman, Peter. "Trading with the Enemy: Security and Relative Economic Gains." *International Security* 21, no. 1 (July 1, 1996): 147–175. https://www.jstor.org/stable/2539111.

Lynch, Megan S. *Budget Reconciliation Measures Enacted into Law: 1980–2010.* Washington, DC: Congressional Research Service, 2017.

———. *The Budget Reconciliation Process: Timing of Legislative Action.* Washington, DC: Congressional Research Service, 2016.

Machiavelli, Niccolò. *The Prince.* New York: Bantam, 1981.

Mackinder, John Halford. *Democratic Ideals and Reality: A Study in the Politics of Reconstruction.* 15th ed. Washington, DC: National Defense University Press, 1996.

MacMillan, Margaret. *The War That Ended Peace.* Toronto: Allen Lane, 2014.

Mahan, Alfred Thayer. *The Influence of Sea Power upon History,* 1660–1783. 15th ed. Boston: Little, Brown and Company, 1949. http://dx.doi.org/10.1017/CBO9780511783289.

———. *The Interest of America in Sea Power: Present and Future.* Boston: Little, Brown and Company, 1918.

"Making Reform Happen: Structural Priorities in Times of Crisis." *OECD.* 2010.

Maruthappu, Mahiben, et al. "Economic Downturns, Universal Health Coverage, and Cancer Mortality in High-income and Middle-income Countries, 1990–2010: A Longitudinal Analysis." *The Lancet* 388, no. 10045 (2016): 684–695. https://doi.org/10.1016/S0140-6736(16)00577-8.

Marx, Karl. *Das Kapital.* Gateway Editions, 1867.

Mason, Jeff and Makini Brice. "Trump Blasts Proposed U.S. Restrictions on Sale of Jet Parts to China." *Reuters,* February 18, 2020. https://www.reuters.com/article/us-usa-trade-china/trump-blasts-proposed-restrictions-on-china-trade-wants-china-to-buy-u-s-jet-engines-idUSKBN20C1ZV.

Mauldin, John. "The End Game of the Debt Supercycle." *Forbes, June* 19, 2010. https://www.forbes.com/sites/investor/2010/07/19/the-end-game-of-the-debt-supercycle/#56f430fc6691.

McGregor, Richard. "Size of CIA's Budget Slice Revealed in Edward Snowden Leak." *Financial Times,* August 29, 2013. https://www.ft.com/content/31997218-10f6-11e3-b5e4-00144feabdc0.

Mearsheimer, John J. *The Tragedy of Great Power Politics.* New York, NY : W. W. Norton & Company, Inc., 2001.

Morrow, James D. "When Do "Relative Gains" Impede Trade?" *Journal of Conflict Resolution* 41, no. 1 (February 1, 1997): 12–37. https://www.jstor.org/stable/174485.

Mullins, Lisa. "Who Is Leading Libya's Revolution." *Public Radio International,* March 21, 2011. https://www.pri.org/stories/2011-03-21/who-leading-libyas-revolution.

Noor, Poppy. "Trump Is Trying to Stop People from Seeing This Ad on His Response to Coronavirus." *The Guardian,* March 27, 2020. https://www.theguardian.com/world/2020/mar/27/donald-trump-coronavirus-response-us-advertisement.

OECD Economic Surveys: Yugoslavia 1990. Paris: OECD, 1990. https://www.oecd-ilibrary.org/content/publication/eco_surveys-yucs-1990-en.

Olson, Mancur. *The Logic of Collective Action; Public Goods and the Theory of Groups.* Cambridge, MA: Harvard University Press, 1965. http://catalog.hathitrust.org/Record/001109264.

Parker, Matt. *Humble Pi: A Comedy of Maths Errors.* New York: Penguin, 2019. http://www.vlebooks.com/vleweb/product/openreader?id=none™ isbn=9780141989136.

Petrovic, Pavle, et al. "The Yugoslav Hyperinflation of 1992-1994: Causes, Dynamics, and Money Supply Process." *Journal of Comparative Economics,* http://yaroslavvb.com/papers/petrovic-yugoslavian.pdf.

Pifer, Steven. "The Mariupol Line: Russia's Land Bridge to Crimea." *The Brookings Institution,* March 19, 2019. https://www.brookings.edu/blog/order-from-chaos/2015/03/19/the-mariupol-line-russias-land-bridge-to-crimea/.

Pramuk, Jacob. "Trump Endorses NATO's Mutual Defense Pact in Poland, after Failing to Do So on First Europe Trip." *CNBC, July* 6, 2017. https://www.cnbc.com/2017/07/06/trump-us-stands-firmly-behind-nato-article-5.html.

Pueyo, Tomas. "Coronavirus: Why You Must Act Now." *Medium,* March 10, 2020. https://medium.com/@tomaspueyo/coronavirus-act-today-or-people-will-die-f4d3d9cd99ca.

Putnam, Robert. "Diplomacy and Domestic Politics: The Logic of Two-level Games." *International Organization* 42, no. 3 (June 1, 1988): 427–460.

Reich, David and Richard Kogan. *Introduction to Budget "Reconciliation."* Washington, DC: Center on Budget and Policy Priorities, 2016.

Remnick, David. "Going the Distance: On and Off the Road with Barack Obama." *The New Yorker,* January 20, 2014. https://www.newyorker.com/magazine/2014/01/27/going-the-distance-david-remnick.

"Rise and Fall of Genex: To Have and Not to Have." *Transitions Online* (April 25, 1988). https://www.tol.org/client/article/18198-rise-and-fall-of-genex-to-have-and-not-to-have.

Rodrik, Dani. *Premature Deindustrialization*. Working Paper No. 20935. Cambridge, MA: National Bureau of Economic Research, 2015.

Ross, Lee and Richard E. Nisbett. *The Person and the Situation*. London: McGraw-Hill, 2011.

Scannell, Kara. "FASB Eases Mark-to-market Rules." *Wall Street Journal,* April 3, 2009. https://www.wsj.com/articles/SB123867739560682309.

Shiller, Robert J. *Narrative Economics. Princeton,* NJ: Princeton University Press, 2019. https://www.jstor.org/stable/j.ctvdf0jm5.

Silver, Nate. *The Signal and the Noise: Why SO Many Predictions Fail … But Some Don't*. New York: Penguin Books, 2015.

Sinn, Hans-Werner. "Why Greece Should Leave the Eurozone." *New York Times,* July 25, 2015. https://www.nytimes.com/2015/07/25/opinion/why-greece-should-leave-the-eurozone.html.

Smith, Matthew. "By 48% to 35% Britons Would Rather Have No Deal and No Corbyn." *YouGov, August* 17, 2019. https://yougov.co.uk/topics/politics/articles-reports/2019/08/17/48-35-britons-would-rather-have-no-deal-and-no-cor.

Snidal, Duncan. "Relative Gains and the Pattern of International Cooperation." *American Political Science Review* 85, no. 3 (September 1, 1991): 701–726. https://www.jstor.org/stable/1963847.

Soros, George. *The Alchemy of Finance*. Hoboken, NJ: Wiley, 1987.

Steinberg, Bruce. "Reforming the Soviet Economy." *Fortune* archive, November 25, 1985, https://archive.fortune.com/magazines/fortune/fortune_archive/1985/11/25/66654/index.htm.

Stevenson, Alexandra and Jin Wu. "Tiny Apartments and Punishing Work Hours: The Economic Roots of Hong Kong's Protests." *New York Times,* July 22, 2019. https://www.nytimes.com/interactive/2019/07/22/world/asia/hong-kong-housing-inequality.html.

Stiltsky, Rumpel. "1984 NBA Finals Game 4: Celtics at Lakers (McHale Clotheslines Rambis) Larry Goes to Hollywood Pt. 2." YouTube video, 1:02, July 22, 2017. https://www.youtube.com/watch?v=qmIA61zEcfg.

Stratfor. "Dispatch: Egyptian Elections in Doubt as Violence Returns to Tahrir." YouTube video, 4:21, November 21, 2011. https://www.youtube.com/watch?v=bI7Mv0vlaK8&app=desktop.

Tharoor, Shashi. *Inglorious Empire*. London: C. Hurst & Company, 2017.

Tetlock, Phillip E. *Expert Political Judgment*. Princeton, NJ: Princeton University Press, 2005. http://portal.igpublish.com/iglibrary/search/PUPB0000181.html.

Trump, Donald J. *National Security Strategy of the United States of America*. Washington, DC: The White House, 2017. https://www.whitehouse.gov/wp-content/uploads/2017/12/NSS-Final-12-18-2017-0905-2.pdf.

Tyrovolas, Stefanos, et al. "The Burden of Disease in Greece, Health Loss, Risk Factors, and Health Financing, 2000–16: An Analysis of the Global Burden of Disease Study 2016." *The Lancet Public Health* 3, no. 8 (August 2018): e395–e406. https://doi.org/10.1016/S2468-2667(18)30130-0.

U.S. Customs and Border Protection. "Section 232 Trade Remedies on Aluminum and Steel: Active Section 232 Product Exclusions in ACE." *U.S. Department of Homeland Security,* February 10, 2020. https://www.cbp.gov/trade/programs-administration/trade-remedies/section-232-trade-remedies-aluminum-and-steel.

Vasovic, Aleksandar. "Serbia Imposes Night Curfew, Orders Elderly Indoors." *Reuters,* March 17, 2020. https://www.reuters.com/article/us-health-coronavirus-serbia/serbia-imposes-night-curfew-orders-elderly-indoors-idUSKBN2143XR.

"Verbatim of the Remarks Made by Mario Draghi." *European Central Bank,* 2012. https://www.ecb.europa.eu/press/key/date/2012/html/sp120726.en.html.

Weber, Eugen. *Peasants into Frenchmen: The Modernization of Rural France, 1870–1914. ACLS Humanities*. Stanford, CA: Stanford University Press, 1976. http://hdl.handle.net/2027/heb.01321.

Weiser, Stanley. *Wall Street. Film. Directed by Oliver Stone*. Century City: Twentieth Century Fox Film Corporation, 1987.

Williams, Ernest Edwin. *Made in Germany, Reprint ed*. Ithaca: Cornell University Press, 1896.

Willimon, Beau. "Let's Not Pretend to Be Naïve." *House of Cards*. TV series. Directed by Carl Franklin. Netflix. Season 2, episode 6.

Wu, Joseph T., et al. "Estimating Clinical Severity of COVID-19 from the Transmission Dynamics in Wuhan, China." *Nature Medicine* (March 19, 2020). https://www.nature.com/articles/s41591-020-0822-7.

Zegart, Amy. "The Self-inflicted Demise of American Power." *The Atlantic,* July 12, 2018. https://www.theatlantic.com/international/archive/2018/07/trump-nato-summit/565034/.

Index